Out in the Storm

THE NORTHEASTERN SERIES ON GENDER, CRIME, AND LAW

Editor: Claire Renzetti

For a complete list of books that are available in this series, please visit www.upne.com and www.upne.com/series/NGCL.html

Gail A. Caputo, *Out in the Storm: Drug-Addicted Women Living as Shoplifters and Sex Workers*

Michael P. Johnson, *A Typology of Domestic Violence: Intimate Terrorism, Violent Resistance, and Situational Couple Violence*

Susan L. Miller, editor, *Criminal Justice Research and Practice: Diverse Voices from the Field*

Jody Raphael, *Freeing Tammy: Women, Drugs, and Incarceration*

Kathleen J. Ferraro, *Neither Angels nor Demons: Women, Crime, and Victimization*

Michelle L. Meloy, *Sex Offenses and the Men Who Commit Them: An Assessment of Sex Offenders on Probation*

Amy Neustein and Michael Lesher, *From Madness to Mutiny: Why Mothers Are Running from the Family Courts—and What Can Be Done about It*

Jody Raphael, *Listening to Olivia: Violence, Poverty, and Prostitution*

Cynthia Siemsen, *Emotional Trials: Moral Dilemmas of Women Criminal Defense Attorneys*

Lori B. Girshick, *Woman-to-Woman Sexual Violence: Stories of Women in Prison*

Karlene Faith, *The Long Prison Journey of Leslie van Houten: Life Beyond the Cult*

Jody Raphael, *Saving Bernice: Battered Women, Welfare, and Poverty*

Neil Websdale, *Policing the Poor: From Slave Plantation to Public Housing*

Lori B. Girshick, *No Safe Haven: Stories of Women in Prison*

Sandy Cook and Susanne Davies, editors, *Harsh Punishment: International Experiences of Women's Imprisonment*

Susan L. Miller, *Gender and Community Policing: Walking the Talk*

James Ptacek, *Battered Women in the Courtroom: The Power of Judicial Responses*

Neil Websdale, *Understanding Domestic Homicide*

Kimberly J. Cook, *Divided Passions: Public Opinions on Abortion and the Death Penalty*

Out in the Storm

Drug-Addicted Women Living as Shoplifters and Sex Workers

Gail A. Caputo

NORTHEASTERN UNIVERSITY PRESS
Boston

Published by University Press of New England
Hanover and London

NORTHEASTERN UNIVERSITY PRESS
Published by University Press of New England,
One Court Street, Lebanon, NH 03766
www.upne.com

Printed in the United States of America
5 4 3 2 1

Library of Congress Cataloging-in-Publication Data
Caputo, Gail A., 1965–
Out in the storm : drug-addicted women living as shoplifters and sex workers / Gail A. Caputo.
p. cm.—(Northeastern series on gender, crime, and law)
Includes bibliographical references and index.
ISBN-13: 978–1–55553–695–4 (cloth : alk. paper)
ISBN-10: 1–55553–695–6 (cloth : alk. paper)
ISBN-13: 978–1–55553–696–1 (pbk. : alk. paper)
ISBN-10: 1–55553–696–4 (pbk. : alk. paper)
1. Female offenders—Pennsylvania—Philadelphia. 2. Shoplifting—Pennsylvania—Philadelphia. 3. Prostitutes—Pennsylvania—Philadelphia. 4. Women drug addicts—Pennsylvania—Philadelphia. 5. Drug abuse and crime—Pennsylvania—Philadelphia. 6. Female offenders—New Jersey—Camden. 7. Shoplifting—New Jersey—Camden. 8. Prostitutes—New Jersey—Camden. 9. Women drug addicts—New Jersey—Camden. 10. Drug abuse and crime—New Jersey—Camden. I. Title.
HV6046.C285 2008
364.3'740974811—dc22 2008001417

To Jill

In loving memory of my sister
Deborah Caputo, always an angel,
and Gerhard O. W. Mueller, my skipper.

Contents

Acknowledgments

I am forever indebted to the women in my study. Mothers and daughters, sisters and friends, they are deeply spiritual and hopeful women who are grateful for the little they have. By letting me know them, their darkest secrets, and their dreams for tomorrow, these women changed my life and my attitude on almost every matter. I think about them every day. Gewn Wilks at New Directions for Women in Philadelphia was instrumental in this study, welcoming me as a researcher and even my dogs to visit. Many thanks to Karen DiDonato, Robin Mirua, John Bealle, and the staff at University Press of New England for their work on this project, to Rachel Shteir, Sherry Pisacano, and my colleagues in criminal justice at Rutgers, especially Drew Humphries and Michelle Meloy for their support. My family is the reason for everything I do. Thank you dearly Mom, Dad, Betty, Terry, Susan, Chris, and Howie for your understanding and confidence. Annie, Sara, Lucy, and Lily were at my side through the writing; without any doubt, the girls helped too. Finally, I am grateful for Jill Breidenbach who has been there for me through the home stretch in so many ways.

Out in the Storm

1. *Introduction*

I've been out there in the storm. That's what it is; it's a storm, it's a hurricane, it's a tornado. Drugs will wipe you out because you can't wipe it. It'll clean you; it'll take everything you have because once you do one, that's it. —Ronni

The course of a woman's criminal career is like a ship's journey. It originates at some particular time and place and proceeds through a series of contingency markers or waypoints in time and place that can shift the direction of her criminal involvement—often numerous times—until that point when she reaches her final destination, and her criminal career is complete. Throughout this journey, she navigates imposing and unpredictable waters, making decisions—bounded by her status as a woman and other vulnerabilities—using only those resources immediately available to her.

Acting as a snapshot in time, this book carries the reader through parts of this journey for thirty-eight drug-addicted women earning a living from shoplifting and sex work (i.e., street-level prostitution) in and around poor urban neighborhoods in the greater Philadelphia area.[1] This book is not about drug addiction per se, but about women's reliance on crime to finance drug addiction. Based on three years of ethnographic research, narrative life histories form the basis of the book, which seeks to explain these women's criminality and, in doing so, contribute to our broader understanding of female criminality in general. Using their voices, this book takes the reader back through drug-related and crime-precipitating events in these women's early lives and toward the present to their criminal involvement. The book has three main objectives. The first is to narrate, from the perspective of women, the etiology of the women's criminal behavior by pointing out how the lives of shoplifters and sex workers before their criminal involvement are both similar and different. The second is to explain how shoplifters and sex workers manage and carry out their criminal activities—to characterize how the women similarly situated as drug addicts and bounded by their status as women and other influences are able to make their particular crime work for them using neighborhood and personal resources, which are sometimes very similar and sometimes different. Tied to this explanation of how women manage crime, the third objective of this book is to expose how women approach the particular drawbacks of a criminal specialization in shoplifting and sex work, including apprehension and violence.

Why Shoplifting?

I have always had an interest in how women negotiate the world, including the world of crime. Originally, this book was to concentrate exclusively on shoplifting,[1] to extend a study of shoplifters and treatment for them that I began more than a decade ago, far from the streets of Philadelphia and its neighboring city of Camden, New Jersey. Shoplifting is one of the crimes associated with women but little is known about the particular crime itself. In large part, my aim was to conceptualize the linkages between gender and this crime by studying male and female shoplifters, but as I explain later in this introduction, the research evolved to compare and contrast the lives of women shoplifters with women who chose a different crime, sex work. In part, my aim was to bring the study of shoplifting and shoplifters into the mainstream of criminological research, to make the case that shoplifting matters.

Shoplifting has traditionally been a subject of psychology, psychiatry, and consumer behavior, often sociology, but rarely criminology. Extant literature is informative about how shoplifters may differ from one another using typologies or classification schemes, about kleptomania, about loss prevention strategies, and about psychological and psychiatric treatment for shoplifters, but it leaves unanswered questions and problems that criminologists should address. This study attends to some of those unanswered questions about shoplifting: What are the precursors to a career in shoplifting? How do drug addiction, gender, class, race, and other personal circumstances and sociological forces mix to explain who engages in this crime and how? Why do some drug-addicted women shoplift to support themselves financially when others do not? How do female shoplifters make the crime profitable compared to women who choose other crime work? How do shoplifters contemplate the crime and negotiate its risks compared to women who engage in other crimes?

One reason for the conspicuous lack of in-depth study of shoplifters and shoplifting may be the perception that it is not important enough, not problematic enough. To be sure, shoplifting is problematic not only for retailers and consumers, but also for communities, the criminal justice system, and for shoplifters themselves. Shoplifting is one of the most common crimes in the United States, with upward of one million shoplifting offenses occurring each year.[2] However, most shoplifting goes undetected. Survey research reveals that shoplifting is much more extensive than reflected in the documented number of offenses reported to police, estimating that between 10 percent and 40 percent of all consumers shoplift.[3]

Economic losses from shoplifting affect consumers through increased prices to offset retail losses, well into tens of billions of dollars annually.[4] Retail theft prevention (usually termed "loss prevention") is a profitable growing business, and stores continue to develop specialized personnel units, technologies, and methods to detect and control theft, but the suitability or effectiveness of these strategies is still unknown. For example, store security cannot monitor every shopper all of the time and must decide which consumers to monitor closely and which to detain at the exit. Without science driving these practices, how can we know whether they are suitable or biased?

Its high rate of occurrence makes shoplifting a particular drain on the criminal justice system because of the need to spend scarce resources on the processing of so many offenders. Depending on the dollar value of merchandise appropriated, the type of merchandise, and the offender's criminal history, shoplifting offenses can result in minor charges resolved with a payment of a fine, or result in prosecution for misdemeanors, or even felonies carrying long prison terms. Civilly, retailers may ban shoplifters from their stores. Fines and probation are normative sanctions for shoplifting and are less costly than incarceration, but the financial and social cost is much greater when mandatory, punitive sanctioning (incarceration) for the recidivist shoplifter comes into play. In Pennsylvania, for example, a shoplifter convicted on her third offense is a third-degree felon subject to imprisonment for up to seven years, regardless of the value of merchandise she acquired. Compare this to prostitution, for which the third offense is a second-degree misdemeanor. Criminal justice systems process hundreds of thousands of shoplifters each year, yet policies and practices for dealing with shoplifters and correctional sanctioning including treatment programming appear fragmented and largely untested.[5] For these reasons, shoplifting matters.

Extant literature has not addressed pathways to shoplifting, the sociology of the crime work itself, or the lives and criminal careers of shoplifters.[6] Typically based in survey research, the literature does offer insight into shoplifters' personal characteristics and potential triggers for their involvement in the crime. Many studies focus on youth. One study on adolescent shoplifting published in 1990 reported that 37 percent of youth shoplifted at least once and most shoplifters are male. A factor analysis revealed four reasons for shoplifting based on the perceptions of students: desire to experience the crime, peer involvement and approval, attraction to a product considered contraband (cannot legally buy, told they cannot have), and finally economic reasons (cannot afford).[7] Another survey of adolescents examined the role of peer influence on male and female shoplifting. While fewer than half of the 1,750 youths admitted to shoplifting, results indicated that exposure to friends who shoplift increases the likelihood a girl or boy will also shoplift. Youths, on the other hand, who do not associate with deviant peers have a strong attachment to their parents, minimizing their exposure to negative peer influences and therefore decreasing the likelihood of shoplifting.[8]

According to a survey of adult shoppers in Washington, the typical shoplifter is female and White, but men and minorities characterize shoplifters in contact with the criminal justice system there. Ethnic minorities represented 21 percent of arrestees, compared to 8 percent of shoplifters in the general population sample. Looking to shoplifters as a group, the authors reported more shoplifters were unemployed over the previous year (18 percent), had family income below $5,000 (24 percent), and were concerned about owing money (71 percent) compared to "regular shoppers" (7, 8, and 50 percent, respectively). Economic hardship and associated psychological stress are, according to the authors, the primary motivation for shoplifting.[9] In another study, researchers used hidden cameras in a drug store to profile shoplifters. Results showed significant high male, minority, and lower economic class involvement, but considering gender and race combinations, White women were the least likely to shoplift and Hispanic women the most likely, even when males were considered in analysis.[10]

Other studies have reported different motivators for shoplifting, including reactions to personal crises, resentment toward merchants, low self-control, drug use (identified as a characteristic but left unexplored further by the literature), antisocial attitudes and behaviors, economic stress, divorce and separation, thrill seeking, and even headaches, backaches, and eating disorders.[11] For example, a study by Moore of three hundred criminal court-involved shoplifters finds women and the economically disadvantaged to be overrepresented (57 percent and 72 percent) and that many shoplifters (48 percent) have "character defects" (self-serving, self-indulgent, manipulative, and prone to personal gain at the expense of others) that predispose them to shoplifting.[12]

Disciplines like psychology and psychiatry have dominated the study of shoplifting and define the crime as a function of an underlying condition such as antisocial personality disorder, uncertain self-concept or low self-image, depression, anxiety, impulsivity, anger, and vengeance. Kleptomania is another psychiatric explanation, a subject with its own body of literature.[13] On psychological and psychiatric correlates, Beck and McIntyre reported that shoplifters compared to individuals who never shoplifted fit the profile of psychopath; female and male shoplifters compared to non-shoplifters displayed higher levels of psychopathic deviance, mania, and masculine orientation.[14] Another study using the Minnesota Multiphasic Personality Inventory on a sample of convicted shoplifters reported depression, anxiety, and confusion as likely causes of shoplifting.[15] A survey of college students found that moral beliefs correspond to shoplifting. Students who judge shoplifting to be just or fair, to correspond with peer group approval, and who support the notion of ethical relativism (a behavior can be ethically correct depending on the situation, group, and time) are more likely to support shoplifting than other students.[16] Another study compared undergraduate students, psychiatric patients, and individuals with eating disorders and reported that shoplifting in all three groups was associated with low self-esteem, depression, and purging behavior.[17] In a study of thirty two shoplifters, 50 percent of the females and 42 percent of the males had financial problems, 9 percent were psychotic, and many had hospitalizations for medical problems. Furthermore, stress at home was very high for both females and males leading authors to conclude that shoplifting is a retaliatory and hostile act that relieves crises and produces relief from stress.[18]

Several studies have investigated shoplifting events. From a psychological perspective Katz's "sneaky thrill" model characterizes how shoplifters who steal for excitement go about the crime. In short, potential shoplifters enter stores often with the idea of shoplifting, and when "seduced" by an object they "reconquer emotions" so as to produce an appearance of normalcy.[19] Successful shoplifting produces psychological pleasure, a euphoric thrill. Dabney, Hollinger, and Dugan found that shoplifters display certain behavioral clues like a visual scanning for security and fiddling with products.[20] Another prevalence study observed shoppers in a small department store, noting characteristics of shoplifters and items they stole. Of the nine shoppers observed taking merchandise without paying, most were female and part of a group. Shoplifters minimized their chances of detection, according to the observations, by scanning the scene for security, stealing small and low-cost items, and purchasing goods during the crime.[21] Weaver and Carroll assessed shoplifting opportunities from the perspective of potential offenders and found that shoplifters select targets purposefully; they identify targets that can benefit them and that are accessible to them. During their contemplation of the crime, shoplifters also consider opportunities around them for completing the crime successfully and call off the crime when they see store personnel and security devices.[22]

Along the lines of surveillance, one study sought to understand why honest shoppers would report shoplifting taking place in front of them. Placing researchers in stores to shoplift in the presence of other shoppers the simulation revealed that gender had no significant effect on reporting; male and female shoppers reported shoplifting to store security at the same rates and the shoplifter's gender made no difference in reporting. The appearance of the shoplifter did matter in the reporting behavior of shoppers. Shoplifters dressed in "hippie" attire (soiled jeans, scuffed shoes, dirty denim jacket, long unruly hair, unshaven, no makeup) were handed over to security significantly more often than were "straight" shoplifters in neat, dress attire (shirt and tie, dress or skirt, fur coat, styled hair, clean-shaven, and makeup). Furthermore, shoppers rarely hesitated to alert security when the shoplifter was a hippie but thought much more carefully about the decision when the shoplifter was straight. The authors conclude that the label of "hippie" or "straight" is a master status, a central trait structuring perceptions of individuals. A hippie status increases the likelihood of stigmatization as deviant simply because a hippie looks like trouble. On the other hand, a man in a business suit and a woman in a dress with makeup presumably are signals of conventionality and honesty.[23]

A survey by Tonglet on motivations for shoplifting concluded that shoplifting is a function of moral beliefs, rational choice, and opportunity.[24] Adults and youth, females and males engage in shoplifting, according to the findings, when they believe the behavior is morally acceptable and when they think benefits such as free merchandise and approval from peers outweigh costs such as apprehension or shame. With pro-shoplifting attitudes in place, individuals usually shoplift when they see an opportunity inside a store take something. In other words, a situational opportunity to shoplift increases the chances that shoplifting will occur for individuals with pro-shoplifting attitudes. On the subject of opportunity, a study in geography reported that teenage shoplifters consider the size and location of stores and the time of day when they think about shoplifting. While the desire to experience a thrilling behavior motivated many of the subjects, so did opportunity. The best opportunities to shoplift occur at large stores far from home during the afternoon and on weekends.[25] My own analyses using survey data gathered as part of the current study looked at opportunity for shoplifting. I was able to identify salient conditions inside the retail store setting that create opportunities for shoplifting in the eyes of students who shoplift: Shoplifting is likely to occur when individuals identify merchandise they define as valuable, mobile, visible, and accessible and is less likely to occur in the presence of formal sources of control (police and store employees).

There are more studies, and while this body of scholarship is diverse, it lacks a solid conceptual base and gets at just the fringes of what shoplifting is really all about. Nothing, it appears, has been written about the work of shoplifting from the perspective of shoplifters committed to the crime. New research on the criminogenic patterns can drive effective programmatic intervention and can help us understand how shoplifting really matters in criminology. Such an approach would consider all aspects of shoplifting, including its etiology, its integration into other parts of an individual's life, its organizational and technical dimensions, its place in criminal subcultures, and its fit into illicit and legal economies. This study takes a step in that direction.

Individuals from all social and economic groups shoplift, but what is especially troubling is that shoplifting involves so many women. Most of the shoplifting research reports that women shoplift more than men do, with few studies discounting this contention and noting that men are more often involved, or that women and men engage in the crime at similar rates.[26] Minorities seem to be overrepresented among shoplifters as well.[27] Getting a handle on who really shoplifts is complicated by limits of research; most studies use selective samples such as college students and criminal-justice-involved shoplifters, namely, those arrested—but more likely those convicted and serving probation terms or mandated to treatment.

While women's overrepresentation is probably valid given the amount of support in the literature, it may not be as profound as many studies have shown. Conceivably, other factors can explain, in part, their overrepresentation (and that of minorities). It is plausible that women behave in a manner that draws attention and increases their chances of detection, for example, in their attempt to acquire particular objects, to use certain methods, or to target certain stores at particular times or on specific days. It is more reasonable to assume that store security personnel observe women (and minorities) more closely than they do men (and nonminorities) by training (doubtfully informed by empirical research) and personal presumptions. Even if women and men and minorities and nonminorities shoplift at similar rates, gender bias and other factors such as racism and classism may result in unequal treatment by the criminal justice system—higher rates of arrest and convictions for women and minorities—and therefore a higher than actual estimate of involvement among women and minorities. Is shoplifting a crime for women and minorities, and if so, to what extent and why? Is the overrepresentation of women a by-product of store security and criminal justice practices? These questions are critical ones for future research.

When women commit relatively minor crimes, those in line with what we would expect (for example, prostitution and shoplifting), they tend to receive more lenient sentences from the criminal justice system than women whose criminal behavior steps out of anticipated gender roles, such as those who commit violent and serious offenses.[28] As a result of my long conversations with the women in this study, I am aware that the women, including the sex workers, have had many contacts with the police and courts but have been handled as nuisance offenders, treated almost with disregard. They have had citations to pay and been scheduled for court proceedings, but they often have their cases dismissed. When sentenced, fines and probation are the norm, even short terms in jail, but they are rarely, if ever, offered any treatment until it may be too late. The system's handling of them is not unique to the women in this study—other shoplifters, sex workers, and many others in trouble with the law for low-level offenses are dealt with similarly. Even though the penalties handed down for their offenses are relatively minor, many women in this study almost never pay the fines ordered and almost never report to court or to probation. Then they are on the run, with warrants out for their arrests. Incarcerations have largely been a result of warrants that have caught up with them, and many of the women have been in and out of jails and prisons because of this, but again without treatment. Thus, they have lived these lives of crime feeding their addictions, but they always wanted a different life. This is not only a problem with shoplifters, but also with sex workers and other low-level offenders that the system does not take seriously enough. It is for these reasons as well that shoplifting matters.

Evolution of the Project

Considering empirical criminological knowledge on shoplifters seriously deficient, the existence of conflicting positions on the extent of women's involvement in the crime compared to men, and limited treatment intervention for shoplifters, I set out to conduct new research in 2003. I planned to incorporate survey research with in-depth interviews of shoplifters. The study began with a quantitative survey of 410 college students on their perceptions of factors inside a retail setting that facilitate and impede shoplifting, risks and rewards of the crime, motivations for shoplifting, and various aspects of their own involvement in the crime. After noting differences in women's and men's responses, I set out on a national survey of shoplifters, but the project ended almost at the start as the organizational partner providing access to subjects pulled out of the research.

While my intention had been to incorporate this survey research with in-depth interviews with shoplifters themselves, I knew that a survey could reveal only so much, and deeper understanding required listening to shoplifters' stories. Thus, I set aside the survey research component and planned a new approach—to conduct in-depth life history interviews of shoplifters from the communities in and around

Camden, New Jersey, where I live and work. My goal was to interview adult shoplifters who are not under criminal justice supervision and to include shoplifters from different socioeconomic groups—middle-class shoplifters and their urban poor counterparts. I sought out research subjects using posted advertisements and flyers handed out in busses coming in and going out of Camden, in department stores, malls, and transportation centers in the greater Philadelphia area, and on the streets of Camden. I soon learned it was an ambitious presumption that active shoplifters would readily submit themselves to study, and immediately the research took another turn. Subjects responding to these advertisements were a select group, mostly drug-addicted male shoplifters living through crime in and around Camden in neighborhoods well known for drug-selling and drug-use activities. Some were women similarly situated. In order to increase participation of women shoplifters from the five women who initially responded, I eventually turned to the criminal justice system. I interviewed two women incarcerated at Camden County Jail and the remainder at New Directions for Women, a correctional halfway house for drug-addicted women in Philadelphia. New Directions functions primarily as a prisoner release program intended to ease women's transition from life behind bars in Philadelphia County prisons to productive lives in the community. It is a twenty-five-bed facility where women stay for between nine and twelve months. Both in house and through referral, women receive a variety of services and programming for drug and alcohol addictions, mental health issues, educational and vocational training, and job placement.

The halfway house proved to be the best source of subjects for my research. After I conducted two or three interviews with women who identified themselves as shoplifters, most of the women there wanted to participate, even women who did not shoplift, but who used drug-selling or sex work to finance their addictions. They heard good things from the interviewees—namely, that I could be trusted and that I cared, that I was not there to condemn them, but to bring to the world their lives, to validate them. At first, I turned away these other women, but as I listened to the shoplifters' distressing life stories, I became less specifically interested in documenting the ways in which men and women shoplift and wanted to further explore women's life experiences and criminality. After conducting several interviews with sex workers and hearing similarities and differences on their entry into crime and on how they worked their crimes compared with shoplifters, I knew this group should also be included in the research. Doing this would enable me not only to explore female criminality in general, but also to add diversity to the study—to compare and contrast experiences of both groups in a study of etiology and crime management among women. Including the sex workers in my research allowed me to identify turning points in the women's journeys that may have led to specialization in one crime or the other, to identify commonalities and differences in how women make their crimes work, and how they manage risk. This is probably the most important scholarly contribution of this book to criminology.

I am confident that the stories revealed in this book are true. I was accepted and trusted. The women remarked on how I was different from other researchers wanting information from them. They rarely talked to the others, and when they did, they gave only those details that would not make them feel vulnerable. With my continued presence at the halfway house when conducting the study and when visiting and in my demeanor I gained their trust and acceptance. I tried hard to show them in my words and mostly in my actions that I am not better then they, that I care about them, that this book is about them, for them; it is their book. Our long interviews and informal conversations were very emotional. They revealed many events in the lives of the women and feelings they had never uttered to anyone before but that they had trapped inside for so many years. For them, I know that talking to me was therapeutic simply because I cared enough to listen. Certainly, this is an indication that they felt comfortable with me and confident that I would represent them as who they are. I know their tears were real and words genuine and that our embraces were comforting to them. Before and after interviews, and on other days and in the evenings, I would visit with them. We would sit together in the dayroom or the dining room and talk about the day, about their families, about the weekend plans, and about my life too. My dogs visited often, so the women could experience some diversion from the monotony of their days and from their sadness. They were concerned about me too, asking about my health, about my family, about the "girls" (my dogs), telling me that they missed me last week, and asking whether I wanted to read from their journals or hear about their progress in education, their visits with children, and their feelings about partners they missed; our interactions became conversations between friends. My task here is to represent them, to tell their stories.

By getting out from behind the spell of quantitative methodology—survey research—and face-to-face into the lives of women troubled by addiction and other circumstances beyond their conflict with the law, this study brings into light the human consequences of social and economic marginalization, abuse, drugs, and the absence of care at so many levels. Francine, a fifty-eight-year-old shoplifter in my study shares her view on the importance of the qualitative method, of listening in order to understand:

Now, what can you do Gail? What you're doing, what you're doing right now and that's to get into the heads of people, and you appear to be a caring person, that you are really interested in why we do the things we do and it's important to be understood, ya know; like the person that arrests you in the store, to them it's like you doing it because you can or you doing it because you don't give a shit about nobody else and that's not all it. It's more, there's other things involved than going in there and taking other people's shit. Ya know, some people it means this to them, I mean, what are you gonna do. But if you got somebody like yourself that's going to take the time and try to go inside a person's head and heart and find out why they do what they do, it makes a difference and you go through it and you'll come up with a solution.

Far from the confines of a desk and closed office door, I have entered into real life. One may envision—even expect—a researcher to be a dispassionate scientist. In my view, this is unnecessary and counterproductive. Individually we can do only so much to produce meaningful changes in policy and in the larger social world that can heal criminal offenders in need and rectify the systems and structures that continue to marginalize and oppress them. My hope here is to do more than report and analyze. My task is to bring to life these women, to validate them finally, and to inspire change for women like them and women who will become like them.

The Sample

The stories told in this book come from thirty-eight women, all of whom identify themselves as drug-addicted shoplifters or sex workers. None of the sampling here was done randomly; rather, it was done purposively to interview addicted women who shoplift and those who use sex work to earn a living. In large part, it involved snowball sampling; many subjects were inclined to participate after hearing about the study from those I had already interviewed. I could have continued sampling, adding new subjects to the study, but through collecting and interpreting the data from interviews, I felt that I reached a point of diminishing returns and that my research objectives could be met using data from the existing subjects. All of the women were in recovery for drug addiction or were still drug addicted actively working their crimes, and nearly all of the women were on some form of criminal justice control as prisoners in Camden County Jail or residents of New Directions for Women. The findings in this book represent these women alone, not addicted women, shoplifters, sex workers, or female offenders generally. Table 1 displays selected characteristics of the sample organized by fictitious names of the women used throughout the book.

The women are primarily of racial or ethnic minority (71 percent with 66 percent of the sample African American), and most of whom were raised in the poorest, most disordered, drug-infested, and violent urban neighborhoods in and around Philadelphia and Camden (68 percent) and have lived adult lives in similar areas. At the time of our interviews they ranged in age from twenty-three to fifty-eight; the average age of the women was thirty-nine. Their drugs of choice were primarily cocaine, crack, and heroin (pronounced hĕŕon by most of the women), but also include PCP (or angel dust), crank, marijuana, and alcohol. Two points are important to note about hard drugs. First, the women rarely described marijuana mixed with PCP, crack, cocaine, and other substances (or "wet weed," as it is known in Camden and Philadelphia) as "hard" drugs. Marijuana, wet weed, and pills are soft drugs to most of them. Soft drug age refers to the first use of soft drugs defined by women themselves. Heroin, crack, and cocaine are hard drugs according to the women in my study, and these are the substances to which they were addicted. Because this book is written from the perspectives of women in the study, I do not redefine soft and hard drugs to coincide with conventional, outside definitions. Second, I did not use any clinical measure of addiction but let the women themselves specify as best they could the time in their lives when drugs became a problem for them, when they believe their addictions began. Some said addiction to drugs happened at the very start of their hard drug onset with the first "hit," others pointed to their regular use of a particular drug, and still others described a social

Table 1
Background Characteristics of the Sample

Name	*Age*	*Race/ethnicity*	*Socioeconomic class*	*Crime specialization*	*Past sex work*	*Past shoplifting*	*Drinking age*	*Soft drug age*	*Hard drug age*	*Primary drug*	*Drug and crime pathway*	*Physical abuse*	*Emotional abuse*	*Incest*	*Rape during youth*	*Neglect/abandonment*	*Violence in home*	*Alcohol in home*	*Drugs in home*	*Runaway*	*School dropout*	*Adult entertainment*
Alice	32	Black	Working	Shoplifting	Y		8	13	26	Cocaine	Childhood	N	N	N	N	N	N	Y	N	N	N	N
Bernadette	33	Black	Lower	Sex work		Y			15	Crack	Childhood	Y	N	Y	N	Y	N	Y	Y	Y	Y	Y
Candee	43	Black	Lower	Shoplifting	N		15	15	23	Crack, cocaine	Adulthood	N	N	N	N	N	N	N	N	N	Y	N
Carmela	39	Hispanic	Working	Shoplifting	N		16	16	29	Heroin	Adulthood	N	N	N	N	N	N	Y	N	N	N	N
Cheryl	27	White	Lower	Sex work		Y	12	16	16	Heroin, crack	Childhood	Y	N	Y	Y	N	Y	Y	Y	N	Y	N
Claudia	44	Black	Lower	Sex work		Y	15	17	17	Crack	Childhood	Y	N	N	N	Y	N	Y	Y	Y	Y	Y
Edwina	42	Black	Lower	Sex work		Y	13	16	15	Crack, cocaine	Childhood	Y	Y	Y	Y	N	Y	Y	Y	Y	Y	Y
Eileen	38	White	Working	Shoplifting	N		13	13	16	Cocaine, crack	Childhood	Y	N	N	N	N	Y	Y	N	N	N	N
Estelle	53	Black	Working	Sex work		N	16	16	35	Crack	Adulthood	N	N	N	N	N	Y	Y	N	N	N	N
Esther	52	Black	Lower	Shoplifting	Y		13	13	17	Crack	Childhood	Y	Y	N	N	Y	Y	Y	Y	Y	Y	N
Eva	41	Asian	Lower	Sex work		N	13	13	16	Cocaine, crack	Childhood	Y	Y	N	N	N	Y	Y	Y	Y	N	N
Francine	58	Black	Lower	Shoplifting	Y		6	13	19	Crank, cocaine, heroin	Childhood	Y	Y	N	N	Y	Y	Y	N	Y	Y	Y
Harriet	46	Black	Lower	Sex work		N	8	12	22	Cocaine, crack	Childhood	Y	Y	Y	Y	N	Y	Y	Y	Y	Y	Y
Jarena	39	Black	Lower	Sex work		N	10	10	15	Cocaine, crack	Childhood	N	Y	N	Y	N	Y	Y	Y	Y	Y	Y
Kelly	41	White	Middle	Sex work		N	16		16	Cocaine	Childhood	N	Y	N	N	N	Y	Y	N	Y	N	Y

La Toya	23	Black	Lower	Sex work		Y	3	10	14	Crack	Childhood	Y	Y	Y	N	N	Y	Y	Y	Y	Y	Y
Lauren	41	White	Lower	Sex work		Y	13	13	14	Crack	Childhood	Y	Y	Y	Y	Y	Y	Y	Y	Y	Y	Y
Lee	27	White	Working	Shoplifting	N		13			Heroin	Childhood	N	N	N	N	N	Y	Y	N	N	N	N
Loretta	44	Black	Lower	Sex work		N	12	12	20	Crack	Childhood	N	Y	N	N	Y	Y	Y	N	N	N	N
Marguerite	42	Black	Lower	Sex work		N	13	13	19	Cocaine	Childhood	Y	N	Y	Y	Y	Y	Y	Y	Y	Y	N
Nannie	38	Black	Lower	Shoplifting	N		15	16	22	Cocaine	Adulthood	N	N	N	N	N	N	Y	N	N	N	N
Nikki	41	Black	Lower	Sex work		N	11	14	16	Cocaine	Childhood	Y	N	N	Y	N	Y	Y	N	Y	Y	Y
Patricia	26	White	Working	Sex work		Y	13	13	15	Cocaine, heroin	Childhood	N	Y	N	N	N	N	Y	Y	N	N	N
Pauline	24	Black	Lower	Sex work		N	13	13	15	Cocaine	Childhood	Y	N	N	N	Y	Y	Y	Y	Y	Y	N
Prathia	47	Black	Lower	Sex work		Y	8	13	17	Cocaine, heroin, crack	Childhood	Y	Y	Y	N	N	Y	Y	N	Y	Y	N
Quenelle	38	Black	Lower	Sex work		Y	15		17	Crack	Childhood	Y	Y	Y	N	N	Y	Y	Y	Y	Y	Y
Renita	37	Black	Lower	Sex work		N	13		15	Crack	Childhood	Y	Y	Y	Y	Y	Y	Y	Y	Y	Y	Y
Ronni	45	Black	Lower	Sex work		Y	15		22	Cocaine, crack	Childhood	Y	Y	N	N	N	Y	Y	N	Y	Y	Y
Rose	42	White	Middle	Shoplifting	N		16	16	36	Heroin, crack, cocaine	Adulthood	N	N	N	N	N	N	N	N	N	N	N
Sailie	44	Black	Lower	Sex work		Y	9	15	26	Cocaine, crack	Childhood	Y	Y	Y	N	Y	Y	Y	N	N	N	N
Sandy	30	White	Middle	Shoplifting	N		13	13	19	Heroin	Childhood	Y	N	Y	N	N	Y	Y	N	N	N	N
Shay	37	White	Lower	Sex work		Y	15	15	22	Heroin	Childhood	N	Y	N	N	Y	Y	Y	N	Y	Y	Y
Shirelle	31	Black	Lower	Sex work		N	10	10	17	Crack	Childhood	Y	Y	N	N	Y	N	Y	Y	Y	Y	Y
Tanisha	39	Black	Lower	Sex work		N	13	13	13	Cocaine, crack	Childhood	Y	Y	Y	N	N	Y	Y	Y	Y	Y	Y
Tracy	26	White	Working	Shoplifting	Y		14	14	21	Cocaine, crack, heroin	Childhood	Y	Y	N	N	N	Y	Y	N	Y	Y	N
Val	43	Black	Lower	Sex work		Y	12	12	16	Cocaine, crack, heroin	Childhood	N	Y	Y	N	Y	Y	Y	Y	Y	Y	Y
Veronica	47	Black	Middle	Shoplifting	N				35	Cocaine	Adulthood	N	N	N	N	N	N	N	N	N	N	N
Zeleste	40	White	Working	Sex work		N	13	13	22	Cocaine, heroin, crack	Childhood	N	Y	N	N	N	N	Y	N	Y	Y	Y

Note: Socioeconomic class, defined by the women, refers to family economic and social position during youth. Drinking age and soft drug age refer to onset of alcohol and soft drug use. Hard drug age refers to onset of problematic or addicted hard drug use, as defined by the women. Drug and crime pathway refers to the period of life when the women link their addiction and criminality. Physical abuse, emotional abuse, incest, rape during youth, neglect/abandonment, violence in home, alcohol in home, drugs in home, runaway, and school dropout refer to youth experiences. Adult entertainment refers to employment as stripper, dancer, or escort.

setting in which their addictions soared (such as at strip-club work). While most of the women had used alcohol and marijuana early in their lives, their troubles with hard drug use usually began in late adolescence and early adulthood; the youngest age reported at the onset of regular hard drug use was just thirteen and the oldest thirty-six.

Since the start of their drug use, these women's lives have revolved around getting and using drugs. For them, shoplifting and sex work generate financial earnings to sustain their drug addictions and most basic needs. To be clear, their economic need has been the determining factor for the women's persistence in criminal behavior over the course of their drug addictions, which have been as short as five years and as long as thirty-nine years. The women made decisions to live through crime. For them, shoplifting or sex work is an occupational choice that is more suitable to their situations, more appealing, more immediately profitable, and more accessible than any conventional occupation or any other criminal behavior. Carmela, a thirty-nine-year-old Puerto Rican woman who began shoplifting two years prior to our meeting after losing her occupation, her home, and her savings to drugs, remarks about her decision to rely on criminal behavior as her means to support both her drug habit and other needs. Like the other women, Carmela is involved in crime solely as a means of economic survival.

I barely just survived by shoplifting. I tried to go on welfare, looking for a job; nothing was coming through. I was on the streets, didn't know what to do. Somebody showed me how to do it [shoplift]. . . . It paid everything for me. It got me a place to stay. I was eating. I got clothes, everything, my drugs. I have a drug habit, heroin, so it paid for the heroin habit. . . . I've come to realize I don't like my life right now with the shoplifting. I'd rather be working, but this is where I'm at right now and it gives me a roof over my head. I eat, I got clothes, I got all the necessities, for now. . . . It's what I have to do to survive right now. I'm not gonna sit on the street, not shower, not have nothing ya know. It's not like something I'm proud of doing, it's not something I want to do as a career. It's something I have to do to survive right now. It's really all about survival.

Clear lines of crime specialization are apparent among the women in this study. Crime specialization is that which the women in this study defined themselves as their primary or exclusive means of generating financial earnings. I asked the women directly to explain their means of financial support over the course of their addictions. While they may have received welfare or money at times from men or other women in their lives or through work, shoplifting and sex work are the chief sources of income. Numbering twelve women, shoplifting specialists make up 32 percent of the study group. Sex workers account for the remaining twenty-six, or 68 percent. Half of the sex work specialists had engaged in shoplifting for financial earnings off and on in the past, but very few (six, or 23 percent of the sex workers) told me they still shoplifted occasionally to supplement their earnings. One third of the shoplifting specialists had prostituted in the past, but almost never after their involvement in shoplifting. While their primary or exclusive criminal behaviors are shoplifting and sex work, some of the women have shown versatility in their offending patterns by engaging in low-level theft offenses such as credit card theft or check forgery and did so most especially during the early years of their addictions before they settled into specialization; they knew how to hustle. Val identifies as a sex work specialist, but over her twenty-seven-year use of heroin, crack, and cocaine she has engaged in other income-generating crimes: "I did everything; I stole credit cards, I shoplifted, I sold my ass, I sold drugs, whatever."

The most common crime the women have incorporated into their specializations is drug selling: 29 percent of the women (who are all but one sex worker) have sold drugs periodically and always in the short term when they seized opportunities, which came to them usually through their intimate relationships but which they rarely sought out. When these women did sell drugs, some continued to engage in their specialized offense; others temporarily desisted because they reasoned that "the money coming in was good enough, I didn't have to 'trick' (for some) or 'boost' (said by others)." Francine, a shoplifter by specialization, sold drugs exclusively for a period of months. When that enterprise was interrupted, when she no longer had access to this crime, she returned to what she had depended on in the past—shoplifting:

I met a guy, and he was a big time dealer, bigger than I knew; they called him the Godfather. He took a liking to me and of course I took one to him; he had the money and the drugs and he and I hung out. We hung out until we got intimate and naturally he started taking care of me and he sold heroin and I was selling it with him. . . . I had stopped the stealing. I wasn't stealing at all. I had stopped. . . . The police came to the house, and we had like crack and the heroin and money and a gun on the dresser, all right; he had a record and plus he was wanted. I never been to jail or nothing, the honorable thing for your woman to do is take the case and that's what I did. When it came time for me to go to court they was talking about giving me two years so I went on the run. Now, in between during the time I was on my run, he eventually went to jail and that left me defenseless. This is when I started stealing again.

Shirelle sold drugs too for a period of months for her lesbian partner, but incorporated this with her employment as a dancer and stripper at a go-go bar and with her sex work there. After she moved her sex work exclusively to the street, she sought out an opportunity to sell drugs for a group of men who rented an apartment on the floor above hers and again integrated that crime into her specialization. In this narrative, Shirelle describes her first involvement in selling drugs and her reasoning for incorporating it into her existing work.

The girl I was seeing was selling crack for this guy. She would go to the bars and she was selling it to the dancers. They didn't want her in the bar because she was a woman. It was bad for business to have dykes in the bar. And then she asked me to take the drugs in there. The first time I slept with a guy for money was at the bar [a strip club or go-go bar]. This guy offered me money, and I thought he was joking. He said to me, "Hey, I want that." I said, "You ain't got the money to pay for it." I said, "A hundred and fifty dollars." He said, "Here, I'm gonna give you the hundred now and I'll give you fifty when we get out there." He put a hundred dollars in my hand. I wasn't gonna pass that money up. We went to his car, and it was over in like five minutes. Five minutes I had a hundred and fifty bucks. That's when I started dating, which is trickin'. You're in a bar and a guy says, "Can I get a shot of that?" And they offer you like fifty dollars, you go right up the street to the room, ten minutes it's over and you got fifty dollars in your pocket. . . . And it worked out pretty good. I could sell the drugs and I could still work and still get paid off the drugs and still get paid off my dancing and trickin'. I was in love with it.

Shoplifting and sex work are not accidental choices for financing addiction; they are specializations conditioned in many ways by class position and neighborhood culture, early life experiences, opportunity, and personal as well as neighborhood resources. Furthermore, while the women in this study had little or no control over conditions and traumas they experienced, especially early in life, they did make choices to improve their lives, although bounded by situational and structural forces and the limits and opportunities of their particular situations. This book positions women neither as passive agents made powerless by victimization and oppressive forces nor as unrestricted actors who create criminal opportunities to benefit themselves. Rather, it takes a middle-ground approach. While profoundly affected by life experiences and limited by drug abuse and criminal options open to them, the women in this study are adaptable in their criminal behaviors; they manipulate resources available to them and create strategies for crime to be most profitable, manageable, dependable, and enduring. They are constrained, yet they are agents in their own survival.

The Literature

A very important point to note is that the shoplifters in this study are among a special class of known shoplifters. The women in my study who shoplift are different from most shoplifters; they can be categorized as "professionals." The term "professional" connotes a level of expertise, distinguished skills, and commitment, which is sometimes the case, but the term itself is a label used in the shoplifting literature to identify shoplifters who are engaged in the crime chiefly as a way of earning income.

Although limited in scope and methodology and using selective samples, much of the sociological research on shoplifting has endeavored to distinguish among shoplifters, particularly in terms of their motivations. The idea of devising typologies or classification schemes originated with Mary Owen Cameron's groundbreaking 1964 study of apprehended department store shoplifters in Chicago.[29] Cameron identified shoplifters as "boosters" or "snitches." Boosters shoplift for economic gain, are involved in other illicit behaviors (for instance drug abuse and prostitution), and associate with criminal subcultures. These professionals made up about 10 percent of the shoplifters in her study. The 90 percent, termed "snitches" or "pilferers," shoplift items of little value for personal use and consumption, are unaffected by poverty or mental illness, and are not committed to criminal values or criminal subcultures. The booster or "commercial shoplifter" is the professional shoplifter who steals as a means of economic gain. Boosters use their connections with criminal subcultures to sell merchandise they shoplift in an underground economy. Boosters can be "heels" or "ordinary boosters." Heels are the most professional of all shoplifters because their criminal behavior is limited to shoplifting, while ordinary boosters are involved in other forms of crime and deviance.

Contemporary research on shoplifters including my own has supported much of Cameron's findings and extended this line of scholarship with new and refined typologies.[30] Moore's 1984 typology is the most comprehensive and detailed. From research on three hundred convicted adult shoplifters, Moore identified five distinct groups of shoplifters using criminal justice data and interviews: the "amateur" shoplifter (56 percent of Moore's sample), the "semi-professional" shoplifter (12 percent), the "occasional" shoplifter (15 percent), the "impulse" shoplifter (15 percent), and the "episodic" shoplifter (2 percent). Moore distinguished these groups by their frequency of shoplifting, use of stolen merchandise, motivation, and attitude. Amateur shoplifters steal frequently, often on a weekly basis, and when they perceive an opportunity to shoplift (for example, when merchandise is not guarded or the risk of detection seems minimal). They are not professionals, however, since they fail to form a lifestyle around theft, use more simplistic tools than professionals, and steal goods for personal use. For semi-professional shoplifters, shoplifting is a normal part of life. Opportunity inside the retail store setting (such as limited surveillance) determines whether semi-professionals will actually shoplift. Unlike amateurs, these shoplifters use more sophisticated technologies to help them shoplift (see the following paragraph for examples), may plan shoplifting excursions, and do not see shoplifting as morally wrong. The merchandise semi-professionals acquire is often sold; the motivation to liquidate stolen goods and the commitment to theft as a way of life suggest that the semi-professional is most like Cameron's booster and therefore most characteristic of the professional thief. The occasional shoplifter steals less frequently than the amateur and semi-professional and pursues shoplifting mainly for peer approval, excitement, and thrill. Occasional shoplifters usually target merchandise of little or no value, which they will most likely consume themselves. The impulse shoplifter does not plan thefts but reacts to temptations within the retail store setting. He or she has very little experience with shoplifting, is often arrested on the first or second attempt, and usually expresses guilt, embarrassment, and remorse when arrested. Finally, the episodic shoplifter steals periodically due to severe psychological illness.

The simplest way to distinguish among people who shoplift is to organize them as either professional or nonprofessional (also termed "amateur") shoplifters. Most shoplifters (upward of 90 percent) are nonprofessionals (or amateurs) who are normally committed to conventional lifestyles and shoplift for various reasons that are always unrelated to earning incomes—during a tempting opportunity, for thrill or excitement, to provide material goods for themselves or others—but rarely because they are kleptomaniacs. In a previous study of shoplifters, for example, I found that most shoplifters were nonprofessionals or amateurs who generally do not plan their crimes but who act with some level of rationality, steal for their own consumption or to give away merchandise to others, and are infrequently involved in shoplifting and other crimes.[31] Nonprofessionals often rely on simplistic methods to steal (such as concealing merchandise in their clothing), their planning of theft is limited, and they consume or give away merchandise they shoplift. However, they can also be quite skilled and efficient, planning shoplifting events and stealing frequently, cycling in and out of the crime—characteristics of an adept shoplifter. The most important point about nonprofessionals and the way to distinguish them from professionals is by their lack of commitment to financial earnings through the crime.

Professionals are motivated foremost by economic gain. They may take "orders" and then carefully plan the shoplifting events (the place, time, and target) or steal marketable items in large quantities and then return or resell the merchandise for profit to friends, acquaintances, and others. Professionals usually work alone, but not always.[32] When shoplifting, they may use simple tools to carry away merchandise (their clothing and shopping bags, for example), or they may use sophisticated technologies such as "booster boxes" or "tag bags." A term coined by Cameron (1964), the "booster box" is a cardboard box used for packaging and mailing that allows the shoplifter to conceal merchandise through a false side or bottom. Tag bags (also called sensor bags) are similar to booster boxes, but may also be shopping bags provided by stores (such as Gap), filled with materials (such as polyurethane foam and aluminum) that incapacitate the electronic detection devices at store entrances and exits.[33] Some professionals make shoplifting their occupation, while others use the crime to supplement their earnings. Professionals are also typically involved in other criminal and deviant behaviors (such as credit card fraud and drug use). Professionals make up a small proportion (about 10 percent) of all shoplifters.

The drug-addicted shoplifter has not been a focus of the extant literature. When fitted into a typology, shoplifters who are drug-addicted are usually considered nonprofessional, as there is a certain level of rationality implied of professional shoplifters (they are free of conditions within themselves or in their lives that affect their ability to make informed choices about shoplifting). However, I have pointed out in my own prior research that drug- and alcohol-addicted shoplifters engage in this crime for economic gain or sustenance. Thus, in their drive to use the crime to provide earnings and sustenance, drug-addicted shoplifters are professionals, but their lives are different from what one might expect of a professional thief. In this study, the women who are shoplifting specialists are drug-addicted professionals whose rationality is bounded foremost by their drug addiction and then by other conditions in their lives. My objective is to expand on the current literature by looking closely at these drug-addicted, professional shoplifters.

There is an extensive but somewhat less complicated literature relevant to the women in this study who choose to specialize in sex work rather than shoplifting. In their drive to earn money through crime, these women who use sex work to earn a living share the motivation of most other sex workers, particularly street-level sex workers who are drug-addicted. While some women may be enticed by the nature of the work itself, the large body of literature on prostitution and sex work has established that the primary motivator for sex-work involvement is to earn money to survive.[34]

Analytic Method

My research method and analysis in this book are guided by critical criminological traditions, most notably feminist inquiry that takes an intersectional approach to subject matter and is somewhat akin to the grounded theory method.[35] This book does not endeavor to test any theoretical explanation for why or how women engage in crime, nor does it propose a new theoretical model. Rather, it seeks to expand on our understanding of female criminality in general and, more importantly, to develop new conceptual knowledge of how female offenders behave and how they are diverse among themselves—how shoplifters and sex workers are similar and different before and during criminal involvement.

The key to both method and analysis is to let the women speak, to listen carefully and to communicate for them their thoughts and lived experiences; women are experts on their own lives and I, the researcher, tell their stories with scientific criminological analysis. To this end, more than one hundred hours of open-ended life history interviews yielded more than two thousand pages of transcripts. Most of the interviews were quite lengthy, some more than four hours long, and most of the women were interviewed two or more times. I proceeded with a general outline of questions to ask for the various topic areas under study and let the women's explanations guide my inquiry into new themes that unfolded. These data were gathered and analyzed systematically and simultaneously. Coding of the interviews once transcribed into written form followed constant analysis and comparison, concentrating on important themes voiced by the women. These themes include pathways and turning points to crime; ability to make a specialization work within a mix of environmental and personal constraints; management of crime itself, including risk; and self-perceptions, future prospects, and reflections on how others might avoid criminal careers.

Interweaving the meanings that women assign to themselves, their lives, and their behaviors using the narratives of their spoken words with my analysis brings forth this new understanding of female offenders and their criminality. This interweaving necessitates a critical eye to the forces underlying the women's important experiences, as voiced directly by them, that have structured their lives. From the feminist and critical criminological traditions, these forces—termed "social status arrangements" or structures (labels that distinguish or discriminate)—including gender, class, and race, operate in a mix: They intersect to influence the lives of women offenders and their nonoffending counterparts in most every way. Just as addiction affects women's lives, gender, economic, and social arrangements shape choices about crime and specialization in shoplifting or sex work. The ways in which women experience the world are generated from these interwoven forces and provide the foundation for analysis throughout this book.

Gender is a critical component to my analysis. As a group, the women in this study share the social status as female, a socially derived definition affecting life in every way, beginning in childhood socialization and carrying through the life course. Gender lends insight into traumatic life experiences a girl or woman may encounter, how she may cope, and how she makes difficult decisions. Gender also helps to explain limits and opportunities for her involvement in crime, for example. Through established patterns of inequity, gender produces sexism manifested in so many ways for offending and non-offending women alike. For the women in this study, sexism unfolds in traumatic abuses they suffered in childhood and limits options open to them for earning money through crime. While essential for documenting ways in which men and women differ in how they view themselves and experience the world, including crime, a strict gender analysis would tell only part of the story here. It would say nothing about how female offenders are different from one another: for example, why some drug-addicted female offenders attribute their onset of drug use and crime to serious and chronic abuses in their youth and others do not, or why some women shoplift and others do not, even when similarly situated as drug addicts.

A deeper, more meaningful understanding of female criminality requires a multifaceted approach, including into analysis other factors that can expose differences among criminal offenders. Beyond gender, these status or structural factors can include race, marriage, sexual identity, and mental illness, for example. Drug addiction is a status factor that all of the women in this study share and to which they attribute their criminality. While my work incorporates the etiology of substance abuse, I do not give special attention to the character of their addiction, the drugs they chose, or consequences of drug abuse beyond criminal involvement. Especially important to analysis is class structure and the social, cultural, and economic arrangements of neighborhoods (such as the presence of an urban drug culture), which act upon individuals and communities and which condition life therein, including crime. My work acknowledges that just as women are agents and products of change, so are families and neighborhoods. For example, broad changes in society over time (such as decline of industrial and manufacturing employment, decline of human, social, and economic capital, development of concentrated poverty areas mostly occupied by racial minorities) affect neighborhood milieus in once-thriving industrial cities such as Philadelphia and Camden, New Jersey and in turn these neighborhoods affect quality of life and criminality. Socioeconomic class (which usually determines one's social location) and neighborhood milieu are critical factors in pathways to and involvement in shoplifting and sex work and represent a central analytic focus in this book.

My methods are also informed by the sociological study of work and occupations, positioning women as workers in crime.[36] Forty years ago, Polsky commented on the benefit of this approach.[37]

> *Criminologists stand to lose little and gain much in the way of sociological understanding if, when studying people dedicated to an illegal occupation, they will overcome their fascination with the "illegal" part long enough to focus on the "occupational" part. After all, any theory of illegal occupations can be but a special case, albeit an important one, of general occupational theory.*

The tradition of research in the sociology of deviance positions crime as work, as occupational and professional, drawing parallels between conventional occupations and criminal work on subjects like vocational entry, skill, and risk management. Taking such an approach, positioning criminal offenders as workers rather than as outsiders affords a fuller, more complete understanding of crime and its participants. Failing to authenticate shoplifters and sex workers as occupationalists only serves to diminish them and further stigmatize them as different, controlled, and entrapped, which only discredits their identity. Informed by this tradition, I listened closely to how shoplifters and sex workers carry out their business of crime, including technical aspects and organizational management as well as interacting structural forces, to convey what they have to say about shoplifting as work and sex work as an occupation.

Overview

Chapters 2 and 3 contribute to the existing body of literature on early life experiences and coming of age in criminally involved women. Shoplifters have never been a focused subject of criminal pathway research; thus, findings in this book on pathways to the crime are new, as are the comparisons of shoplifters to sex workers. In these two chapters, I seek to point out how the women in this study are both similar and different in their early life experiences before crime by comparing and contrasting lives of shoplifters and sex workers.

Chapter 4 focuses on crime specialization among the women. From the viewpoint of women in this study, shoplifting and sex work offer viable means of generating income to provide for life's necessities and to support drug addiction. However, not all women follow the same path. Some gravitate toward sex work, perhaps seduced by the pull so strong in their neighborhoods; others exploit broader networks to shoplift in lucrative arenas outside of their neighborhoods. I provide analysis of ways in which the women make their specialization work for them within the context of socioeconomic class and neighborhood character, particularly how the neighborhood drug culture limits women and provides them opportunities and mechanisms to finance their drug addictions through shoplifting and sex work. While caught up in structural constraints, the women exert their own agency to manage the business of their crimes.

Chapter 5 addresses risk management in shoplifting and sex work. Positioning crime as work, I explore how the women specialized at shoplifting and those at sex work perceive the dangers inherent in their crimes and how they negotiate their offenses and their involvement with the law, psychologically and behaviorally, to overcome fear, to reduce risks, and to maintain business. While shoplifters have to work harder to make their specialization work for them, they are not at risk for violent victimization, as are sex workers, but face stiffer penalties when apprehended.

Chapter 6 summarizes findings, with an emphasis on contributions to the field and to policy. One of the unanswered questions in criminology concerns differences in offending patterns among women, often similarly situated in addiction. This study reveals the effects of personal experiences and structural forces, including social class background and neighborhood milieu, early life trauma, and decisions made in adolescence in shaping crime specialization among addicted women. My research on specialization demonstrates that urban drug cultures sustain both shoplifting and sex work and that shoplifting is a viable and reliable source of income for addicted women, as is sex work, correcting the overly sexualized portrayal of women's income-producing criminal activities. Even though women in the sample are among the most disadvantaged in their cities and in this country, my research on managing criminal careers reveals that these women are actively involved in shaping their lives, avoiding dangers, and maximizing their benefits, which include a reliable source of drugs. Finally, crime is work. Women in my study survived their troubled pasts and drug addiction and they have lived through crime, but for them, crime is an occupational choice embodying work ethic, habit, skill, and other marks of occupations both deviant and conventional.

2. *Early Life Trauma*

I was born and raised in an abusive, bad alcoholic family. My father was really bad alcoholic, my mom's a bad battered wife. He didn't like smack my mom, right, he beat her, literally. There was always liquor around, and I started just drinking as a kid. I was physically and sexually abused from age six until I was twelve. . . . We was always afraid. A lot of times we ran from my father so we spent a lot of time living in motels and living in the car, just everything to run away from, you know. I went to a lot of different schools. . . . By the time I was thirteen I thought I was grown already, I would drink and smoke weed. I started hanging around with people from Camden, trying to impress other people, I guess for attention. I had like a facade on. I acted like a bully; I did a lot of fighting just so people wouldn't pick on me. When I was nineteen I started doing heroin . . . shoplifting to support the habit and everything else. . . . I've tried to commit suicide three times. I'm on a lot of medication now. My self-esteem comes from a little blue bag, from heroin. —Sandy

The sentiment expressed by Sandy in the preceding quote captures the retrospective appraisals of most women in this study: Childhood trauma occurring within the home resonates as the first important part of women's journeys to drugs and crime. These traumas include emotional maltreatment, substance abuse socialization by caretakers very early in life, and witnessing domestic violence. While life in a substance-abusing home can be dangerous, accounts by the women suggest some caretakers were also directly malignant. Revealed in the stories of their childhoods, chronic abuses included not only physical and sexual abuse—the most visible, intrusive forms of traumas noted in the literature—but also the invisible suffering of emotional abuse, neglect, and abandonment. While the types of abuse they suffered as girls may have differed among the women (strangulation by their mothers or rape by their fathers, for example), the essential nature of the abuse was the same: continued infliction of power, dominance, degradation, and dehumanization. This triggered a wave of negative reactions, a misdirected coming of age during the women's adolescence that would carry through life. They would embrace their caretakers' addictions, relying on early drinking and early drug use habits as a means to escape troubles, employing other destructive coping mechanisms, and engaging in crime to survive.

As their childhood stories unfolded, it became quite clear that early life trauma is overwhelmingly present among sex workers and women who described home lives that classified them as growing up urban poor. These women, who reported such early life traumas and underprivileged childhoods, are primarily African American. For the most part, women specialized in shoplifting were raised in working- or middle-class areas and they experienced much less early life trauma than those specializing in sex work (especially shoplifters who never prostituted before settling into their shoplifting specialization). As a group, the women in this study tag home experiences when they were girls as events and conditions that would eventually define them, though it seems that those who specialize in shoplifting tend to view themselves as somewhat less shaped by childhood experiences than by things that happened to them as adults. In this chapter, I seek to point out the similarities in early childhood and adolescent experiences among women who turned to crime as a way of life, but more importantly, I want to convey the differences in these experiences between those who chose to specialize in sex work and those who chose shoplifting as their primary criminal behavior.

Note that in the material given in these women's voices, any questions inserted in italics within square brackets are my own, as part of the interview conversations.

Inside and Out, the Underprivileged and Sex Workers Suffer Most

While most of the women in this study spent their childhoods in poor urban environments, it became clear when listening to their experiences and to those of others who grew up in working- or middle-class areas that social class and neighborhood milieu played a critical role in their childhood experiences and pathways to crime. "Social class" is that economic position and social location in which the women characterize themselves as being raised—as urban poor, for example, in tenement buildings or housing projects; in row homes or apartment buildings as lower middle class or working class; or as middle class, usually in single-family homes outside of the urban center of Philadelphia and Camden, New Jersey. "Neighborhood milieu" refers to the cultural feel of an area, the normative social interactions, expectations, and arrangements among its inhabitants and businesses alike. A drug-infested, violent, and disordered urban neighborhood is different from a middle-class suburban neighborhood in many ways. In the middle-class area, for example, residents, including children, have more sustained interactions with the broader conventional society, while others differentially situated in the lower- or working-class environments experience a separate world, one more isolated from conventional society and its behavioral norms.

Women raised as part of the urban poor suffered disproportionately not only inside their homes, but outside; violence, disorder, and drugs were normal features of the childhood social worlds of women raised poor. The women raised poor are overwhelmingly members of racial minorities (88 percent) and sex workers (85 percent). The women who turned to sex work as a crime specialization tend to recall the most violent and disordered childhood surroundings—neighborhoods in North and Southwest Philadelphia and Camden, postindustrial centers destroyed by the closing of factories and disappearance of manufacturing jobs, by the flight of working-class and White residents, and by severe economic and urban decline. Camden is a striking example of urban blight[1] marred with poverty and crime. While New Jersey boasts a high median household income ($61,672) that is consistently higher than the United States median income ($46,242), the median income in Camden is among the lowest in the nation ($18,000). In Camden City, 44 percent of families (and 58 percent of children) lived in poverty during 2005, compared to 8.7 percent of all New Jersey residents and 13 percent of Americans.[2] With a 2005 crime rate of 75.2 per 1,000 residents, Camden is also a dangerous place. In this small city of about 80,000 residents living in nine square miles there were 34 murders, 47 rapes, 704 robberies, 901 aggravated assaults, and 2,297 instances of domestic violence known to the police in 2005. Twenty-one in every 1,000 people in Camden were victims of murder, rape, aggravated assault, or robbery. Compare this to a statewide violent crime victimization rate of 3.6 per 1,000 New Jersey residents. The nonviolent crime rate over that year was 54.2 per 1,000 residents compared to a statewide rate of 23.4 per 1,000 residents.[3] This means that an estimated 54 people out of every 1,000 in Camden were victims of property crimes, such as burglary and motor vehicle theft, but across the state of New Jersey, just 23 people out of every 1,000 were victims of property crimes.

The crime rates in the city of Philadelphia are lower than in Camden, but high compared to the United States as a whole. According to Uniform Crime Reports statistics, there were 22,883 violent crimes, including 406 murders and 62,616 property crimes reported to the police in the city of Philadelphia during 2006. An estimated 15 out of every 1,000 people were victims of a violent crime and 42 were victims of a property crime. Across the United States, the violent crime rate in 2006 was 4.7 per 1,000 people and the property crime rate was 33 per 1,000 about 5 people in every 1,000 were victims of a violent crime and 33 in every 1,000 were victims of a property crime.[4]

Ronni, a woman who relies on sex work to support herself financially and shoplifts for food, occasionally remembers life in late 1960s North Philadelphia, once White and working class but now predominately poor and minority:

I grew up in the heart of North Philly, between 19th and Diamond and 19th and Fontaine, but I was not allowed to play outside. I do remember during that time, that there were a lot of gang war days there, a lot of street fights. I do remember one time there was a whole gang of guys on this side, and another whole gang was coming this way and I remember my grandmother coming outside, saying, "Get in the house, get in the house." . . . So, every time we went out we used to sit down on the step.

Prathia, also a sex worker and occasional shoplifter, was afraid as a child in her North Philadelphia neighborhood of row homes, Kensington, during the 1960s. Known as the "Badlands," parts of this neighborhood are still in ruin, crime- and drug-ridden: "I came from Kensington. Drugs were real prevalent in my neighborhood. Houses be falling apart and burnt down and people walking around looking rough. They were rough around the edges. You know, it was scary. To me it was scary and I didn't want to stay there."

Edwina, also a sex worker, lived most of her childhood in Southwest Philadelphia in a neighborhood today referred to as University City but then known as "Black Bottom"—a reference to the racial and class status of residents living there. Gang wars were common in that part of the city during the late 1960s and 1970s. Children had good reason to fear for their safety.

It was gang warrin', a lot of rapes goin' on. . . . The children would go get hurt as they be playing, we go in these little parking lots and get hurt . . . in the abandoned houses where they found a couple bodies in there. . . .I was just walkin' down the street one night on to my grandmom's and out of nowhere this guy come runnin' up behind me and hit me in my head with a brick. For nothin', for not reason at all. I was just walkin' down the street.

Inside their homes and outside in their neighborhoods, women of the urban poor were socialized into a drug culture early in life. In their neighborhoods drug selling and drug use were so commonplace, the women remember, even conventional businesses joined this illicit economy. Lauren recalls a deli near her home in Kensington: "A couple blocks away, there's a deli where they sold drugs but my block. [*So it was a drug area?*] All areas are drug areas as I was growing up."

This neighborhood exposure coupled with familial socialization into alcohol and drug use no doubt facilitated their own early substance use among the women when they were girls and enabled them to acquire drugs in their own neighborhoods. Renita remembers a candy store where children in her elementary school would buy candy and drugs before school in the 1980s. At that deli in Fairmount (North Philadelphia), marijuana sold for three dollars, a good price then:

There was this candy store . . . and they sold weed at this store. He was selling three-dollar bags, that was good back then. . . . A lot of people at school knew about that place, everybody went there in the morning. That store, he used to make sure his store was open just before school time, and it be crowded, kids getting candy and weed. He made his money.

Shirelle recalls drugs as ever-present in the North and South Philadelphia ghettos where she lived as a child in the 1970s and 1980s, knowledge she would rely upon as an adolescent and adult when in search of these drugs:

Every neighborhood that I lived in there were drugs and I knew where they were at. Crack, powder, and weed. You know and all the other stuff, the purple haze and all that crazy crack to powder, I mean the syrup . . . I would see bottles all on the street.

When they were girls, the women who grew up urban poor and their families tended to move residences frequently. Nikki moved with her family at least twelve times during her childhood and adolescence. They sought safety:

We moved to North Philly, back where it was all tore up and stuff like that. One day, when we came home, somebody had broke into the apartment. So, my mom just packed all our stuff up and we moved to my aunt's [who's] got eleven kids in a three-bedroom house. . . . Then my mom finally found an apartment around the corner so we moved in there. . . . We stayed about two months. There was a lot of rats, rats like this, tails this long. We used to come downstairs sometimes in the morning and you see two or three big rats on the floor. . . . Then, we moved into a house, but in the wintertime it was cold so we stayed there about two months. . . . Then we moved back down North Philly, but the people around here, they was goin' crazy around here. They were bustin' people's windows out and stuff. . . . Then we moved 'cause the ceiling in that house had fell in the back then, it got cold and the pipes bust. Water was runnin' everywhere so my mom had to move again. That's when we went to the [housing] projects.

Limited by their economic and social class positions, the women and their families never escaped these neighborhood problems as they moved within the poorest urban areas, not away from them. Edwina describes this instability as a child moving within and across neighborhoods in Southwest Philadelphia and Camden.

Like every six months we'd move to different houses, different neighborhoods, ya know, things happening in the neighborhood between my family and other families. But those problems was still there wherever we was. . . . Once, my stupid-ass father shot somebody and killed them and their family wanted to deck our family.

Women from other environments remember stable childhoods without fear of the outside world. Rose, a shoplifter raised in Northeast Philadelphia ("the Northeast"), remembers a peaceful childhood, as did most others who were raised middle class in safer areas such as Cherry Hill, New Jersey, and the Philadelphia suburbs. "I grew up in upper-middle-class neighborhood. It was nice and my parents spent a lot of time with us; we had a nice home, we were always vacationing, we were always going places."

All but two of the twenty-six women raised poor (92 percent) said their abuse early in life was the trigger to their addicted and criminally active lives, compared to 67 percent of working- or middle-class-raised women. Furthermore, all but one woman who attribute addiction and criminality to adult experiences (rather then early life experiences) are shoplifters. For the small group of women in my research with unremarkable and stable childhoods, victimization by intimate partners in adulthood and other trauma trigged drug addiction leading to crime. Veronica's comments illustrate this point:

I can't speak for other women but myself; my childhood wasn't bad at all. I had a very good childhood and a very good life, a sheltered life. My mother works for the Philadelphia school board, my dad works for the city. They sent me to school; I graduated from Wesley College in Dover, Delaware. I went to St. Joe's College for organic chemistry. Yes, ma'am, it was not my background at all. It has nothing to do with it. I chose to do drugs at the age of thirty-five. I did it on my own because I was introduced to it by friends, so only thing I can say I had a poor choice of friends I turned to when the abuse that I had with my husband. I waited so late to be a bride, I was a virgin until I was twenty-six when we married. We stayed together nine months. Nine months, that's all, it was nine months of agony. I was very abused. During that time, I had a hysterectomy; he crushed my pelvis. . . . He had these steel-toed shoes and right in front of a Beverly police officer, he kicked me, and then after I went to the hospital; I had to stay 30 days. . . . I had a best friend that I considered my best friend and we started snorting cocaine and then I started, then she introduced me to the smoking of crack cocaine. . . . I was working at the time, I worked at the hospital for fourteen years. When he left, I had to pay all of the rent. Because I was dressed fairly decent and wanted to keep this image I could no longer afford, I started stealing, and that's where it began.

Rose experimented with marijuana and after high school occasionally used methamphetamine "really for energy 'cause you know you could be like super mom, you could have the house cleaned and dinner and take the kids out all day and do, do, do all day long." But she claims she was not a regular user and maintained steady employment. It was not until the death of her lover when she was thirty-six that she began to abuse drugs, first prescription pain relievers, then crack. She turned to drugs as a means to cope not with abuse, but with loss.

Well, what really put me into heroin was, well that's only been for like three years I've been doing it because I was with my boyfriend for eleven years and then he had gotten cancer and then he was in remission and he had gotten it back and it was pretty much throughout his body. I was doing his prescription OxyContin into my hand. I just had my Vicodin for my back because I waitressed so you know but I starting to do a little more than I should. It was like watching your best friend slowly die in front of you, ya know; I was trying to kill my own pain. I was with him for like eleven years and watching him go from three hundred pounds to like a hundred and eighty pounds, losing his hair, I mean just the whole thing, and then he passed away and then that's when I really started going into heroin. We had all our friends and then when he passed away, I didn't really see a lot of people because, well we hung out as a couple and now it was just me. I hadn't seen like all my friends that I had grew up, but I was still in contact with my best friend. She was a heroin addict. . . . My kids were teenagers and they were in school and working. You know, teenagers at that age, they're in their own thing, their own friends. A lot of it was boredom too. The kids weren't around, they didn't need me because they were off doing their own thing.

Nannie, also a shoplifter but raised in a poor environment in North Philadelphia, remembers a good childhood, a stable growing up.

I had a wonderful childhood. I can look back and say there was a lot of love and it was like every day. I had fun, I had Christmas, I had bikes, I had skates, I had ropes, and I was jumping ropes and I had jacks to play with. A lot of things to keep me occupied as what a child should have at the time. I used to play soccer and tennis. . . . My mother she wasn't on drugs at all. She don't smoke, she don't do anything. I had support all the time from my mom. . . . But as you get older different things occur.

Like Veronica and Rose, Nannie's path to criminality was a result not of early life abuse, but of traumatic events in adulthood. In this regard, she is one of the exceptions among other women in my study who were raised poor. A mix of stressors occurring later in life (late adolescence and early adulthood) that compounded one another led her to drugs and crime:

I had to take care of my grandparents because my mom was at work doing a lot of overtime. I was also working at the University of Pennsylvania doing dietary work. I had to change my shift to part-time because I wanted to be there all day to wash my grandparents and feed them, but it didn't matter because I loved my grandparents. I had to watch my brothers and sisters too. . . . I could never like really take care of myself the way I wanted. I might have got what I wanted but that wasn't the point, the point was that I never got no sleep; I was stressed and depressed a lot. . . . Hospitals always cut back, so when they did cut back, I was the first one laid off, but when they called me back, I had broke my wrist during a fall. I couldn't take care of my grandparents. Then I started running away from the problems and I kept going out, and then I started going around my friends and they was doing drugs, cocaine and marijuana. I started smoking blunts [marijuana and crack], I thought it was relieving my stress and depression and the pain from my body, but I knew that the pain would still be there but not as much. So I'd smoke constantly every day; it started controlling me. That's when I started shoplifting because I wanted to make more money because my unemployment wasn't enough for what I was making at my job. I was missing that money, and I was also missing the career that I had.

Another exception among those women raised in a poor urban environment is Candee, a forty-three-year-old African American woman raised in Philadelphia. Married to a minister, Candee remembers abuse in adulthood and a nervous breakdown, followed by her loss of two unborn children as the triggers for her addiction and consequently her shoplifting.

I was twenty years old when I got married. I was married to a Muslim minister, twenty-five years older, who supplied my habit. He supplied my habit and he also supplied me my pills too. In Muslim, the husband is allowed to have four or five wives and stuff like that; he had girlfriends. But he mentally and physically abused me. He used to put guns to my head, telling me he was going to kill me. I cover my head around everybody. I wore a scarf everywhere I went. Because that's what he wanted me to do and I did it. I was afraid of him, when I tried to leave him, I stayed out all night. He said, "I'm gonna kill or shoot you, then I'ma shoot myself." I got on my knees and kept beggin' him not to kill me 'cause I think he was serious about shooting me. What he did was he smacked me in my face and told me I could go head out. I left and I went to a hotel. He found me. My friends set him up and he sold to an undercover cop and he went to jail. That's how they got him.

I started using drugs after my son died in 1984. I miscarried him about eight months, I had a nervous breakdown and I got into a severe depression; I had suicidal thoughts. He [husband] put me on some Xanax, and he told me I should smoke [crack]. The first hit I took I thought you smoke this like you smoke a joint, so I took one hit and I passed out, I just remember hitting the floor and I passed out. I was told when I woke up that my heart had stopped and they had me laying on the bed with nothing but water around me; I was told my heart had stopped. I think I stopped for about two or three months. . . . I had five seizures in one day before I lost my daughter. She lived for a couple of days, but I dropped into a coma after that and I never got a chance to see her alive.

Among the women raised poor, the disordered and violent environments surrounding their homes mirrored in many ways what they experienced inside their homes as girls. Seventy-seven percent report a history of physical abuse, 69 percent said they suffered emotional abuse, 50 percent said they were neglected or abandoned by caretakers, and 50 percent were victims of incest. Conversely, only 25 percent of the women from working- or middle-class areas were physically abused, 33 percent were emotionally abused, just one was a victim of incest, and none were neglected or abandoned by caretakers; just one (Estelle) transitioned to new guardians at a young age but for reasons other than neglect or abandonment. As previously discussed, compared to shoplifters in my sample, sex workers were more often products of poor urban environments and more often victims of abuse. Early life trauma still affected shoplifters, but to a lesser extent, with 58 percent (seven of the twelve shoplifting women) recalling early life trauma as their initial pathway to drugs and crime (as opposed to twenty-five of the twenty-six sex workers, or 96 percent of sex workers). Further distinguishing between women who have ever sold sex clearly shows that child victimization interacting with social and economic class is a risk factor for sex work. Among women ever involved in sex work (including four current shoplifters), 80 percent were raised in the poorest environments and 93 percent suffered a direct abuse (physical, emotional, sexual, neglect/abandonment). Comparatively, 25 percent of women never involved in sex work were raised in poor environments and 25 percent were abused directly.

They Drank, So I Drank

A substance-abusing, violent, and negligent family system laid the foundation for multiple traumas women in my study would experience as girls. A common experience among them was early exposure to alcohol. All but three women (92 percent) in my study lived in homes with alcohol-abusing caretakers when they were girls. Compare this to 16 percent of American families on average exposed to alcoholism in the home.[5] The three women not exposed to alcohol abuse early in life reveal adult pathways to drugs and crime. Furthermore, among women raised in alcohol-abusing homes, more than half (51 percent) remember parents, guardians, and caretakers abusing other drugs including marijuana, cocaine, crack, and heroin.

It is important to note two important points about exposure to alcohol and other substance abuse in the home early in life. First, socialization into drug and alcohol use and abuse by caretakers played a pivotal role in many of the women's early drinking behaviors. Women raised by alcohol-abusing caretakers and those raised by multiple drug abusers began drinking in the home at similar ages (12.5 years and 11.8 years on average).[6] However, the influence of exposure to multiple drug use is clearly a factor in problematic hard drug use (namely, heroin, cocaine, crack); women raised with alcohol- and drug-abusing caretakers developed hard drug use problems much earlier in life (age 16 on average) compared to women raised by caretakers who abused alcohol and not other drugs (21.7 years on average). Second, exposure to multiple substances is a lower-class phenomenon linked to crime specialization.[7] Ninety-four percent (all but one) of women reporting abuse of multiple substances in the childhood home were raised in the lower socioeconomic class and all have been sex workers; just one shoplifting specialist (who was previously a sex worker) recounts parental use of heroin, crack, cocaine, or other hard drugs in the childhood home.

Precipitating their own alcohol use was not so much their exposure to substance abuse but, more importantly, behavior modeled by parents and caretakers. Alice's recollection illustrates the experience of the women I interviewed. She perceived persistent alcohol use as a normal part of life and began drinking wine and liquor regularly as a child, with her parents' permission. She defines abuse as loss of control, an interpretation repeated throughout the interviews. Alice is a shoplifter; her exposure to alcohol and not drug abuse is one important difference between other shoplifters and sex workers, who were more often exposed to multiple substance abuses.

My dad, he considers himself an alcoholic, but he still drinks, but I mean, he doesn't attack anybody, or, you know, so I guess I don't consider them alcoholics. . . . I started drinking at a young age, like eight or nine 'cause my parents always had alcohol in the house. In the beginning, it was just more so like picking up people's glasses, like my mom or dad, if they had friends come over, if they turn their back, I may pick up their glass and drink out of it. I always drank, and I did get drunk. Maybe just, you know, maybe a glass of wine or liquor or something every day. But they [parents] didn't see it as a problem when I drank.

One of Nikki's after-school tasks was to mix drinks for her mother. Curious, she secretly began to mix herself drinks as she bartended, sensing that this behavior was wrong. Then when Nikki was eleven years old, her mother said the drink was "just a milkshake" and invited her to join in:

My mom, she used to drink sloe gin and milk. . . . When she said go make me one I was making me one but I was making mine and putting it in the corner and I was sippin' it and watchin' them dance. Then after a while, she was like "Come here, it looks like you're makin' yourself one," I was like, "I only had one." She was like, "Go make one [for yourself] and make me one." She said, "It's not liquor; it's like a milkshake." That's what it tasted like to me, a milkshake. When you mix it with milk, it look like strawberry milkshake. . . . So, whenever she be like, "Go in there and make me a drink," when I made her one, I made me one.

As explained earlier, early exposure to both drug and alcohol use is a factor in what specialization the women chose. Shirelle specializes in sex work. She talked of wanting to be like her mother but also sensed that using drugs was not okay for a child. Her mother nonetheless allowed it, redefining right and wrong behavior for her child who, at the tender age of ten, began using marijuana in the home.

She didn't fall down drunk, you know, so I wouldn't consider her to be an alcoholic. She would sit on the phone, smoke her little joints, and it was like, she was poised. You know, and it was like sophistication, that's what I got out of her smoking weed and drinking. 'Cause, she was sophisticated, legs crossed, on the phone, glass of wine in this hand, joint in this hand, song. I thought that was how people were supposed to act. I thought that that was how it was supposed to be, and when I got older, umm, like ten, I started smoking marijuana, and she wasn't mad about it.

Harriet's parents also provided her alcohol as far back in her youth as she can remember, first as a childcare strategy. Then at the age of thirteen her "allowance" came in the form of liquor and drugs. Her exposure to alcohol and drugs by all of her family members preceded her own substance abuse at a very young age, her early criminal behavior, and her entry into sex work in late adolescence.

What led me to prostitute was drugs. What led me into doing drugs was drugs was in my family, all my life. I was given four-ounce bottles of beer at the age of four months so that I didn't know night from day. She had eighteen children, and I was the baby. She had a lot of laundry to do, this, that, and the other. I would sleep all day and be up all night. That was her way of giving me a sedative to put me to sleep so that she could function during the day because she be up all night with me and working all day. And I got an allowance, you know most children in high school got maybe like ten dollars or five dollars allowance. My father would give me a bag of weed and half-pint of corn liquor. My parents was bootleggers, ya know, so drugs was in my life all, ya know, it was there all my life. My brother was a big-time drug dealer, ya know, he used to work for the Black Mafia and, ya know, he used to sell a lot of drugs, he used to keep pounds of weed in the basement. Every Sunday we smoke weed and eat cabbage and I was at the time, I was like twelve, thirteen years old. . . . Most of my brothers and sisters they sold drugs. They sold weed, crack, heroin and all that so that I got into smoking weed and sitting on the step doing hair all day because I braid hair. I would do hair all day, smoke weed, drink Harvey's Bristol Cream [Sherry] and all that. I started selling drugs in school.

Why would the women as girls take part in drinking and drug use at such young ages? Most of them recalled a desire to be a part of their families, even though they were often victims of abuse and neglect by their caretakers. This bonding to alcoholism is one reaction children generally have to alcoholic parents. Another, not apparent among the women in this study, is to separate themselves from the alcoholism, the parent.[8] Take Cheryl, a sex worker whose mother was an abuser of alcohol, crack, and heroin and whose brothers and stepfather abused alcohol, methamphetamines, and heroin. In part, these persistent influences led her to crack addiction before age seventeen (she was also a victim of sexual and physical abuse). Other women exposed to multiple substance abuse in the home began drinking and using drugs at younger ages than women exposed to alcohol abuse alone (and they reported higher rates of sexual, physical, and emotional abuse, neglect, and abandonment). While initially resistant to become involved in alcohol or drugs, Cheryl forced herself to connect to her family that way, something she would later recognize as a misdirected sense of loyalty:

I was raised by drug addicts. . . . My stepfather would do meth. He was a heroin addict, that's how he died. He overdosed in front of me . . . He was speedballing and his heart stopped . . . they were all drinking, my brothers and my mom and it was like her boyfriend was the biggest, like the ringleader of it so it was constantly people getting beer and smoking weed. . . . My mom was also smokin' crack then got into heroin and gradually died. . . . I started drinking as a kid. I would like force myself to drink because everybody else was. . . . And smokin' pot with my mom when I was twelve. I remember the first time my mom offered me a joint, I was like no. But yeah, then I started smokin' weed like every day and then I started doing other stuff. I was sixteen when I smoked crack with her. It took me about a year before I started shootin' up [heroin] with her.

No Safe Haven

Witnessing violence among parents or caretakers was a defining element in the childhoods of the women I interviewed; 71 percent recount witnessing chronic physical partner violence against their mothers and female caretakers perpetrated by fathers, stepfathers, and other men in their lives. While not directly intended to punish them, witnessing abuse no doubt thwarted these women's emotional well-being when they were girls. This violence created anxiety, constant worry, and fear. Tracy, a shoplifter raised in a home with alcoholism, remembers:

There was always arguing and yelling in the house. I remember one time when I was a small child my dad tried to smash my mom in the head with a log. We were always afraid and had to stay out of the way.

The women's stories reveal a linkage between violence in the home among caretakers and crime specialization; 81 percent of sex workers and 50 percent of shoplifters remember such violence as trauma. Loretta, a sex worker, remembers her mother and stepfather were both "bad" alcoholics, creating a dangerous combination together. Living with violence among caretakers deprived her of security and safety.

My mother and stepdad were bad alcoholics. He would fight her, fight, fight, fight, fight. Me and my younger brothers had to get out of the way, but I would always get in the way. I got hit in the head with an ashtray once.

Trying to stay out of the way—under the table, head in the pillow, out on the step—was sometimes not enough. As children, there was nothing for the women to do to end the violence, as Val recalls: "As a child I watched my dad do a lot of bad things to my mother, and when you're a kid you can't help. There's nothing you can do; you can't help."

While socially and economically underprivileged women were most vulnerable to violence among caretakers in their homes as children (81 percent), women from working- and middle-class areas were not immune; one half of the women raised outside of poverty also witnessed domestic violence. While her house was located within a pleasant New Jersey suburb, Kelly's home was chaotic and violent, causing her anxiety and depriving her of peace.

I just remember a lot of chaos going on in the home all the time. Always fighting and me and my brother would sit on the step and listen. . . . I was always worrying about everybody, always worrying about everything. My life was great from the outside. Everything was just perfect on the outside, but I hated my life.

Despite her nonminority and middle-class socioeconomic status, Kelly eventually turned to sex work as a means of supporting her drug habit, but she is an exception. Most women raised outside of urban poor environments in my study who witnessed abuse are shoplifters.

Violence in the home had no limited, situational effect; its effect has carried through the women's lives. It affects Tanisha still today:

When I was young, my father was very abusive to my mother and I watched it, and from the very first time I could remember I was always under the table. As I got older, my uncle did it to his wife, and I used to watch that and I said to myself I would never let that happen and I still carry that with me now. I had watched my father beat up some of his girl-

friends and my grandmother, his mother lived around the corner. When I was younger, I had watched it my whole life, he would kick them and hit them with radios and things like that. I have watched him my whole life up until today, he hasn't changed, and it has took a toll on me.

Estelle also remains troubled by the continued beatings suffered by her aunt, whom she loves deeply.

I was raised by my aunt and uncle. She was just our whole life. He would come home and get to drinking. He would fight her and fight her, for no reason. And um, I was an only child, but I was raised with their son who was four years older than I was. And sometimes we stand up and watch him like bump her head into the ground and stuff like that. I just can't be a happy-go-lucky person because that had an impact on me.

Most of the women growing up in these violent homes were not only witnesses to abuse, but also victimized. Domestic violence extends throughout families, as Cheryl remembers:

[My stepfather] would come home and accuse my mom of cheatin' on him and doing this and that, that she was hiding people in the house like men, and he would beat her up; he would beat us all up, he would beat me and her the most because I guess because I wasn't his kid.

Turtlenecks in Summertime

Physical beatings and confinement were reported by 61 percent of the sample. Sex workers report higher rates of abuse (69 percent) than shoplifters (42 percent). Women economically disadvantaged as girls were more likely to suffer physical abuse (77 percent, compared to 25 percent raised working- or middle-class). Unlike the male-perpetrated domestic violence witnessed by the women in my study, both female and male caretakers committed abuse against children. Sometimes the abuse occurred for no reason, the women explained, but sometimes it was a punishment for misbehavior. This violence and other, co-occurring abuses, especially within alcohol- and substance-abusing homes, forced them to make decisions that led to drug addiction and trouble with the law. Like many others, Shirelle was subjected to corporal punishment, a disciplinary tool used by her adoptive mother. She narrates herself as a victim with agency, who ran away to survive.

I can remember one time when I was nine, she tied me to the chair in the basement, and she beat me with an extension cord. The funny thing about it is the more beatings I got, the more beatings I got. I mean can you understand, all right; I would get in trouble, get a beating, turn around and the next day, get in trouble again and get another beating. You know it was like the more I did the more I got, and I just kept doing more shit. And it was like I just didn't care, I mean I cared to an extent that I knew I was gonna get a beating, but I just didn't care cuz, I couldn't stop just stop myself, I just kept doing it. . . . You know, but as I started getting older, and I'm in high school now, I didn't feel that I should be getting a beating with extension cords, you know, having to go to school with the lies. . . . I was constantly getting beaten and in summertime I would wear long sleeve shirts and turtlenecks to hide the bruises for me being embarrassed and not participating in gym because I had welts all on me. Come on now, that just didn't make sense to me, so I ran away.

By comparison, Alice, a shoplifter from a working-class background, had very strict parents but was never abused by them.

I grew up in Philadelphia in a middle-class neighborhood. We was like one of the only black families. I was raised by both of my parents; they're still married, they've been married for thirty-seven years. I have a brother. I went to Catholic school; I was raised Catholic. I had very, very strict parents, but they never hit us or anything.

Women who suffered childhood physical abuse recall harsh corporal punishment and violent confrontations. Tanisha made the mistake of coming home a little too late one night.

One particular night I said to my mother I wanted to get something to eat. I came in a little late. She told me to go ahead and sit down and eat my dinner. He [father] said I'm going to throw it in your face, and I laughed about it and I went to pick up the fork to eat it and the next thing I knew the plate was broken in my face and hot food all over and I was going in the kitchen and getting a meat cleaver and me and him was going to go at it. I think I was thirteen. . . . Yeah and not too long after that, I tried to commit suicide because I felt that I was hurt, you know.

Was the thought of suicide a strong reaction to this event? Surely, but Tanisha suffered in other ways. She lived in a violent home with a mother who abused crack and a father, a "bad" alcoholic who tortured her mother and who physically and sexually abused Tanisha. Her reaction was a cumulative response to these traumas. At thirteen Tanisha was drinking corn liquor and began freebasing cocaine and smoking marijuana with angel dust. She was "put out" by her father at fourteen. That's when she began to use her only resource to survive—she would trade sex for things she needed.

Skipping school and hiding bruises with long-sleeved shirts or turtlenecks in summertime helped to mask the embarrassment and shame, but only over the short term. Ultimately, escape meant the girls had to leave the home. Francine lived her childhood in the slums of North Philadelphia near the campus of Temple University with an alcoholic father who abused his wife and children. Francine marks chronic physical abuse as the powerful force leading her to leave home.

Now that I'm older I have a lot of wisdom about my father. I guess he tried to teach me lessons [through physical abuse] 'cause he would get sick of me. But what he did was totally wrong; he was a monster. Things that he was doing when I was a child I didn't understand, but I wasn't going to tolerate either. . . . I ran away when I was like thirteen . . . because the school sent a letter saying I hadn't been coming to school and my mother didn't stand up for me, ya know, and tell my father that she told me to stay home to help Pearl with the baby; she didn't say anything. . . . He kept an extension cord and a belt on top of the china closet. So that night I seen him headin' towards that china closet and I seen him with that extension cord coming back so I turned around, I said, "I'm not gonna get beat no more," and he said, "You come back here," and I said, "Hell no," and I ran.

Like many others who ran from abuse, Francine would try living at home from time to time until she left for good as a teen. She worked as a dancer in a go-go bar, a familiar line of work in her neighborhood, at age thirteen and then again at sixteen, once she finally left home for good. Years later Francine exercised her will again, seeking out alternative means to support her addiction. Shoplifting became more profitable and efficient for her than sex work. In her movement away from sex work to shoplifting, she is an exception to most other sex workers.

I Ain't Never Been Shit

While it leaves no physical scars, emotional abuse can be just as harmful to the psyche and spirit as physical abuse. It is more than feeling unloved or deprived of affection and warmth in parent–child relationships, feelings reflected in remarks made by many of the women I interviewed. Intended to harm, emotional abuse comes in many forms, including mistreatment of a child's feelings, self-worth, and emotional needs. Just over half of the women described themselves as having lived with chronic emotional hurt perpetrated by mothers and fathers alike (58 percent). As with other forms of abuse, sex workers were disproportionately victims of emotional abuse (73 percent, compared to 25 percent of shoplifters), as were women raised within the urban poor (69 percent, compared to 33 percent from other environments). Some women remember criticism and rejection they perceived as unfair, while others recall unprovoked ridicule, shame, and humiliation by the caretakers they loved. Many internalized the abuse, defining themselves as shameful, undeserving girls and women, even to the present. When they were girls, all of the emotional abuse victims sought escape through drugs or alcohol. Harriet remembers how she felt disgraced first by her family and then by strangers as a consequence. She, like the majority of the women, was a victim of multiple abuses occurring directly within her home. Here she describes both emotional and physical abuse. Her internalization of abuse is evident in the first words of her story:

I ain't never been shit. . . . My mother nagged me, told me I'm still never gonna amount to nothing, don't be good about your self-esteem attending school. . . . I used to go through this constantly every day. . . . I used to ask when can you feel good about me because I always was trying to be accepted because when I was nine I heard her and my father arguing saying that they never wanted me. Ya know, so I carried that with me my whole life. Ya know, so I tried to be something that they would approve of. It's like I still was never able to be accepted because I was, every time we come home from school, oh the bitches is home, the boys are home, ya know, for a while I thought bitch was my name because that's all I was ever called. They would ridicule me.

They would dress me as a boy, I could never have dresses. I had to wear nothing but jeans, hats, pants, coats, jackets, shirts, shoes, and pocket-

book. Then I used to constantly get into fights to protect myself, and I would come home and she would beat me for fighting to protect myself because they didn't allow us to fight. So see the children knew that so they would pick on me just so I know if I fight, I would fight back, I used to come home with black eyes, beat-up clothes.

When I was in school, it's like for four years they thought my parents were deceased 'cause I told them my parents was deceased; see I didn't get in trouble but I didn't have to prove that until my first suspension. I was in eighth grade. I had to have a parent bring me back and that's when my father and my mother found out, that's when the school board found out that I did have parents because I was too ashamed to want nobody even know that they were my parents, ya know, because things that should not happen to me. Ya know, and getting high was my way of covering up all my pain. Yeah, I still have a lot of pain.

Shay remembers constant ridicule by her mother as a child. Looking back, she makes sense of her reactions:

My mother played a part in it I guess not wanting to hear being put down. Yeah, my mom would tell me that I'm never going to amount to anything, I'm never going to be shit . . . I had to be like nine or ten at this time. Ya know, she did favoritism them [brothers and sisters] a lot, and I didn't feel a part of them at all. I was always told I was never going to amount to anything. . . . I guess I wasn't happy and I had found a few friends and wouldn't come for a few nights at a time. Then it started weeks at a time. School was really going downhill. . . . Well see I really couldn't comprehend it then, but I understand now why I did what I did.

To feel insulated from emotional abuse, many of the women tried to disassociate themselves emotionally from their parents when they were girls and to seek shelter in social networks outside of the home. This would be a decision sending them on a direct path to addiction and, for some, continued victimization.

He Molested Me; She Let Him

Childhood sexual victimization is one of the most striking differences between sex workers and shoplifters. Half of the twenty-six sex workers all from the poorest Philadelphia and Camden neighborhoods were victims of rape in their own homes by male relatives (incest), compared to just one shoplifter (8 percent), who is also the only victim from a middle-class background. Sadly, sexual abuse was chronic and co-occurred with physical and/or emotional abuse. Always perpetrated by men, these experiences conveyed yet another message to the girls that they were unimportant, objects for oppression. Incest caused great harm.

For Harriet, rape by her father and his invited friends was a normal part of her childhood development. Harriet is a sex work specialist, as are all but one of the women who remember experiencing sexual assault as children. She explains the abuse and how her own father "pimped" her:

I was an abused child, my father was raping me, and he used to tell me that his friends would pay me to do deeds [sex acts] for them. I was eleven years old. They used to come in my room and fondle me, ya know, and everything, trying to play with titties that I don't even have. From the age of eleven to sixteen I used to sleep with two or three layers of clothes. I used to sleep in my closet. I used to sleep under my bed because he would come in and I would tell my mom that he was bothering me and he would say "She's dreaming; it's five o'clock in the morning; she's dreaming."

Why did Harriet seek to protect herself by hiding and building an armor of clothing? No one cared. The next logical step to self-protection for her was to escape, to numb her feelings through alcohol and drugs because this is what she learned through her parents' behaviors. She is not alone. This is a common survival strategy. Harriet continues:

I used to cry to my mom, "I need a lock on my door so he don't come in." She would say "You're dreamin'; you ain't putting no holes in my furniture. I pay the rent here." So then I had to turn around and prove to her that I wasn't dreaming [about the abuse]. *So one day I hid in the closet when he went to the bathroom and as he went to pass the door in my room, when he went in my room naked, I shot him with a BB gun and he screamed and hollered and running through the hall. So that was my proof to my mother; I said "Why was he out there if he's not messing with his child, ya know."* [What did she do?] *She told us, it was like, as long as it stayed in the house, she didn't say anything. The only one that she took action was the ones* [children] *who went outside the house with it and so they got beat.* [Your brothers and sisters were also abused?] *My sisters and I had a problem with it because I thought after eighteen children, out of nine girls it should have never got to me. . . . I covered up my pain by getting high, which I was getting high since I was a child because that's all I was given.*

For a while, ya know, I fought back with him because he always told me if a person touch you in this kind of way how to react and how to do this and then he did it and taught me how to fight back with him. When I turned fifteen I shot my father with a BB gun. Ya know, and that was my beginning to try to change my life at least I thought, ya know, because the first time I got pregnant he beat me with a suitcase and made me lose my baby, told me I was a bitch because I didn't give it to him first and then put me out the house. Well, he kicked me out, bare feet, pregnant. I had no shoes on, no socks, he put me out the house bare feet and pregnant because he told me I was a horny bitch and didn't give it to him first so he said until I give it to him, I no longer can live in his house.

Raped by her brother, Marguerite turned immediately to escape mode; alcohol was ever present in her home, and she drank to numb her emotional pain.

I started drinking when I was thirteen after my brother raped me. . . . There was always liquor in the house 'cause my parents always had wild parties on the weekends. . . . I would sit in the cellar and drink wine or Schmitz [beer] by myself just so I could escape.

Seeking comfort and shelter from their mothers or other caretakers always proved futile for the women. La Toya describes two occasions of abuse by her stepfather, how her calls for help went unanswered, and what she did.

My stepdad stepped into the picture, but I didn't know that he was going to play a big part in my life. Like I'll be getting out the tub and I'll be going in my room and he'll come out and I'll be running in the bare or whatever and he'll peek over and stuff like that; I didn't know, me being young I really didn't know, I didn't know if it was a problem. I didn't know how to react to it, but I just knew something was wrong with him. I had a funny feeling something was wrong with him. . . . One particular night my sister was in her bed and I was in my bed and he came in the house. He took off his clothes and he got in the bed with me. I ran out the room and ran into my mom's room and said, "Mom, he's in my bed, he's in my bed." She said that he didn't mean it. I couldn't believe it. . . .

My mom had went over my stepdad's mother's house and he was home. He just came home from work and I was coming home from school. He said, "Come here," and I said, "What?" and he said, "Come here, sit right here, I need to talk to you for a minute." When he said sit right here, I thought he was saying sit right here next to the bed. He was saying sit on his lap. Okay, mind you, I'm twelve years old and I'm like what's going on, and he took my hand and he made me touch his penis. From that day on I was just scared, I just didn't know what to do, he said, "You better not tell your mom; if you tell your mom this is going to happen, she's not going to believe you, she's not going to give you no allowance, you know your mom love me, she's not going to believe you anyway." So if you tell her, it really don't matter. . . .I thought she wasn't going to believe me; I thought she would beat me. [Did you tell your mom?] *I told her. She didn't believe me, I couldn't believe it. I thought it was my fault, ya know, I didn't know how to react to the situation; I just started being real rebellious in school, and then I finally left home.*

La Toya's mother was a crack user who also drank poisoned liquor:

She was so sick from drinking, she couldn't even get up. . . . She was drinkin' a fifth of liquor every day. And the man that was selling her the liquor was cuttin' the liquor with real alcohol. He would pour some of the liquor out and pour rubbin' alcohol in it to make it, he was trying to stretch it . . . she started getting sick . . . spittin' blood in the buckets. . . . That hurt me a lot 'cause she wasn't there for me like I don't matter none.

La Toya got the impression that crack and liquor were more important than she was. Sadly, she was not alone in this feeling. While mothers never directly sexually abused their daughters, their actions and failure to act fed the abuse, the women claim. Perhaps because of their own victimization or oppression, addiction, denial, fear, uncertainty, or simple indifference, failure by mothers and other female caretakers to protect reinforced the experiences of violence and dominance. Failure to care can also be illustrated in the case of Edwina, whose mother not only allowed incest but also taught her daughter to trade sex for money. Edwina was first a victim and then a victimizer, acting with agency to protect her interests. It is no wonder Edwina has been a sex worker ever since.

I had a rough life at a young age. Yes, because when I was a little girl my father molested me. I have four sisters and five brothers. Not only did my father molest me, my brothers did too. I got through that. My mother always told me and my four sisters never lay down with a man, I don't care if it's your husband, without him giving you money. So, my father every morning, while my mother was downstairs ironing our clothes, he used to call me upstairs and he used to molest me. . . . He would put his penis between my thighs so after hearing my mother telling us about that, I thought why is he touching me and mommy downstairs? That was a thought I was asking myself so I started eventually going into his pants pockets taking fifty-, hundred-dollar bills and change whatever, because my mother told me never let a man touch me without getting paid for it. So I started taking money from him from six years old; the molestation didn't stop from him till I turned thirteen, until I started running away from home. So then, I started taking care of myself, prostituting and working in peep shows. I've been prostituting myself my whole life.

Left to their own suffering and having the abuses, the exploitation, and oppression reinforced by their caretakers, the girls reacted by internalizing blame then and throughout their lives, rebelling, and detaching through alcohol and running away, often with siblings. Prathia blamed herself for the abuse she suffered, drank, began stealing, and ran away from home. Her reliance on taking things of value from others is ironic.

I've been drinking since I was eight years old. I've been drinking for thirty-nine years. Started when I was eight after my dad first molested me the first time, I started drinking. My father sexually molested me and my sisters. I started drinking with my sisters. We would go in the closet and take some of daddy's wine. Then it became a everyday thing; we'd go in his closet 'cause that is where he kept his stuff that he drank. It tasted good. It numbed my feelings. I didn't think about what I had to deal with on the outside as to when my father came home or what he was going to do, it didn't bother me because half the time I didn't feel it anyway. I just put it to the point that I guess this was something that grown-ups did to kids; you couldn't tell me any different 'cause I'm eight years old, what am I supposed to know except my father's hurting me and nobody'll listen to me. But, that dared me to be out there on the street, I ran away from home; I constantly ran away from home. . . . Everybody reacts in different ways and out of all of my parent's children, we all had some drugs, alcohol, some type of addiction. And we've all stolen; we've run away from home. It led me to drinking a whole lot, it led me to stealing, not only was it to get the alcohol, the drugs or whatever I set out for, but it always resorted into taking something from someone. I blamed myself for a long, long time.

All of the women who report child abuse, including incest or rape, have some psychiatric diagnosis—most commonly depression and posttraumatic stress disorder. About half of them attempted suicide at least once in their lives. Cheryl did so several times, and as she explains, heroin and crack ease the pain she suffers because of sexual abuse.

Holding it in just screws you up, like that really screwed me up really bad. I mean I tried to kill myself and everything a few times. It was so easy for me to just get high and not think about it. I felt shitty enough where it was like I want to feel better, and the drugs got me to feel better, so of course, you're going to keep doin' them. I didn't like the person that I was because of what happened [the abuse]. The drugs make you feel like somebody that I wanted to be. Everything was all right. It didn't really matter. Like I never told anybody about being raped for years and years and years. . . . It was just like the more drugs I did, it seemed to go away. To me, it would go away.

Women who had been abused sexually and in other ways report using hard drugs at much earlier ages than women who did not report sexual, physical, emotional abuse or neglect. Women directly abused began to drink at twelve years, use soft drugs at thirteen years, and hard drugs at seventeen years on average.[9] Women not directly abused started drinking at fourteen years, using soft drugs at fifteen years, and hard drugs at twenty-nine years on average. Early life abuse is a pathway marker to early life drug addiction.

Lauren began using crack at fourteen, but her initial reaction to abuse (incest by her brother) was to shoplift cosmetics to feel pretty, a facade for her shame:

My brother he raped me when I was seven. I told my mom and nobody did anything about and I had that sense of, I mean, I thought I was the bad one because nobody did anything about it so I began to steal from stores, like fingernails to make myself look older. You know makeup. They used to have five-and-dimes on the avenue and I would go in there and steal things that I wanted because my mom wasn't really there to give me anything that I really needed, like money and stuff like that 'cause she was too busy getting drunk. . . . [Why do you think you wanted to look older?] *I don't know. No. Not really maybe to look older, but to feel pretty, basically to feel pretty. I would put like mascara on. I still wear mascara today. But I would put the false fingernails on, the lipstick and makeup to make myself feel pretty.*

Several of the women talked about self-mutilation as a method of coping with abuse when they were girls, and some as adults. Sailie hurt herself as a child then as a woman by burning, cutting, and carving her skin because of the abuse. She carries the trauma of abuse and abandonment with her today to the "bed which they laid me," the halfway house for prisoners. She explains:

I was given away at birth 'cause my mother was too young to take care of me. I was raised by this man and this lady that my mom gave me to, and they were both very abusive. She was physically abusive. She beat me a lot, um, he sexually abused me as a child and actually went into my adulthood. . . . I hurt myself sometimes when I was six years old. Well, when I was little I didn't used to cut myself; I used to bang my head a lot. And bite myself, pull my hair and stuff like that. When I got older, that's when I started cuttin' myself. I started burning myself with cigarettes. It progressed when I felt angry or sad or lonely or frustrated, whatever feeling I would just hurt myself. I still do sometimes. I went through a lot of abuse, that's how I started drinking; that's how I ended up on the bed which they laid me here.

Sailie could never completely detach herself from the sexual abuse she was suffering, even in her adult life. Drugs and alcohol eased her pain: "Getting high was the only thing that made me happy. It was the only thing that made me feel good. It was something so I didn't have to think about reality. I know towards the end of my addiction, it was definitely an escape." Finally, she did fight back to end the abuse.

When I was thirty-seven . . . I found out I was pregnant again; this time it was my dad's baby. . . . I went in and out of the hospital during my whole pregnancy from depression. . . . By now, I'm a little sick of my foster father, I mean, I got this kid by him. He still doin' things to me and so I stole a gun. I stole a gun from a friend of mine. I went back to my foster father's house and tried to shoot him. He called the cops on me and they arrested me for stealing the gun and attempted murder.

They Left Me, They Gave Me Away

While caretakers who are substance abusers may be emotionally absent to children, they can also be neglectful of their physical care responsibilities as parents. Neglect and abandonment was not a common experience of the group as a whole (34 percent), but women victimized in this way were most likely to be victims of multiple forms of abuse and trauma (physical abuse, emotional abuse, sexual abuse, drug-abusing caretakers). They were all from impoverished urban neighborhoods. More sex workers report neglect and abandonment (11 or 42 percent of sex workers) compared to shoplifters (2 or 17 percent).

Neglect of their most basic needs often necessitated criminal involvement. Lauren found herself in a reverse role, expected to become parent in the absence of her alcoholic and drug-abusing mother. At age ten, survival necessitated crime.

I took care of my younger sister . . . my mom was too busy getting drunk. I took care of the house. I learned how to cook at a young age, whatever I could learn how to cook, when there was food in the house. . . . I was stealing to take care of me and my sister, stealing like t-shirts and socks and underwear and stuff from a little store on the avenue, somewhere where I knew I could get away with it where I knew I wouldn't be caught. . . . I conned the guy at the corner store, tellin' him that my mom would pay the bill . . . started a bill at the store. . . . I had wrote a note and imitated my mom's handwriting when I learned how to do cursive and I took the note around to the store and the guy believed it was my mom's and I started a bill at the store. That my mom didn't know anything about so I could get cigarettes and sodas and lunch meats and stuff for me and my sister.

Consumed with their addictions and the pursuit of their own self-interests, as the women explained, some parents and other caretakers failed to see the girls as a part of themselves, as their responsibility—leaving them alone and vulnerable. For Renita and her sister, neglect by substance-abusing parents meant they too were without food, but they were vulnerable to other dangers as well.

I didn't have no childhood. My dad and my mom was alcoholics and my dad was abusive to my mom. And they would leave me and my sister in the house all the time. Either they was out working or out doing their thing and they would leave us pretty much in the house by ourselves all the time. . . . Well, I can't remember how I felt but maybe afraid but anyway with no food, nothing to eat so we like more ate off of this bread. . . . And there was a time when me and my sister was playing at the window and she fell out the window, but she didn't die, she's still alive. I was about nine and we had went into foster homes because no one was home; our parents were unfit and nobody was at home. And then when I was about thirteen we got moved to my aunt and my uncle and my cousins. . . . We wasn't treated very good. It's like basically they only wanted us there for the money and stuff like that. . . . So our grandmom she had wanted us and my dad lived there too so we had moved in . . . and it wasn't right there either because our dad, that's how I think I get my ways from him 'cause he's always intoxicated, he won't talk to you. He never tells us that he loved us . . . he was abusive to his girlfriend and us . . . they didn't feed us enough, my sister kept getting molested . . . we ran away.

Women remembering neglect by parents or other guardians when they were girls told me they were abandoned and forced to reside with new guardians. These transitions were often informal arrangements involving payment to a new caretaker, most commonly grandmothers and other family members, but sometimes they were simply "given away" to "these people" or "this lady," acquaintances of biological parents. Loretta was taken away from her parents for her own good, to improve the quality of her life, but separation from her loved ones leaves her still feeling abandoned and separate.

I grew up in Columbia, South Carolina, with my mother and stepdad until the age of eight. I had two younger brothers and sisters. I was brought here to my two great-aunts who had my other brothers and sisters; they were older than me. They were a lot older 'cause my mother instead of her giving them up for adoption, she gave them to somebody in the family. Back in them days, they could do that. They would give them to somebody in the family and they would take care of them. . . . [Why didn't you stay with your mom and stepfather?] *'Cause my mother was a bad alcoholic. She would fight; her and my stepdad would fight, fight, fight, fight. . . . My mother would leave us in the house, go to work; she would go drinking and she would leave us in the house alone all the time with nothin'. . . .* [Was it better with your great-aunt?] *Well, we was poor, we lived in the projects, but I never went a day without food. I never went a day without clothes. My great-aunt was a lovely woman. . . . But I never saw my baby brother. I'm fourty-four now. It's a long time. I had a sister [who] would always run to see me. She was with my other great-aunt. My older brother was with my aunt, her sister. So I had two older sisters. She did everything she could do for me. I was trying to get one of those talk shows to see if I could get in touch with my baby brothers. I haven't seen them. We grew up. . . . I haven't seen my baby brothers in thirty-seven years. I think about him a lot. I have three daughters; I got two grandchildren that he's never seen.*

Even while her addicted parents left Renita and her sister alone at home without protection and without food, the absence of a relationship with her mother devastates her:

I still have a problem with that, ya know, when I was growing up. I remember one time when I was little my mom had walked us to school; the only thing I remember with her, she was walking in the cold and walking back and going back, that's the only part I remember. From this day, I don't even know how my mom looked. Nobody had no pictures of her; they had pictures of her but they can't find no pictures of her. I still have a problem with that, ya know, when I was growing up. It still hurts me now.

Sent to live with her grandmother to avoid harms of life with a drug-addicted mother, Pauline felt unwanted, left by her mother.

I was about six, six or seven. That's when I know my mom was getting high, smoking crack. I noticed the difference in her that she was getting high on crack and she wasn't taking care of us like she was supposed to. She gave us to my grandmother, but that didn't help. She [mother] wasn't there for a long time; I think that took a lot effect on me so I paid for her pain. So at the age of thirteen I ran away and that's when I started getting high and doing all this stupid stuff.

Looking back, Val does not blame her mother for being an absent parent or a drug abuser, but she does believe these factors led her to seek emotional warmth from strangers outside of the home and through drugs.

You always have that loyal love for your mother, and I don't care what they do to you, you still do. I used to see my mother hurt so much and I used to always say that when I grow up I'm going to make sure my mother never have to suffer again, you know, and as I grew older it seemed like watching her go into her addiction and alcohol, it made me feel like she didn't care about nothing but alcohol, you know. I used to start looking for love from other people, like my mother drink all day she was drunk, she didn't care what we was doing, you know, we could stay outside until all hours of the night and like I used to look for love from the lady down the street, you know, and in a way I believe I grew up too fast, you know, and slowly but surely I started smoking weed.

Esther and her siblings were "given away" by her mother, and separated into different foster homes. Sent away again, and again, Esther finally met her sister, enabling her to reunite with her mother, but with painful results.

My mom gave us away as kids, you know, 'cause she couldn't take care of us cause of the drugs? So I came up in foster home, but they never treated me right. At ten years old they figured as though it's about time. They called me down this agency and my case manager told me, she said, "You're not getting along here; we're going to have to take you out of your home and put you somewhere else!" And, um, it was horrible. It was just horrible. . . . I stayed there [at the new foster home] for a while then after a while they had tooken me to a new foster home. They told me, they said guess what, you have real sisters and brothers and a mother . . . so they arranged one day for me to meet my sister; I'm thirteen and she was something like fourteen. To see somebody walk in the room that look just like me . . . That night I ran away from home. She [sister] said "Come on, I'm taking you home with me," and we ran away to her foster home. I said "Do we have a mother?" . . . She took me one day to my mother's house. . . . And she [mother] just looked at me and said, "You're Esther, huh?" It was on since then, you know what I mean. 'Cause that was when I was introduced to the drug life then 'cause she was a drinker and she didn't mind if the kids drank. [Did you stay there with your mom?] *I was there for a while until she didn't want me. It was hard. . . . They sent us back [to different foster homes], but we ran away again and got locked up. I was fifteen and we tried to break out [of jail] so they sent us up state road [to a juvenile correctional institution].*

Their feelings of abandonment and experiences of loss were reinforced, as the women explain, when they were moved two, three, four, or more times between guardians at young ages. Sadly, like others, Shirelle suffered in childhood; she wanted to grow up fast. There was nothing for her in the foster care homes where she was sent; she took consolation in drugs and then directed her own life, independent of adult caretakers on the streets.

I remember one time, this really hurt me when she said it, she said, "I wish I would have never adopted you." I was a little older, about twelve maybe eleven. . . . She took me to the department of services . . . Then I was like in different foster homes, they just kept shipping me around to different foster homes. I didn't wanna stay. Things like that hurt. . . . I kept running away. . . I didn't like them, I was there for a month and then I'd leave . . . I've been in group homes. The longest I've ever been in one place at one time has been for like maybe five months. You know, I wanted to be grown up, started smoking weed, and I kinda liked it. I smoked, and smoked, and smoked, and smoked, and smoked, and smoked, you know.

Maternal abandonment and separation of siblings left enduring wounds for these women and placed them in grave danger. Take Lauren, whose mother always had chosen drugs over her girls—her unwanted baggage, as Lauren described herself and her sister. Cutting all ties finally, Lauren's mother shipped them to live with an acquaintance. Having lived a life punctuated by an absent mother, multiple relocations, abuse, and sexual assault, Lauren sought refuge with her sister in the unknown, on the streets, because this option seemed to her healthier than any other one.

Then when I was eleven my mom had met this guy, and she didn't want to take me and my sister with her. I don't know what was going on in her mind at the time, but she said that we couldn't go with her . . . I didn't really understand it at the time. I was just so, like, wow, she had me and you didn't want me. . . . So me and my sister lived with this lady. I was stealing to support us there too because the lady didn't really have any money and the money that my mom was givin' wasn't enough. . . . The lady couldn't take care of us anymore because my mom had stopped making payments, so we had to move out of there. . . . My dad split me and my sister up and had taken me to live with a friend of his that he worked with, but it didn't work out there because her husband was very violent. My sis-

ter was sent away [to father's female cousin and her husband] and used to get molested there. She was like eight, seven or eight; we were separated, and she wound up getting molested . . . her husband molested my sister and she tried to kill my sister . . . wrapping a telephone cord around her neck. My father's cousin tried to kill my sister sayin' that it was her fault that her husband did what he did to my sister. . . . I got my sister and ran away.

Consequences of Early Life Trauma

Scholarship on female offenders and substance abusers reveals quite a lot about the lives of addicted and criminally involved girls and women. This scholarship is diverse, based on a variety of methodologies including ethnographies, retrospective and prospective studies of girls and women, surveys, and clinical research of girls and women in the community, educational settings, jails and prisons, and treatment programs. While feminist criminology generally positions criminal involvement as a product of multiple, usually intersecting forces (structural and status inequities) that carry negative consequences—such as racism, classism, and gender bias—it also recognizes that girls and women are not always similar to one another.[10] Feminist pathway research then does not specify a chain of events that characterizes the typical female offender's journey through crime. Rather, it endeavors to illustrate common patterns among female offenders that are usually different from nonoffending women, and certainly from males. While sex workers as a group and other particular types of female offenders have been the focus of pathway studies, shoplifters have not.[11] This line of research, including studies of sex workers, has produced a substantial body of scholarship, which tells us that criminality is best explained by early life experiences, including misdirected coming of age in adolescence (which I discuss in Chapter 3).

Early childhood experiences play a critical part in girls' and women's journeys toward lives involving substance abuse and crime. Childhood trauma is their stepping-off point, setting the stage for how girls and women view themselves and how they experience the world. The early life experiences revealed by women in my study are the most important developmental influences on substance abuse and key markers in the lives of women in crime. Substance abuse is the reason for crime clearly articulated by the women in my study and for so many other women in crime; as many as 81 percent of women in state prisons have substance abuse problems.[12] It is no surprise that many of the same themes in the etiology of female criminality are fundamental for understanding drug addiction.

Exposure to parental alcoholism and drug abuse during childhood is common among substance abusers and a critical element in the etiology of substance abuse. Girls with parents who abuse alcohol and other drugs are at an elevated risk for alcohol and substance abuse than others, and they tend to begin using alcohol and drugs earlier in adolescence than others. One study found that compared to children raised without substance abuse, children of alcoholics had higher rates of substance abuse and emotional distress.[13] A study of 454 children by researchers in Virginia also supports this idea that parental use of alcohol and drugs socializes children to use early in their lives. That research showed that heavy alcohol use among children of alcoholics was significantly greater than among children in families with no alcoholism.[14] A national survey found that living with parents who abuse alcohol or drugs doubled the changes of children in these families using alcohol or hard drugs compared to children not raised in substance-abusing households.[15] A study in Oregon of 645 adolescents even showed that substance use of parents was predictive not only of when daughters started to use alcohol and drugs, but of the particular substance used.[16]

My study shows that girls exposed to hard drugs began to use hard drugs earlier in life than girls exposed to alcoholism alone. They also used the same drugs as their parents. Other researchers document that the particular substance used by parents socializes the child into use of the same substance. Findings of research by Biederman and his colleagues at Harvard showed that when parents drink, girls are likely to drink, and that when parents use illicit drugs their daughters are also more likely to use these same drugs.[17] In a longitudinal study of family factors influencing substance abuse of adolescents, other researchers in Oregon were able to identify marijuana use by parents as a significant predictor of a girl's own marijuana use. When a parent used marijuana, girls were more likely to use the same drug compared to girls whose parents did not use marijuana. Furthermore, as the rate of marijuana use increased by parents, so did the rate of use by girls, and this was especially true for younger girls compared to older girls.[18] Other research found increases in substance use by parents can also predict increases in use by their children. For example, following a sample of 4,200 children over a five-year period, researchers at

RAND found that increases in drinking of adolescents from grade seven to grade twelve are predicted by increases in alcohol consumption by an important adult in their lives.[19] Studies of female offenders have produced similar results that highlight parental substance abuse as a precipitator of drug and criminal involvement.[20]

Exposure to domestic violence marks early life experience of substance abusers and female offenders. Children who witness this violence are likely to use alcohol and drugs themselves to cope with the stress brought on by living in such an environment. In a national survey of adolescents aged twelve to seventeen, exposure to domestic violence was identified as one of the most important risk factors for the onset of substance abuse in adolescence. Girls living in substance-abusing homes exposed to violence in the home used alcohol and hard drugs more than girls not exposed because they suffered emotionally from the environment of abuse.[21] Research of female offenders tells the same story.[22] One example is a study of 102 female offenders jailed in California, 60 percent of the women tied their problems, in part, to witnessing the abuse of their mothers by their fathers when they were girls.[23] A recent study in Hawaii showed 58 percent of female juvenile offenders were witness to domestic violence, a percentage significantly higher than of male juvenile offenders.[24]

Research has quite convincingly linked child abuse to female criminality and drug use.[25] Sadly, research reveals how girls and women involved with drugs and the law have had childhood lives marked by multiple and chronic abuses. For example, a 1993 study of 294 California female inmates reported 71 percent were physically abused as girls, 41 percent suffered incest, and 85 percent were emotionally abused.[26] A 2005 study of 403 women imprisoned in Georgia found that 57 percent came from homes marked by domestic violence, 43 percent were abused sexually, and 38 percent were physically abused.[27] Compared to their nonoffending counterparts, girls and women criminally involved usually have experienced higher rates of abuse.[28]

Gender differences in abuse histories of male and female offenders are striking.[29] In a study of 281 delinquents in Ohio, Belknap and Holsinger found significant difference in the abuse histories of girls and boys incarcerated. Girls were significantly more likely to be verbally abused (66 percent, compared to 55 percent of boys), to be physically abused (75 percent, compared to 63 percent of boys), to witness physical violence among caretakers (49 percent, compared to 31 percent of boys), and to be sexually abused by a family member (60 percent, compared to 19 percent of boys). Girls were also more likely to be sexually abused repeated times. Girls were significantly more likely than were boys to identify these abuses as a trigger for their delinquency (56 percent, compared to 40 percent).[30] The Hawaii study of youth incarcerated reported 50 percent of girls were physically abused, 35 percent were neglected in their homes, and 38 percent were sexually abused, compared to 41 percent, 25 percent, and 8 percent of boys.[31]

Sexual abuse is especially relevant to female criminality, identified by many research studies as a critical early life event distinguishing male and female offenders and sending girls toward delinquency.[32] According to research, rates of sexual abuses are highest among female offenders than females in the general population and males across the board. In the general population, a 1994 review of nineteen surveys on the prevalence of child sexual abuse in the United States by Finkelhor estimated at least 20 percent of women compared to just 5 percent to 10 percent of men have been sexually abused during childhood.[33] Comparing male and female criminal offenders, the Bureau of Justice Statistics estimated child sexual abuse for females between 23 percent and 37 percent, compared to just 6 percent and 15 percent for male offenders.[34] Studying women sexually abused as girls and a comparison group of women not abused, Siegel and Williams estimated a twofold increase in the chances of a crime arrest for a girl sexually abused. According to that research, 20 percent of women sexually abused were arrested for a violent offense, compared to 14 percent of women who were not abused. In adulthood, 20 percent sexually abused were arrested, compared to just 11 percent of those not abused.[35] A recent study in Michigan of 204 girls found significantly higher rates of depression, suicide attempts, problems at school, and use of alcohol, marijuana, and hard drugs for girls sexually abused than for girls with no history of sexual abuse. Being sexually abused also predicted involvement in theft and other crimes.[36]

Childhood sex abuse is a particularly important risk factor for entry into sex work for girls and women.[37] Research by Silbert and colleagues in San Francisco on 200 sex workers reported 61 percent of the sex workers were abused sexually as children.[38] Interviewing 1,272 female inmates in Chicago on their experiences of sex abuse and sex work, McClanahan and her colleagues at Northwestern University found that sex abuse has a lifelong effect on entry into sex work. Women who were sexually abused (35 percent) were almost twice as likely than those never abused (65 percent) to become involved in sex work at any time in their lives (44 percent, compared to 29 percent).[39] Study in Colorado showed sex workers were abused as young girls more than twice as much as women who never worked in the industry (32 percent, compared to 13 percent).[40]

In a longitudinal study following 1,196 boys and girls into adulthood, Widom and Kuhns found that girls abused and neglected were far more likely to become involved in sex work during their youth and in adulthood than were girls with no history of abuse or neglect. Comparisons of boys and girls showed that abuse and neglect had no influence on crime of boys, supporting the large body of literature positing early life victimization as a highly influential factor in female delinquency and crime.[41] Most research positions sex abuse and other traumatic experiences in childhood as first elements in a chain of events that lead girls into a life of crime, including sex work. Running away, for example is poised as an intervening event linking prior sexual abuse to entry into sex work. Research by Simons and Whitbeck of forty adolescent female runaways and ninety-five homeless women in Des Moines reported differently. Multivariate analyses revealed a direct effect of sexual abuse on entry into sex work independent of other events, such as substance abuse and running away from home.[42]

Substance abuse is a consequence of child abuse.[43] A national survey that compared girls from substance abusing homes with other girls found that 81 percent of girls who used drugs were more often physically or sexually abused than other girls (57 percent) indicating alcohol and hard drug use is a coping mechanism for abuse.[44] One study looked at substance use and other negative outcomes for teens exposed to alcoholism at home or sexual abuse and a comparison group of teens. Those sexually abused or raised in alcoholic homes showed more negative outcomes, including substance use, than teens with no alcoholism at home or abuse. In that same study, rates of substance abuse were highest among teens who suffered multiple traumas.[45] A National Institute on Drug Abuse research study of 1,411 adult twins from Virginia found that drug abuse was higher among women sexually abused as girls than those with no sexual abuse. In fact, those women abused sexually were almost three times more likely to become drug addicted. While sexual abuse often co-occurs with other problems, such as family dysfunction, to help explain why girls develop alcohol and drug abuse problems, these researchers were able to show that sexual abuse in itself had a direct effect on substance abuse.[46] Research has also identified gender differences in alcohol and drug use as a response to abuses suffered in childhood. A study of 696 addicts from the San Antonio area compared men and women on type and degrees of child abuse (from no abuse to extreme abuse). Differences in minimal and moderate emotional, physical, and sexual abuses were slight, but women drug abusers compared to men were far more likely to have been severely or extremely emotionally abused (35 percent of women and 19 percent of men), physically abused (39 percent of women and 23 percent of men), and sexually abused (44 percent of women and 12 percent of men).[47] Another example of research that looked at gender differences is a study at Rutgers University in New Jersey of the long-term effects of sexual victimization as well as neglect and physical abuse on alcohol problems of men and women. Compared to their counterparts not victimized as girls women abused as children were more likely to abuse alcohol, but men who were victimized were not any more likely than other men to abuse alcohol.[48]

Mental health problems, addiction, and criminal involvement are linked in the lives of girls and women.[49] For example, a meta-analysis of forty-nine studies of drug-addicted women at Harvard Medical School found that childhood trauma is highest among drug addicted women with mental health problems compared with their general population counterparts. From 55 percent to 99 percent of women in that research reported a history of physical or sexual trauma that occurred primarily in childhood compared to 36 percent to 51 percent of women in the general population. Analysis also showed that when looking at women drug users as a group, those abused physically and sexually in childhood became addicted to drugs earlier and used drugs at higher rates than the women who not abused. Women experiencing multiple abuses were at greatest risk of developing psychological problems, two times more likely than women who suffered only physical or sexual abuse.[50] A study of female offenders in Oregon's juvenile correctional facilities revealed high levels of mental health problems among girls compared to boys. According to that study, 81 percent of all females in custody were diagnosed with a mental health disorder compared to 60 percent of males. The young women were more likely than the males to have depressive disorders (74 percent compared to 39 percent) and post-traumatic stress disorder (47 percent compared to 21 percent of the males). Girls compared to the boys had higher rates of co-occurring mental health disorders and substance abuse (57 percent compared to 35 percent). Furthermore, the young women were more likely to have had multiple suicide attempts (18 percent) and hospitalization for mental illness (16 percent) compared to the males (4.5 percent and 6 percent). As much other research has pointed out, the Oregon study also showed that females in trouble with the law and involved with drugs have histories of child abuse; just 9 percent of the young women said they were not ever sexually, physically, or emotionally abused.[51]

Early life trauma creates emotional and psychological pain expressed in substance abuse. A 1991 national survey of 1,099 women conducted as part of a ten-year longitudinal study of alcohol use among women supports other research on the effects of child sexual abuse on alcohol and drug use and mental health. The research found that not only did women sexually abused as girls drink alcohol more regularly than women not abused, they were more likely to be alcohol abusers, use cocaine, heroin, and other drugs, and suffer from mental health problems like depression and anxiety.[52] Girls witnessing violence in the home, socialized into substance abuse by their parents, neglected and abused, cope with the emotional tolls of these trauma by abusing alcohol and drugs. A national study of 4,023 adolescents found posttraumatic stress disorder mediates early life trauma and subsequent drug abuse. According to that project, family alcohol use, family drug addiction, and most especially childhood sexual and physical victimization and being a witness to domestic violence increased significantly the chances youth would abuse hard drugs and would begin use earlier in life than others. All of these precipitating factors create stress and anxiety seen as post traumatic stress disorder expressed in substance abuse during adolescence.[53]

Looking at gender and the effects of childhood trauma on mental health, an Australian study of 1,612 men and women found that when compared to women never sexually abused as girls, women sexually abused were significantly more likely to develop psychiatric problems both in childhood and later in life similar. That research also showed that when compared to men sexually abused as boys, the women abused were much more likely to develop major affective disorder, anxiety disorder, and other mental health problems, indicating that sexual abuse may somehow stir up psychiatric problems more in girls than in boys.[54]

Women in my study raised in the poorest environments (who also tend to be minorities and sex workers) suffered disproportionately in every category of abuse and trauma. They were the only victims of neglect. Consistent with its earlier research, the National Center on Child Abuse and Neglect reported in 1996 that while abuse was no different for racial minorities than for nonminorities, children from lower income families (less than $15,000) were significantly more likely to be abused and neglected than children whose families earned incomes of $30,000 or greater. According to that report, children of lower income families are forty-four times more likely to be neglected, eighteen times more likely to be sexually abused, sixteen times more likely to be physically abused, and thirteen times more likely to be emotionally abused than are children from families of higher incomes.[55] Other research parallels such findings that children from lower socioeconomic families and poor, disordered communities suffer disproportionately from abuse.[56] Using retrospective accounts of adult women, a RAND study of 224 women in Los Angeles found sexual and abuse physical abuse during childhood present for 41 percent of the women raised poor.[57] Comparatively, researchers in New Jersey of 668 women from the middle class found that just 29 percent were abused physical, sexual, or emotionally.[58]

The stories told by the women in this study of the deprivations and victimizations they endured early in life were largely unspoken to anyone until my meetings with them, revealing how unresolved traumas originating in childhood carried through their lives even to the present. While their status as female placed them at risk for sexual abuse, their socioeconomic positions and especially their family milieu conditioned abuses, deprivations, and trauma in their early lives. Family systems defined and organized by substance abuse, as the women explain, laid the foundation for abuses to unfold. There they were subject most especially to malignant emotional abuse, physical abuse, neglect, abandonment, and sexual predation directly within the home. Moreover, socialization into substance abuse and bearing witness to violence in the home were also emotionally abusive to them. Caretakers' corruptive actions created a false sense among the women during their childhoods that drug and alcohol use is normal, leading all from substance-abusing homes to participate in such use at very young ages directly in the home. Living with chaos, tension, and physical violence among caretakers created anxiety, constant worry, and fear, depriving the girls of peace, security, and safety—all forms of silent emotional abuse. These invisible abuses were just as destructive to their emotional and behavioral health as were abuses leaving physical scars.

The traumas experienced by these women as girls occurred at an especially important point in their emotional growth and psychological maturation.[59] During childhood and early adolescence, girls mature in relation to others, defining themselves not as separate from but as connected with family, for example. Emotionally, they need empathic relationships, compassion, a sense of belonging, and care in their own lives. Separation, disconnection, and isolation in their relationships and the neglect of their own nurturance are especially problematic for girls. Lacking care and protection sets the stage for psychological distress. Disconnection, isolation, and neglect, often characteristic of a family system organized by drugs and alcohol, leave girls helpless, powerless, and alone, especially when those responsible for their care victimize or diminish them. For the women in this study, the intentional and unintentional harms to which they were subjected triggered numerous reactions, such as internalization of abuse manifested in blame and self-harm and other reactions including detachment from families (running away); most especially, the drug and alcohol use they were taught early on became their emotional crutch.

My findings show that while shoplifters and sex workers share some similarities in their early life experiences, such as being raised with alcohol abuse and domestic violence, their paths to crime specialization started out and evolved differently in some respects. Women with the highest rates of abuse and traumas that were chronic and co-occurring (witness to domestic violence, multiple forms of child abuse, parental multiple drug use, and a distressing social environment of urban poverty) are primarily sex workers, not shoplifters. They suffered a "multiplicity of abuse,"[60] which compounds the suffering of girls so affected sending them into a tailspin. Shoplifters, who are more often middle class and nonminority, were not completely insulated from trauma, as they are also drug addicted, but the less severe the trauma they suffered no doubt set them in a different direction. These differences between sex workers and shoplifters are then compounded by occurrences and decisions made during adolescence and early adulthood. In the next chapter, I discuss the ways in which the women's adolescent and early adult decisions work with early childhood experiences to shape their paths to criminal specialization in either shoplifting or sex work.

3. *Coming of Age*

Adolescence and young adulthood is the critical period for healthy psychological maturity and social growth for girls as they find their own identities. In this transition, girls begin to rely more heavily on relationships outside of the home, with friends in peer groups, and they move toward independent lives through education for example and career paths. As a group, for the women in this study, early victimization experiences within their own family systems set the stage for misdirected coming of age during this period (i.e., substance abuse and running away, rather than entry into mainstream educational and vocational pursuits). Their responses to harmful early life experiences—often termed "coping mechanisms," "escape mechanisms," and "adaptive behaviors"—represent a set of early contingency markers or turning points, with notable consequences. For example, a girl who runs away from home to put a stop to sexual abuse by her father may find the need to trade sex for housing when she is on the streets with nowhere to go. At some later time and place, women then encounter new contingency points, affected by previous decisions and experiences that can shift the nature and direction of their behaviors. A woman earning money in a commercial sex business as a stripper, for example, who has started to incorporate sex-for-money transactions with her clientele may subsequently decide that working full-time as a street-level sex worker is a better financial alternative.

Comparing shoplifters and sex workers on their experiences in this period of life reveals similarities but also how the two groups lived it differently. Drug use and dependence during adolescence and young adulthood for both shoplifters and sex workers is an expression of earlier life experiences reinforced in their connections to social networks outside of the home. Both groups tended to settled into drug dependence during this transition to adulthood before their entry into crime, with some notable exceptions among sex workers. Differences between shoplifters and sex workers are clear. Growing up in the middle class with few co-occurring child abuses and traumas, remaining at home until late adolescence, graduating high school, and, most especially, choosing work outside of the adult entertainment industry characterizes the adolescent and young adult years of shoplifters as a group. Being raised in a lower socioeconomic class, experiencing multiple forms of childhood trauma, running away from home, dropping out of school, and working in the commercial sex trade are more characteristic of sex workers as a group than of shoplifters.

Transitioning to a Destructive Adolescence

In their transition to adulthood, girls rely less on their parents and more on social networks outside of the home as they begin to form their own futures. Women in my study, like so many other addicted women, had a deformed experience brought forth by earlier trauma and abuses. In their transition between childhood and womanhood, the woman in this group abused in childhood talked of how they sought liberation: not independence necessarily, but escape from chaotic homes that imprisoned them. They continued to take comfort in alcohol and drugs, now primarily outside of the home and usually in the company of friends in violent, drug-ridden, decaying neighborhoods. Most ran away from their homes, while others fled to the streets as often as they could, believing this would improve their lives. These decisions may have produced immediate relief from suffering, at least emotionally, but the effects were never long-lasting and never could have been; the girls were still vulnerable children. Sadly, during this time of liberation, they would become drug addicted and drawn to crime and deviant lifestyles. Seeking liberation meant they would fall deeper into trouble. Experiences during their adolescent and young adult years reveal quite a lot about the paths to shoplifting and sex work.

Take the case of Val. Sexually abused by her own father as a child, emotionally starved by her drug-addicted and alcoholic mother, and raised in an impoverished and dangerous urban area, she sought relief in drugs—her "man," as she describes them. Always feeling unloved, always lonely, and fearful of men, she found that drugs gave her the comfort and peace she desperately needed and never had in her home. As with others, drugs would ultimately destroy her. With hopes of a good life vanished at a young age, Val entered the world of addiction and prostitution.

I think I grew up a little faster than other kids . . . I just was running, I believe that's why I am so good at it now. I ran back then, you know, and that's not a scapegoat. I always run from reality. That's what really got me on drugs to make me feel like I wasn't alone, to make me feel strong and like I can go ahead and challenge the world. As long as I am high on drugs I can do anything. That's been my friend. I really started using when I was like twelve; I started smoking weed and taking pills, you know, me and my girlfriend we used to skip school and smoke weed, take Valiums on the railroad tracks. . . . The crack and the coke and the heroin came later [at age sixteen], and I lost control of my life completely. I was addicted immediately. Yeah, right away, right away, coke for me was like a man for you. It was like my man. . . . I hated men, I despised men. I didn't want them to give me nothing. I didn't want to stay with one you know, and it seemed like all I needed was a friend and I didn't want it to be a man; I wanted it to be a woman. I wanted that relationship that I should have had with my mother and sister, you know what I mean, and right to today I could say I still look for that. But drugs was like so comfortable to me because I didn't have nobody and it was like that was my friend, you know, that's what gave me the strength to know that I could go on the next day. It was so comforting to me. I started doing drugs and selling my ass to get these drugs. It is sick, you know. I've been out there for over twenty years and drugs, that's been my man.

Val moved directly from drinking in the home to using drugs, running away, dropping out of school, stripping and dancing at a go-go bar, and abusing drugs, to periods of homelessness, violent relationships with men, shoplifting, periodically selling drugs, and sex work over the long term. Some other women in the study followed a similar path. The contexts in which the women, as adolescents, began to fall into these addictions differ in some ways, as did the circumstances that drew them into deviant lifestyles and crime.

Drugs, Then Crime

Almost across the board, the women started participating in income-generating crime after their hard drug use became a heavy or daily habit. The comments by Esther who was first in sex work then a shoplifter illustrate this point.

My habit was pretty treacherous. Crack, crack, crack. From a kid, the drug thing, it escalated just like it says it does, you know what I mean? The drugs of choice, first you start off with little drinks, then I tried the marijuana, then up, up, and it gets, you know what I mean, it gets more intense. And that's what it ended up. When the crack cocaine came into play, that was the worstest thing. Ah, whoaa. That was the worstest thing, I started smoking. Listen, the drugs makes you, the drug makes you do anything, I mean, whew, get it and want the most money because it's a, it's a habit that keeps on grabbing at you. 'Cause it don't let you go, it don't let you go. . . . I didn't shoplift until I got older and started using drugs. I wasn't a hustler like that, a street hustler, go get the goods and then go out and, come on that's a double D stealing and then you got to sell it, and all that. Until I got into the drugs, until I got into the drug, with the drugs I was, look, it was like look, baby, I was taking, I would go, I became an expert, just by thinking because this is how this drug had me; this is how hooked this drug had me and how I had to have it. I became an expert at every and anything to get money, without having to lay on the backseat of that car.

Also take Sandy, a shoplifter who never before engaged in crime before her addiction to heroin.

I've worked on and off you should say. I started boostin' about two years after I started using. . . . I've been doing this for ten years . . . there's three hundred sixty-five days a year, there's times I went twice a day. The fear of being sick, knowing that you're physically hooked on drug and being sick is what keeps me going. The only reason I did it was for the habit. If I wasn't using I don't think I'd be going inside the stores at all. Some people say it's an adrenaline rush. I've heard that, some people enjoy it. I don't enjoy it. I do it 'cause I know I have to do it. I wouldn't otherwise 'cause that's the level that I go to go to get the drugs. I'm not gonna go selling my body and do whatever. . . . I need to have the drugs every day. And, I go shoplifting every day, but I, you can't work and get a paycheck every day. It'd take me two hours to make what somebody else would make in forty hours. On a daily basis, this is the only way I know I can have cash.

Edwina is an exception for whom criminal involvement preceded drug addiction. However, as evidenced by her comments, eventually she also saw sex work as a means to support her drug habit.

When I was using, ya know, first prostitution, it was prostitution before crack cocaine with me, and I liked prostitution, for real. I liked doing things for money. I did. [It wasn't to support a habit for you at first?] *Right, at first it wasn't. It was to survive and to have fun and to have money in my pocket and then look good but as time went on, ya know, I was introduced to crack cocaine and it started not being fun no more. Things started getting real desperate, and I started getting desperate. To deal with these nasty men out here, the things that I had to do. I had to go with men that would buy me this funky and filthy and, ya know, it just turns your stomach. That's how bad I was feeling. The worst thing about my past? I told you that I had to prostitute from the beginning. I had to go to with the old and the very young to support my habit.*

All of the shoplifters told me they engaged in crime for earnings once their drug use became out of control, as did the largest majority of sex workers. Some sex workers began selling sex before they were using hard drugs or using hard drugs heavily, but they are the exception. The focus of this chapter is on decisions made by the women during their adolescence and young adulthood that represent splitting-off points in their pathways to shoplifting and sex work. One of the most important decisions is to run away from home.

Seeking Liberation but Moving Deeper into Trouble

A critical turning point in these women's adolescence is the decision they made as girls to seek companionship on the streets. Most ran away from home (63 percent), usually multiple times; the average runaway was just under fourteen years of age. Runaways reported more multiple early life abuses, especially neglect and abandonment, than nonrunaways. As socioeconomic class and early-life victimization are related for women in my study, it would follow that most runaways are from poor urban settings; 88 percent of runaways were raised poor. Runaway girls and their counterparts who did not run away entered into their drug addictions in similar ways. When they fled to the streets to seek happiness and comfort in others, they were prone to adopt the deviant behaviors of their friends and companions, drug users in the impoverished, criminogenic neighborhoods where they lived or sought refuge. For those raised working and middle class, these friends and companions were sometimes schoolmates or neighborhood friends, but more often new people they met in the urban neighborhoods where they purchased their drugs—those neighborhoods where many women who were raised poor lived, such as in Camden or North Philadelphia. The decision to run away from home would be a turning point to crime type; runaway girls were more likely to enter into sex work than shoplifting.

A product of a broken home, like most of the others, Prathia lived as part of the urban drug culture with its attendant violence, urban decay, and poverty. While still living at home, she began to drink at age eight to numb her emotional and physical pain in coping with continued violent sexual abuse by her father. Then at age ten she ran from home to her older sister, in whose company she would learn how to use drugs and where to buy them, the "the hookup," "the 911 old rundown" as she explains it. She dropped out of school, and by her late teenage years she was addicted to heroin and then to crack. Turning to crime was her financial necessity. Sex work was her crime choice.

I was staying with my sister in the projects. I walked the street, I met people. She introduced me to a speakeasy guy that sold liquor, told him if there was anything that my sister wants, come get it, don't worry, put on my bill. So, therefore, my liquor was covered. Then she introduced me to another girl that shot drugs. We became friends so I got the hookup, I got the 911 old rundown. I found out where everything was, and that sent my addiction soaring up the hill. It was the middle of the eighties and I remember when I first had my first crack, and I smoked it and I'm saying, "Ooh, I like the way that feels." I liked the way the rush was, and then everything just drifted right on out. I liked the way it took my cares away from me. I didn't have to sit and worry anymore. That sent me to the races. It was on every corner, bars on every corner. I became an alcoholic, drug-abusing lush. I began to know people, I began going different places, I began doing different things. I learned to suck dick. I learned how to turn some more tricks.

Sandy lived in a middle-class suburb. Sexual and physical victimization early in her life and witnessing violence and alcoholism in the home led her to seek acceptance and companionship among drug users in Camden, New Jersey's poorest, most drug-infested neighborhood, just over the Delaware River from Philadelphia. She remembers why:

By the time I was thirteen I would drink and smoke weed and I thought I was grown already. I thought I was old enough ta hang with the wrong crowd, hanging with people trying to impress other people. You know, I hung around with a lot of people from Camden, knowing I wasn't supposed to be in the area, but I don't know the reason. I guess I got more attention, I would have more attention walking down the street, north Camden on State Street, than I would if you went to, suppose, the Cherry Hill Mall [located in a middle- to upper-socioeconomic-class area]. I was so unconfident in myself that it seems like the area I was in I got more attention there, than I would outside there. I don't know how to explain it. . . . Then I started doing heroin when I was nineteen on a daily basis, but I wouldn't do the drugs there, I took them home. I hooked [hung out] with this guy that used to shoplifting, and he would steal, like, sets of sheets and comforters and take 'em to certain people and sell 'em. Like he would get, like, a $500 comforter and sell it for, like, maybe $150 or whatever, and that's how he supported his habit. So I got myself into it where I started doing it every day. I still continue to do it now. I've been boostin [shoplifting] all my life.

But I graduated from Cherry Hill West. Top ten in my class and there was times in my life I worked on and off; like, I'd work as a cashier for like five years and then I would shoplift to have extra money to support my habit, because I didn't want anybody knowing about the habit. And then I'd work as a waitress, and then all my other money I used as a waitress would go to the drugs. The boosting, shoplifting I did that more 'cause that would get me the money I needed to use without everybody else knowing that I was using. So, I still had money in my pocket to make it seem like I wasn't and then I would still play it off, like I'd have my tips from my paycheck, and then shoplift money I could use for the drugs, which is a lot easier. Then nobody knew about it, that's how I covered my tracks.

Both Prathia and Sandy suffered early life abuses and sought companionship on the streets where their drug addictions soared, but they differ in the crimes they would use to support these addictions. Despite the abuse in her past, like many others who grew up in middle- or working-class families, Sandy chose to specialize in shoplifting rather than sex work to support her drug habit. Like most other shoplifters, she never ran away from home, never dropped out of school, and maintained ties to mainstream society as she continued to live in a middle-class suburb, working on and off in a conventional occupation. Compared with Sandy and others who did not sell sex but who became specialized in shoplifting, Prathia and other sex workers tended to make different choices in adolescence. A critical one is the decision to run away from home and the attendant effects on the women's lives; 81 percent of sex workers, compared to just 25 percent of shoplifters, ran away from home. Running away from home is a risk factor for dropping out of school, for victimization on the streets, for entry into the commercial sex trade, and for sex work specialization.

Ripping and Running, No Time for School

Overall, 63 percent of the women dropped out of school. Compare this to the average dropout rates across the national (5 percent) and in New Jersey and Pennsylvania (3 percent and 4 percent, respectively).[1] Running away is a risk factor for dropping out of school. All but two of the twenty-four runaways (92 percent) dropped out of school, compared with 14 percent of those who lived in their homes until age sixteen years or older. The connection between running away and dropping out of school makes intuitive sense. Girls who did not run away but who fled to the streets for companionship were still living at home, even though these homes were often dangerous places. At least this time off the streets may have protected them from the constant pull to street life. Runaways were most often homeless, "going from pillow to pillow" as one described; thus, most were a part of the urban street culture. In that culture, using drugs and living the fast life, "ripping and running" as several women describe it, is partly exciting and partly therapeutic. Going to school encumbered the girls. Shay, a sex worker, remembers that her decision to drop out of school seemed the right decision at the time, a mistake she now regrets:

I had found a few friends and wouldn't come for a few nights at a time. Then it started weeks at a time. School was really going downhill. I was smoking weed. I started hanging out on corners, staying out late, and I'd get in trouble with the cops and curfew, you know all that. I was smoking weed, not going to school or going to school, signing in, and leaving. I dropped out at the eleventh grade. I dropped out to hang out on the corners. I wanted to be with my friends. I mean it's senseless now but, ya know, it was a big thing then.

Pauline, also a sex worker, dropped out too. Her drug of choice then was to smoke angel dust sprinkled on marijuana. Angel dust is a street name for PCP, an anesthetic with hallucinogenic properties.

At the age of thirteen, that's when I started getting high. I was drinking and smoking angel dust, poppin pills, all that crazy stuff. I never knew I had a drug problem. I thought that was the thing to do. I was around everybody who got high and stuff like that so I thought it was the thing to do. In eleventh grade, I dropped out with my friend that I used to hang with. I guess I like getting high at that time, so to be in school, it took up time for me out there getting high. That's where my addiction progressed. I started smoking more angel dust.

Street-level peer groups are an important part of drug and crime involvement for Pauline and Shay, like the others who fled to the streets from the conventional world and deeper into the street culture.

Dangerous Streets

In addition to increasing the likelihood of dropping out of school, running away places girls at risk for street-level victimization, particularly rape. Seven of the eight women who were victims of rape outside of their homes during their youth were runaways at the time. All were school dropouts (usually from the ninth or tenth grade) and all would become sex workers.

On the run from rape by her father, Edwina was gang-raped at thirteen and impregnated by one of her attackers. She never reported the incident because she was a runaway (hence a law-breaker). She said: "My father abused me and it lasted up till I was like thirteen and that made me a runaway child. I'd be in South Philly, North Philly, and Jersey. Anyway, thirteen years old I got gang-raped by seven guys and that wasn't no fun at all. I got pregnant . . . I was traveling around a little girl lost and confused, but I was a survivor."

Harriet was raped when she was a homeless runaway. She was also a victim of robbery when she was on the run. "I started living on the streets. I was in abandoned houses, in abandoned cars, in people's cars, up-to-date cars of people who didn't want to pay their rent so they was living in their cars. I was out there for a while, and I started getting into fights and getting beat and getting mugged, you know, getting beat for my money."

Sometimes perpetrated by strangers, but usually by befriended boys and men, the sexual assault, now occurring outside of the homes they escaped, again reinforced to the girls just how vulnerable they were to male violence and oppression, especially at the hands of those whom they wanted to trust. Lauren describes being gang-raped by her friends. She still blames herself, it seems. During our conversation she broke down and cried, reaching to me for a comforting embrace. Never, she whispered, had she told anyone of this attack.

When I was a runaway at fifteen, I was raped by ten guys, and, well, I had been drinking. I was smoking marijuana and drinking liquor and that was my first experience with pills. I took, like, a few quaaludes and I didn't know they were that strong, and ten guys took advantage of me and I wound up with this tattoo on my hand. [Were these strangers?] *No, these were guys that I hung out with, partied with in school, on street corners . . . people that I knew, that I grew up with. They called me a whore.* [You didn't go to the police?] *No, I was too scared, you know, back in those days you used to disappear. It happened to me once, and nobody did anything about it, so who's to say that they would do anything about this one.* [Did you get any help?] *Never, it makes me feel ugly, worthless.*

After this rape, Lauren sank further into despair. She, like the others raped on the streets as runaways, never spoke a word of the attacks and never reported them to the police. Faded black, the tattoo covers the back of her hand. It is a crude mix of images—blotches of ink with stars, part of a flower, and arrows within circles. For twenty-six years she has carried this mark. Fear of retaliation was a good reason not to reveal the attacks; fear that no one would believe or intervene was another, since nobody cared in the past; and fear of arrest for running away made sense too. Without medical and mental health care or police intervention, these girls kept pain locked inside with a storm of alcohol and drugs.

You Can Get Anything with Your Body

Most of the runaways managed to find temporary housing with friends, but when forced to find shelter on the streets and in abandoned homes they would come face to face with the dilemma of whether to sell sex. While on the streets—whether for days, weeks, or months—the girls had to survive. This usually meant they would shoplift for food when hungry. It also meant they would be at risk for entry into sex work. It was not necessary for shoplifters to acquire shelter, as in general they were not runaways. Furthermore, among women who had ever sold sex in their lives (runaways and nonrunaways), those who ran away from home became sex workers at younger ages, usually during their teenage and young adult years. Early familiarity with sex work was an important aspect of their commitment to the crime.

Homeless, out of school, and already a heavily marijuana user, Shirelle became a sex worker in her teens.

I was twelve, and I ran away. I wanted to be grown. So I ran away. You know, I wanted to be grown up, started smoking weed, and I liked it. So I stuck to that and I claimed that and I ran with it; I took it, and I smoked, and I smoke, and I smoke, and I figured I'm not hurting myself or anybody else. School wasn't interesting me anymore; all I wanted to do was smoke weed, run the streets with my girlfriends and be grown. That's what I thought was being grown was. I like the lifestyle that I was living, I like being able to get up and go out any time I want. I wanted to be free; I wanna run wild. I was emancipated at sixteen and then I really took off; you couldn't tell me nothing. I started getting high every day and smoking weed and drinking and smoking weed and drinking. I wanted to smoke weed more, and I was just running the streets, sleeping with Tom, Dick, and Harry, not even for the drugs not even to get high, just, and it was to the point where I was sleeping with this guy just to stay at his house. I was out there, I was walking the streets literally, walking the streets in the wintertime trickin' for a place to stay. When I first did it, I didn't like it at all. You know, I couldn't, I didn't, it wasn't any, it wasn't any emotions. I just felt like, I felt dirty, cheap.

Renita, not yet addicted to drugs when she started selling sex for places to stay, tells of a similar experience:

Well, it was a friend next door to us and this guy and he said we could move in with him and, like, this guy and two other guys, older guys that stayed there, and we wind up moving in there with them. We would have sex with them to stay there. I was about fourteen at the time. Then I was out on the streets, out on the streets sleeping around with this man or that man just to have somewhere to stay, just to have a roof over my head. During the day I was with people that I knew, then later on in the night, when the nighttime comes, I knew I can't stay there with them so I get hooked up with a guy.

As Renita developed a reputation as a street sex worker, she met a "trick," a sex work customer, who introduced her to crack and became the father of her first child. She was just sixteen years old when the child was born. Once the relationship ended, Renita resumed street sex work—this time to support not only her housing but also her newly acquired drug addiction. Her experience as a sex worker-for-housing naturally led to her decision to sell sex for money, but her reputation earned on the streets also drew her in. She explains:

No, well, anyway there was this guy I remember; he didn't come out and say, "Well, I know you sleep around," but evidently that's what he probably meant, and he's, like, he introduced me to this guy, which is my baby's father. He was a trick at first and a drug dealer. Basically, he sell me stuff. Yeah, so I started off smoking crack the whole time, but I didn't even know what it was. Ever since that day I smoked it and I liked it so ever since then my baby's father would supply me with it all the time. . . . He had the weed, he had the crack, he had the angel dust; that was my favorite, angel dust. I was still going to school when I was out on the street but not as much until one day I just kept not getting up for school on time, keep being late, so I gave up; I said, "Well, I ain't going to school no more." . . . Then I was back out on the street this time and tricking for money.

La Toya was already using cocaine and angel dust at thirteen and crack at age fourteen. She traded sex for housing, sex for drugs, and sex for money. Then she found another way to earn money and get the drugs she needed:

When I was thirteen and had gotten onto cocaine, I liked it and I knew other people who had it, and of course there were older men and of course I had to deal with them sexually you know so that was another thing. For me it [dancing] just expanded the horizon. I got to meet other people through these men and then going out different places and socializing with them and they liked me, and I knew they had what I wanted and I put myself out there and I would initiate, you know, proposition them; yes, I would, and it was for the drugs and money. . . . They would introduce me or refer me to some of their friends, you know, if they were having a little affair or something and they would call me up: "A friend of mine needs a girl; we're having a little get-together and there's plenty of money," and I said "Sure, when, what time?" and that's what I would do. So I started dancing, doing private parties, and most of the drugs I didn't have to buy them because they had them. They always supplied the drugs.

A Lot Comes with Dancing

Sex work takes on many forms: sex for money, sex for housing, sex for drugs, sex for services, sex for favors, and so on. Sex in exchange for a product is sex work, or prostitution. The objectification of women as sexual beings, sex objects used for entertainment purposes, is just another form of sex work, as the stories of the women in this study reveal. The "adult entertainment industry" is a generic term used here for commercial sex businesses such as peep shows, go-go bars, strip clubs, and escort services. While the women in this study had no control over the conditions and traumas they experienced very early in life, they made thoughtful decisions to enter the world of sex work. Doing so was a clear turning point to crime specialization.

Of the thirty-eight women in the study, eighteen (47 percent) worked in the adult entertainment industry. All ran away from home (representing 75 percent of all runaways). As running away precedes dropping out of school, it is no surprise that nearly all (94 percent) also dropped out of school. Kelly from the middle class was not a dropout. As to socioeconomic class, a very important indicator of both running away and dropping out of school in this study, a much greater proportion of women raised poor entered the adult entertainment industry compared to women from working- and middle-class backgrounds. Among the twenty-six women from the poorest families, 62 percent chose this path, compared to 17 percent of the twelve women not raised poor. The youngest age reported for entering this work was thirteen and the oldest twenty-four; women began stripping and dancing at an average age of eighteen. Their tenure was generally short, just four or five years, but the effects life-altering.

Working in the adult entertainment industry is not just a risk factor for involvement in sex work; it is a clear pathway to sex work specialization instead of shoplifting specialization: 65 percent of sex work specialists chose this path early in their lives, compared to just one (8 percent) shoplifting specialist who began first as a sex worker before establishing herself as a shoplifter. Choosing not to work in this industry seems to insulate a woman from involvement in sex work, setting her path to shoplifting specialization.

The adult entertainment industry is a particularly inviting occupational choice for runaways and dropouts; it is yet another form of excitement they had come to embrace in their street lives and provides "easy money," or in other words a high income to work ratio. Working in these settings seems to have perpetuated heavy drug use and addiction. Most importantly, all of the women sold sex for money within these settings, positioning them on a direct course to street-level sex work. A young runaway and dropout from a poor area, Jarena's comments illustrate these themes: Working in this business is accessible and profitable, drugs and sex are central to it, and sex work on the street is the final destination.

I met other people on the block. I went to the bar; I met a girl. I was seventeen, we stayed together for two years and, you know, she danced, and I had been having a few drinks and did it. It was pretty easy. I like dancing . . . the attention, and the money, and being on the stage. It was faster; making money there was more faster than working a regular job.

I was smoking cocaine and then everything was good. I got introduced to crack cocaine there, that's when it was in the little vials, and the first time I had passed out. I got back up; it didn't scare me away. I said "I'm ready to go." I wish I had stopped, but you know, it was all in fun, you know what I mean, the partying, and the making money; I thought that was it, you know what I mean. I kept on dancing till I was twenty-one, but a lot comes with dancing between eighteen and twenty-one.

I started doing lap dances at bachelor parties, football parties, all the parties, whatever. Then I left dancing and started escorting when I was nineteen. I was introduced to escorting by my boss at the bar, and that made more money. That made more money than working at the bar so I left the bar and went into escorting. I was getting paid good. I had five guys in one day. Maybe the old guys just wanted to talk. Every man, well, they wanted a blow job, but some old guys just wanted to cuddle, you know what I mean?

I escorted till I was twenty-four, and I was introduced to the streets [street prostitution], and I worked on the streets but I was still escorting. I went to a friend of mine, and she lived really bad like I did. We walked up to Frankford Avenue, and she explained to me everything that she was going through, and she explained to me if I wanted to do it [street prostitute] that she would wait for me and what to do, you know. The first time she showed me how to do it, it was crazy, but I was willing because I was desperate. So anyway the first car came up, I looked at her, she said go ahead. Tell him to drop you off right here, and that's what I did for a long time. Cars were coming all the time in North Philly. I started hanging with her, and it seems to me it worked out pretty well. Then something happened. I was in the hotel when two of my friends were escorting, and I went with them in a room and the other one went in a room together with one guy that I saw and when I came out the room, he said to me, "Come back in an hour," and I came back, they didn't come downstairs and there was a lot of cops coming in, and what happened was they got beat, the one girl got set on fire; that was enough for me. I stopped escorting, that was enough for me; I thought I was next so I took it to the streets.

Zeleste is different from most others; she is from a working-class background and spent two years in college after earning a G.E.D. Her drug addiction began with close friends freebasing cocaine. Her drug use intensified after her sister's brutal murder, hence she began to spend more and more time in a North Philadelphia neighborhood to buy and use her drugs. Soon she would leave her job as a model for children's clothing to dance, introduced to the "life" by her new drug-using friends. Like Jarena, Zeleste was drawn to the money, enjoyed the drugs, and eventually became a street sex worker.

I started going out and getting high, and like I said I got mixed up with people who were into this dance life and dancing. I was twenty-two when I started dancing at a club. I did that for like three months and then I started escorting. A friend of mine worked for an escort service and said we should go out and do a call. So, I ended up going out on a call for an escort agency, and when I got done well, look at this money. I made like one hundred dollars for an hour, plus I got a fifty dollar tip; I was like, "Oh yeah, send me on my next one!" So then, I started checking all the time with the escort agency, and it just got easier and easier, going out on dates, making all this money [in exchange for sex]. After a while, I was doing the escorting with a little bit of the street thing. Then after things started dete-

riorating [her life from the emotional and physical addiction to crack], I wasn't escorting at all and I was just doing the street thing.

Partly dangerous, mostly exciting, this choice of work was not a last resort. It was popular and profitable in those poor, disordered, drug-infested Philadelphia neighborhoods. Introduced to the life by other girls and women similarly situated (runaways, dropouts) who were already part of it, the women remember being enticed by the prospect of "fast money, good money" and excitement of life in the fast lane, an especially appealing proposition for runaways. La Toya, a runaway who was already using drugs, began dancing at age sixteen. She needed money and knew dancing was the "in thing" in her neighborhood. Her social class position had a lot to do with it. She remembers when and why she started dancing:

I ran away a lot and then I dropped out in the eighth grade and left home for good when I was sixteen, staying with a boyfriend and back and forth to my girlfriend's house, 'cause I didn't really have no stable place; I was just a kid going from house to house. I started dancing right away. . . . Go-go dancing was in and everybody [girls] was there to get their money to do drugs. The drugs was in the club, the go-go dancing was there, the men was there, the prostitution was there, everything was there, so it was just a big circle. . . . It was in the neighborhood. You could tell, girls ran with stilettos and stuff on their way to the go-go clubs, which was about three, four blocks away from where I lived. I always knew they was around, but I never had the courage to do it until I got the drugs in me, then I was like, whatever. So you just go down and say, "Hey, can I dance or whatever?" All you do is kind of look sexy, put a little bit of makeup on, go down there, and whoever the owner is of the club ask them can you dance, ya know, give them fifteen dollars to get it, it was never no audition before you get on stage; it was nothing like that.

Just released from a juvenile correctional institution for being a chronic runaway and sent home, Shirelle ran away again and started working at a peep show to earn money for housing at fifteen. This peep show was located below an adult bookstore and on the same block as a go-go bar. She explains what working in a peep show involved:

I used to work, as strange as this may seem, at a peep show, down on 13th and Arch. There was a bookstore on top and if you go downstairs, they have live girls. I worked in a booth, my name used to be Champagne. I used to work in this booth and a guy would put two dollars in my thing. Once I saw the two dollars come down I would push the button and the screen would come up and I would just sit there in a sexy pose, you know, talk, play with my pussy . . . whatever he wanted me to do. The window would stay up for like maybe two minutes and then it would go back down. I would try to get them to put more money in.

To be sure, the women were not passive agents in these settings. They wanted to earn good money and learned just how to do it. They knew how to hustle. After Shirelle left the peep show she earned a GED, but decided to return to the industry, this time at a go-go bar. Peep shows earn women just so much money. Go-go bars and strip clubs are more crowded and tips are better. Getting in required only a simple audition (a dance on stage) or a nominal entrance fee. Shirelle remembers her decision to switch from work in a peep show to dancing at a go-go bar:

I used to walk past this club every day. It was like right next door to the peep show and it was a go-go club. Every day the bouncer used to see me and he would say, "Why are you working there; you can make so much more money over here?" He kept saying, "Come on in," and he said, "You have an hour?" I was like, "No, no, no." Then one day I actually went over there and I auditioned and I made the job. That's how I started dancing. . . . It was fast money, easy money, better than the peep show. It was quick money and good money, I could make 'bout five, six hundred easy in a night. . . . I didn't wanna be seen working at McDonald's; that wasn't enough money for me. . . . I wanted to be accepted into my society, like the older girls. I liked the lifestyle, staying out all night, being able to drink in the bars, you know, have different men lust over my body. You know, it was just, I don't know, it just felt kinda good.

Different from most other dancers, strippers, and escorts, Kelly lived in a middle-class New Jersey suburb of Philadelphia. She left home just before she turned sixteen but she graduated from high school. Strip clubs, go-go bars, and peep shows were not located in her neighborhood and her friends were not part of this lifestyle. Further, unlike the women who ran away from home as adolescents, experiences in her adult life led her down the path to sex work. Her intimate knowledge of this line of work came after she was using drugs daily and during her marriage to a cruel man who paid women to prostitute with Kelly for his gratification.

I lived with Jack; that was a crazy abusive relationship. We went down the shore one time and he had a woman come into the room. 'Cause I loved him I did what he wanted at that point; I did crazy things to keep him. I remember when she left I went down to the bar and got totally trashed. From then on in I think he fulfilled every fantasy that he wanted and that everyone else wanted. . . . If he wanted a girl for me, he would call a service and they would come out for an hour or two, or a guy, whatever. Sometimes he called two guys to come out or he'd bring me to the fantasy show bar where I had sex with the strippers in the rooms in the back. . . . I was drinking a lot, strung out. I had to, to have three men on you is disgusting. And I think at that point I did not feel anything anymore because I was everybody's toy. Whatever they asked me to do I did. I did not have any feelings anymore. The roller coaster went on and on like that until I could not take the women and men coming and going so I left and I had no money; so I, after Jack taught me well I guess, from going into fantasy show bars I figured I can go dance. So I went to work at a couple clubs 'cause from going there and getting to know some of the girls, they got me in.

Strip clubs and other settings for adult entertainment, according to the women's accounts, were perfect places for using hard drugs. Quenelle was drinking and smoking marijuana before she started dancing, but her use of hard drugs escalated at the go-go bar. There she began smoking "bowls" or "moodies," which is marijuana laced with cocaine, and then "turbos," which is marijuana mixed with crack cocaine. I asked her which came first, dancing or the drugs:

Dancin' at a go-go bar, yeah, that's where it all began. Mind you we was already drinking and smoking dope. They was lacing the pot with coke; it was called bowls or moodies and then there's turbos that's like the marijuana or weed mixture with crack. I became addicted to the weed, cocaine, turbos, and crack and now along with the alcohol it just topped it off. But Philadelphia, see the thing about the go-go clubs in Philly, it's not like you have to go outside to smoke your weed or nothing like that; it's always in the club. So when we dancing and we givin' them a lap dance, he already smoking weed or whatever he smoking, he could be turbos, bowls, moodies or whatever, passin' something, and you want to fit in and you want to get in with the crowd, you gonna tell him to pass you whatever he got, and along with the money you takin' the drugs too, so you smoking while you're doin' whatever you're doing. So that's what I meant when I said everything came at once; it wasn't like a separate time that I just started smoking, it all came at once.

"It's More Than Lap Dancing"

A few of the women who worked in the adult entertainment industry sold or traded sex before; as runaways they learned sex could get them a night off the streets. Others also knew sex could get them the drugs they craved. With the exception of Harriet and Edwina, who were taught as girls by parents to trade sex for money, the women who worked in the entertainment industry began sex work within that industry, this time for money. In fact, all of the women who ever worked as strippers, dancers, or escorts prostituted with patrons directly within those settings and outside, on the streets, in cars, and in rental rooms available specifically for sex work. La Toya's description of the adult entertainment industry as a business of sex work and drugs epitomizes this theme.

They get their money from the door [cover charge] and from the alcohol, and from the rooms, like if you want to rent a room [in the building for prostitution with a customer]. Most of the profits is from the prostitution. The doormen usually sell weed [marijuana], but it's everything you want, if you want weed, coke, if you want weed, crack, heroin, snorting powder [cocaine], and alcohol is always at the bar. If you get high, you're all right. You won't worry. They sell just about everything in the bars. You ain't got to worry about what you want, like a little world where you get everything you need. That was my little world. It wasn't like I had to go on the outside of the world. I tested my waters when I got into the go-go life before [prostituting on] the street. I just experiment. It don't come with no rule book; you just go with the flow and then as you go on, you just know the tricks of the trade of their lifestyle. You just know. You do this and make four hundred and fifty dollars, like, because he ain't never felt like that before. You know, I made him feel something special so he paid me one hundred dollars more. You know? They [bar owners who owned other clubs in New Jersey] even came and picked me up at a certain time, like twelve o'clock at McDonald's on Broad and Girard, and take me to Jersey to go in them clubs. They had a special bus to pick you up at twelve o'clock at Broad and Girard at McDonald's.

Val gives a similar account of sex work inside the clubs. Dancing and stripping is more than lap dancing; it is about sex work.

It's more than lap dancing, when you first come in, when I first came into the go-go bar, I never like to stage dance. I liked the easy stuff. I give you a lap dance and then you can whisper in my ear and tell me whether or not you want to date. Then we go upstairs and you pay off the owner of the go-go club and you got the night, or you got the room for half an hour or whatever but if you want me for the night then you got to pay me for the night.

Inside the strip clubs, go-go bars, and peep shows women learn quickly they can earn good money and have various options open to them. Bernadette describes the various services she could provide for cash:

When I was dancing, the guys were coming to take the girls, once they pick who they want to see, if they want to pick me and it was a few dollars for a show without touching and it was ten dollars, it was twenty dollars to come in my booth with me and it was fifty dollars for a hand massage, a hundred dollars for a blow job and two hundred dollars for sex so those were the options. I was bringing home about $1,500 a week.

From the Inside Out

Among those holding employment, shoplifters and sex workers similarly turned to crime as an exclusive means to generate incomes; both groups first tended to incorporate their crime of choice into their legal employment. Shoplifters who worked before becoming specialists at the crime used shoplifting to earn money for their drugs, and used their legal earnings for other necessities. Fewer sex workers ever held employment, but those who did used sex work to supplement this income. Without exception, all of the women working as strippers, dancers, and escorts began to incorporate street sex work after work hours with their sex work inside clubs and bars. They were, as many explained, getting "greedy." They wanted the best of both worlds. Inevitably, they would take it to the streets entirely. It was a necessity, they explained; their lives were getting out of control.

Street sex work, as the women explained to me, is just as easy as, sometimes even easier than, sex work in the confines of strip clubs and go-go bars. By "easier," the women mean more directly accessible at any time. And taking sex work to the street means women can keep all of their earnings, when before they gave back part of their earnings to the club or bar. If a woman finds the right neighborhood where drugs and sex work customers are close, she can take care of her drug needs at any time. La Toya left the bar partly because it was dangerous there but primarily since indoor sex work at adult entertainment settings is the less efficient alternative. She took the same path as all the others, leaving the bar setting to trick on the streets.

If I got five hundred or six hundred dollars a night at this one club; I'm not trying to stay here and get robbed because when you leave there you got to have a cab and get where you got to go because there are guys standing out there, there's girls, and they want to rob you after you come out. Robbing and stuff like that always happened. And I got a little greedy. I wanted the best of both worlds. I wanted the go-go life, and I wanted the life on the outside. I wanted a little bit of money that I can get after I leave the go-go club. I wanted to get whoever wanted a trick, whoever knew that I was go-going in my neighborhood where I was living, whoever knew me and China. Then we was done with the go go place when our drugs got real progressive and that's all we could do was smoke and pick up whoever we could pick up on the street. 'Cause when you mix the high into [the dancing] that was never going to work because then you're getting high; that lifestyle is one job by itself.

Like their counterparts working as dancers and strippers, escorts would also transition to free market sex work. After stripping Kelly worked as an escort. She learned to develop a customer base and knew she could keep all profits if she ventured on her own. So she left the confines of the escort service and decided to become her own boss.

So then I met this guy in the club [where she had been a stripper and dancer] who ran what they called an escort business but it is not; it's just a whore business. So I went to work for him, and I started, like ten in the morning he'd call; I'd call him right back with directions to his house and I'd go. I got good money; it was about a hundred and sevety-five dollars an hour, and I get a hundred and ten. I worked for him, maybe six months then went to two other girls after him who had escort services. Then I started getting really greedy for money and I started doing home calls, letting them come to my apartment. I learned about that from the girls; they would say, "You don't have to spend the money in gas and all; just let them come to you." Then I get to keep it all. . . . And I would go out to the bars, drink, and make some more money, like I would get twenty bucks to go in the car and give a blow job.

As La Toya pointed out, using drugs daily is one job by itself. All of the women who worked as dancers, strippers, and escorts supplemented their incomes with sex work inside and out until they decided finally to leave altogether and work full-time on the streets. There were no exceptions. All of the women who made the decision to work in the adult entertainment industry followed this path. Save for one, out on the streets selling sex is where they remained. Work in peep shows, as dancers and strippers in clubs and go-go bars, and as escorts clearly led these women on a distinct pathway to street sex work.

Work and Shoplifting

As touched on earlier, the adolescent and early adult decisions made by women who ended up specializing in shoplifting differ from the decisions of those who specialize in sex work in some important ways. Most of them did not run away from home or drop out of school, and often worked in conventional occupations before later relying on shoplifting as their sole means of financial support. Even when shoplifters did run away or drop out of school, they tended to work at conventional, mainstream occupations (server, cashier, health care worker, and some at skilled labor) before turning to crime to support their drug addictions. Shoplifters and sex workers are similar, as discussed previously, in that most shoplifters first used this crime as a way to supplement earnings from their legal occupations, just as most sex workers first began to incorporate street sex work with their jobs as dancers, strippers, and escorts.

Tracy ran away from home at fourteen, was out of the house permanently by sixteen, and was working with a GED at nineteen. While she shares some characteristics of sex workers—socialization into alcohol use as a child, running away, and dropping out of school—she still lived in a working-class area and worked a conventional occupation rather than living life on the streets, perhaps in part a consequence of her close connection with mainstream ways of life. While she still defines herself differently from other drug users, she too turned to crime as a way of life when her drug addiction became the primary focus of her life.

I was working, and for a while there wasn't any drugs; I didn't even smoke cigarettes. I always kept a job. I always cleaned my house. I always had a car, owned my own houses. When I was twenty-one, I started using crack; when I was twenty-three I snorted cocaine and then went to the oxy. [OxyContin, known as "oxycotton" on the streets, is a narcotic often used to relieve pain in cancer patients. On the streets the pill is crushed and snorted for an immediate and powerful high.] Then I started with the dope [heroin], it turned me into a monster. Then my whole attitude toward everything just changed. I stopped caring; I was antisocial. At work I didn't even want to talk. Everything just got on my nerves. I kept going home early. I started calling out. I just stopped wanting to go altogether.

I started shoplifting with people I hung out with who were already boosting [shoplifting], so it was just convenient. Instead of going to work, it was easier just boostin'. In the beginning, I had the car still so we started riding around to different places to different areas and going boosting. I used to drive and they'd come running out with this whole shopping cart of baby formula, and I'd have the trunk popped and hop in and we'd take off. I liked boostin'. We did it every day. Every day it was a job, a full-time job, every day. We wouldn't get high until we cashed out [sold stolen merchandise for money] everything. . . . Most people are hookers on the street, homeless people; that's not me. They have no morals or respect for themselves or anyone else, no class; they don't shower. I wasn't raised that way. I may have ran away from home, but at least I knew to clean myself; I knew proper etiquette and how to take care of myself, you know.

Alice, an African American from a working-class background, never ran away from home; she graduated from high school, and took a job at a supermarket. She explains her entry into drugs and shoplifting:

I had a little job after school and when I graduated from high school, I started working for Pathmark. I went to Community and took some courses but didn't complete it [degree]. I was definitely scared to steal because I saw them arresting other people there. So, um, I mean down to the little nickel candy, I paid for it. It wasn't until I started using drugs that I started shoplifting. As I said, I started drinking at a young age just for fun; my parents always had alcohol in the house. I had experimented with marijuana, but not until maybe about twenty-six I started using PCP [same as angel dust] and cocaine [rolled in a cigarette paper] with some people that I just met along the way, just hanging out or met 'em through other people. I had to go outside of my neighborhood, 'cause they don't sell it in my neighborhood. So, I started meeting different people. . . . Maybe about a year later I started more cocaine, a few times a week, not every day, sometimes every day, but not consistently, but it was still a problem. So, I think, that's when the shoplifting came in because I wasn't working as much. I actually started stealing from my job; I lost my job due to stealing from my job. . . . I guess I felt it was more respectful to steal I guess than prostitute.

Shoplifters as a group were both less likely to run away from home and less likely to drop out of school compared to sex workers as a group; 77 percent of sex workers dropped out of school, compared to 33 percent of shoplifters. Shoplifters were also more likely to live in working- or middle-class neighborhoods, at first integrating crime with work when they had jobs before their addictions progressed to the point that they relied on crime for earnings.

Veronica's story provides another contrasting example of a shoplifter's path from addiction to shoplifting specialization (instead of sex work). A graduate of St. Joe's University, she had established herself in a profitable career, but in her fourteenth year of that occupation, a newly acquired cocaine addiction began to take hold of her life. She was not in desperate financial circumstances when she started to shoplift; crime supplemented her earnings until drug use became more important than work. She could maintain her financial and social "image" by supplementing her income with shoplifting earnings.

Because I had to pay my bills, that's when the stealing started. Because I needed money for the drugs and to maintain and keeping an image. So I started using and stealing, and because I was dressed fairly decent or keep this image because that's what I was used to, I could no longer afford that, so I started stealing, and that's where it began. I've tried part-time jobs, but then that takes away from me getting high. So I couldn't do that. I've been in my addiction for twenty years, cocaine. . . . I would make a day out of it once I had lost my job. So I was shoplifting every day. So I had all this free time, so I was out, so I planned my day from about eight-thirty until twelve o'clock and that's what I was doing.

Rose kept legal work for a couple of years after her daily use of heroin began. Like other shoplifters, she managed to maintain that tie to conventional life, supplementing her drug habit with profits from shoplifting until getting the drug became "like another job," her primary job.

Well, it was expensive, up ten dollars, a bag of heroin would last all day; then that ten dollars to twenty and then thirty and then forty dollars. It was daily, and it would suck up all my money; I was working every day, and I waitressed, so I came home with eighty or a hundred dollars a day, and still no bills were getting paid. Spending the money on the drugs, the gas gauge on the car was almost empty. It's like spending all my money on it, and then from the heroin you get so tired and then you start buying rock [crack] to wake me up because that was just so readily available. I would just take a drive down the street to another neighborhood. I knew where to go; like it's not in my neighborhood, I live up in the northeast (Philadelphia). I mean you might have to get in a car and drive to it. It became like work, it became like another job. I mean I was getting up, I didn't have to be in work until nine in the morning and I worked all the way in Horsham, which is a far drive, and I used to drive from northeast, down to North Philly in the morning, to Horsham, and then after work I had some more money, so I would drive from Horsham back to North Philly, then all the way back to the northeast. I mean this took up most of my day. I mean this got tough, just so I wouldn't be sick, and it really got to the point where it wasn't about being high anymore, it just got to the point of feeling normal, about being right. I started shoplifting, but I mean I still worked. I was pocketing stuff, but normally I would have never of done that, never. . . . At one point I was getting unemployment and the unemployment ran out, and there was a couple of weeks when I wasn't working and I was like, oh my gosh, what am I going to do now? I even started working at a nursing home, but it got to that point because my house got on sheriff sale.

Life-Changing Decisions

Unhealed early life trauma of shoplifters and sex workers manifested in intensified drug use, typically in the context of social networks outside of the home. Shoplifters and sex workers victimized at home fled to the streets and peers, by running away (sex workers especially) or spending more and more time outside of their homes in neighborhoods where they knew they could get drugs (typically shoplifters). Involvement with other drug users reinforced their own use, contributing to their addictions in adolescence and young adulthood. By their early life trauma and victimization, they followed a path to adolescent female substance abuse established by research. These commonalities aside, sex workers followed an adolescent path more characteristic of the female offender, shoplifters a different one. Running away from home distinguishes sex workers and shoplifters during this period of life. It is both a result of trauma and a predictor of things to come: revictimization, survival crime, entry into the adult entertainment industry, and sex work.

Running away from home is a consequence of child abuse. In a Canadian study of 3,760 nonoffending girls and women comparing those abused and those not abused, researchers identified physical abuse and sexual abuse as important factors leading girls to runaway. Having experienced physical abuse or sexual abuse doubled the chances a girl would run. Consistent with other scholarship, the research also found that girls and women who were victims of multiple abuses were even more likely to respond by running away from their homes during adolescence. In fact, those who were both physical and sexually abused were four times more likely to run away.[2] In my study too, women who suffered sex abuse and additional traumas were the most overrepresented among runaways. An expression of child abuse, adolescent runaway is a risk factor for criminal involvement.[3] For example a survey of girls incarcerated in U.S. juvenile correctional settings indicated that 61 percent were victims of physical abuse, more than half victims of sexual abuse, and about 80 percent ran away.[4] Research in San Francisco with 200 female sex workers reported that 60 percent were victims of sexual abuse before age sixteen, and these girls ran away from the abuse in nearly every case.[5]

The typical woman in my study who ran was just under fourteen years old, abused in her home, was using drugs, and fled to the most problematic and criminogenic neighborhoods of Camden and Philadelphia, where she bonded with other drug users. According to the Office of Juvenile Justice and Delinquency Prevention, the National Longitudinal Survey of Youth shows that about 18 percent of youth in the United States ran away from their homes by age seventeen; 5 percent ran at age fourteen, 6 percent at age fifteen, 7 percent at age sixteen, and 6 percent at age seventeen.[6] While physical and sexual abuse backgrounds factor into the lives of some runaways (about 21 percent), runaways who are considered the most endangered are very young (thirteen years or younger) with a history of abuse at home, use hard drugs, are drug dependent, and flee to crime-ridden areas.[7] Endangered runaways (about 71 percent of all runaways) are at risk for continued harm. They are usually also in the company of others who use drugs (like peers), had tried to commit suicide in the past, were truant, were victimized on the streets, and had exchanged sex for housing, food, money, or drugs.

Girls who run from abusive homes are at risk for new victimization, this time on the streets. One study in Iowa of forty adolescent runaways found that after running away from home, 53 percent of the girls were assaulted with a weapon, 45 percent were raped, 39 percent were beaten, and 23 percent were victims of robbery when they were on the streets.[8] Girls, according to that research, are more likely to be sexually victimized than are boys. Another study of 974 boys and girls in the United States found that 36 percent of girls were robbed, 31 percent beaten, 30 percent threatened with a weapon, and 23 percent raped. Just 7 percent of boys in that same study were also victims of rape.[9] A similar study looked at the effects of sex abuse, length of time as a runaway, drug use, and other factors on the likelihood that runaway girls would become victims of sexual abuse on the streets. Those researchers found that sex abuse in particular puts girls at an elevated risk for sexual abuse when they are homeless runaways.[10]

Running away from home means girls often turn to crime that will earn them a place to sleep, money, drugs, food, and clothing. They might panhandle, shoplift, steal food, and sell drugs, but selling sex is often the best alternative for a young runaway out of school and on the streets. One study using a nationally representative sample found 28 percent of street runaways and homeless youth traded sex to survive on the streets;[11] a similar one, in Montreal, reports a rate of 55 percent for girls.[12] Another study compared sexually abused adolescents with a sample of sexually abused adolescents who prostitute. While both groups were abuse victims, those who would become sex workers ran away from home at a significantly greater rate (77 percent, compared to 44 percent) than sexually abused children not involved in the crime.[13] It was not the decision to run that led to sex work, but rather a mix of consequences stemming from the runaway experience and vulnerabilities carried over from early childhood. For example, Gilfus links childhood abuse and sex work among imprisoned inmates to the decision to run away, which often leads to school dropout, homelessness, few employment opportunities, the need to sell sex for survival, and consequently immersion into street crime.[14]

Poor school performance, truancy, frequent school transitions, and especially school dropout are risk factor for delinquency. The Bureau of Justice Statistics estimated that 68 percent of inmates incarcerated in U.S. prisons over 1997 did not receive a high school diploma, compared to just 18 percent of men and women in the general population.[15] About 70 percent of women in state prisons never completed high school. Similar to results among women in my study who dropped out of school, criminal offenders who are minorities have higher dropout rates than nonminorities; 30 percent of White prisoners in 1997 completed high school, compared to 21 percent of Black and Hispanic inmates.

Shoplifting, sex work, and other street survival crimes of runaways are partly a function of street peer networks. According to research by Hagan and McCarthy set in Canada, children who flee to the streets from abusive homes bond with others in deviant and criminal peer networks, in part to seek companionship, as my research also shows. These networks are also instrumental in shaping the behavior of youth involved through a process of socialization and education that involves a teaching and learning about things such as how to recognize criminal opportunities and how to carry out crimes to survive on the streets. The research revealed significant effects of tutelage in street networks on drug selling, theft, and sex work.[16] When youth embed themselves in these networks, their involvement in crime increases significantly. My findings similarly show that girls on the street learn how to make money by selling their bodies, for example, and working as dancers and strippers. They learned these things from others situated in deviant networks. Years before Hagan and McCarthy, Letkemann described how even when networks are sought out for a sense of belonging and companionship, the process of association that occurs is not simply social. Rather, it involves a learning process in which essential information about available opportunities in deviance and crime (safe cracking, robbery, and burglary in his study) and the range of techniques passes from member to member and from experienced members to newcomers.[17] Another study found that girls who fled their abusive homes were likely to become involved with deviant peers, and these associations not only increased their risk of survival crime, but also their alcohol and drug use as my research also shows.[18] During this transition to adulthood, girls involve themselves with drug-using peers in places where they can easily obtain these drugs, and this involvement reinforces their drug use. For example, a study in Utah on adolescent substance abuse found that, compared to boys, girls are more likely to use drugs in the context of drug using peer networks and that they use drugs within neighborhoods where they think or know these drugs are readily available.[19] "Similarity breeds connection" according to McPherson and colleagues in an essay on homophily in social networks.[20] Homophily in social networks, according to the authors, structures our relationships and our ties to others and to social institutions (peer groups, marriage, work, support systems). Girls, for example, emotionally scarred by abuses in violent homes who use drugs and seek companionship on the street would bond with others who share these commonalities, not with girls who shun the use of drugs, live in affluent, peaceful, protected homes, and are engaged in school and civic activities. When girls socialize and bond with others similarly situated, experiences that occur in these social networks (drug use, for example) serve to reinforce commonalities among members and therefore reinforce connection to these networks.

In my study, women abused during childhood who did not run away still fled to the streets to the same neighborhoods and deviant peer groups that runaways did. Like runaways, they learned where and how to get the drugs they needed and how to earn money through crime in their involvement with street networks. However, many of them did not put crime to work until later. They had more protective mechanisms in place—still living at home, usually graduated from high school, and sometimes working in conventional jobs—and were less embedded in these networks. While they were still becoming drug dependent, they were less entrenched in the street life, less likely to engage in survival crimes, to be victims on the street, to work in the adult entertainment industry, and to enter into sex work.

According to my study, girls from the poorest communities, victims of serious childhood traumas, and runaway girls are at risk of entry into the adult entertainment industry. Furthermore, girls and women willingly engage in sex work during this employment, and their involvement sends them on a fast track to street sex work. Extant research has not focused on these issues specifically. A growing body of scholarship on dancers and strippers covers subjects on the social milieu of establishments,[21] reasons women choose the work, how workers perform, how they manage clients, social stigma, and emotional well-being,[22] and the characteristics and motives of patrons.[23] It suggests women from all social class backgrounds involve themselves in this work and that, like the women in my study, their motivation is primarily financial. Interviews with twenty female strippers across the United States also showed that young women select the work for its entertainment, to practice the art of dance, to remain physically fit, and much less often for reasons related to unresolved trauma of childhood.[24] While women are enticed by the money that dancing, stripping, and escorting can bring, according to research, there are downsides to the work. This includes the stigma women feel and emotional tensions stirred up by their status as dancer or stripper and the men who want more than just to observe. To make this job work for them, according to research, women balance their autonomy and emotional well-being against the demands of work, which can be demoralizing and sometimes abusive. Barton's work on strippers, for example finds that the financial rewards and flexibility of this work appeal to women (who range from middle-class college students to women struggling to survive desperate financial circumstances), but having to deal with negative forces like social stigma and sexual advances by men inevitably harms them emotionally ending their careers.[25] A study of topless dancers in the U.S. Southwest conducted in 1993 and then ten years later characterized topless dancers as women who feel stigmatized, who then create excuses for their involvement, distancing themselves emotionally by redefining themselves as dancers rather than deviants.[26] Women in my study told of different experience in all of these respects.

Research on sex work by women working as dancers and strippers suggests sex for sale is taboo and unwanted by women themselves. For example, a Chicago study that included women working as dancers, in escort services, and in other indoor settings reported that 24 percent sold sex when they were dancers and 18 percent when they were escorting, but researchers framed the study as violence against women, not work.[27] In another study, dancers in Tampa Bay might have earned extra tips by lap dancing, but there would be no selling of sex and full nudity would be out of the question. In contrast, women in my study were expected by management, other workers, and patrons to sell sex, they even performed fully nude sex with one another on stage, and selling sex was a real part of their job.[28]

The character of work the women in my study performed at peep shows, go-go bars, and strip clubs is not burlesque, not art, not dance. Upscale exotic dance clubs depicted in research may retain some of the elements of traditional burlesque, but they are not in Camden or in Philadelphia where women in my study worked.[29] Their bars and clubs were located in and around poor and disordered neighborhoods, along adjacent highways, and near trucking destinations. They were in neighborhoods where the drug culture thrives, serving as another source sustaining that economy and providing outlets for girls and women to use drugs, earn money, and enjoy the fast life. My findings owe partly to the characteristics of my study group and the social setting of their working establishments, but their experiences are doubtfully exceptional.

Like their nonoffending counterparts, women in crime often work two or three jobs to help meet financial needs. For women in my study, selling sex indoors as well as on the streets helped them to meet increasing financial demands of their drug addictions. Shoplifters previously employed had the same sort of experiences, first incorporating crime earnings into their legal occupations, and then shifting the balance to crime work. Over time, both groups left the legitimate working world, immersing themselves into life in crime. Other researchers have noted how offenders rely on dual sources of income in two parallel economies, one legal and one criminal, and how many make the move to crime work. For example, a nearby study of women's transitions through the legal and illicit economies found that women supplement legitimate earnings with crime, and once seriously drug dependent, they abandon legitimate employment for crime.[30] Set in New York, the life history research with drug-addicted women found that when dissatisfied with their low pay, many young women began to incorporate crime earnings into their legal wages, through drug selling and theft, for example. Some even used workplaces as stations to carry out crimes. At work in a hospital, one woman earned money by stealing truckloads of supplies and selling them. Other women balanced both, earning income through a legitimate job and then through crime during off hours. Earning a very low wage at a department store, another woman began work for a drug dealer after her regular workday. As a group, the women lived entirely through crime once they became deeply entrenched into the drug world. Fagan and Freeman connect decisions to incorporate illegal work with legal work and decisions to shift to crime work as a function of monetary returns as well as time considerations.[31] Reliance on dual economies (legal and criminal) is especially important for youth and adults living in inner cities (and arguably the less educated, drug dependent, and youth entrenched into the street life), in part because they have fewer options in the legal sector for stable jobs promising personal and professional growth, job security, and increasingly higher earnings. Money through crime can come more rapidly, over a shorter duration, than earnings through legal work, another benefit of crime over alternative low-paying jobs. These decisions, according to Fagan and Freeman, are rational ones.

Stripping, escorting, and dancing, sex work, and shoplifting are occupational choices. Certainly, patriarchy and a cruel economic system, the disease of addiction, and troubled lives frame the availability of choices, but women resolve dilemmas of work by exercising choice. Some research offers a different view, particularly when it comes to dancing, stripping, and sex work. According to Farley, women selling sex indoors and on the streets are victims of oppression harmed by paid rape who must "tune out the poison" inflicted upon them by men.[32] Raphael and Shapiro refer to women who no longer involve themselves in sex work as "survivors of prostitution,"[33] as do other researchers studying violence against women. However, sex workers tend to define themselves as workers and their position as work. Consistent with my findings, Canadian researchers learned from workers in strip clubs that it was "neither duress nor despair that lead these women to make this choice, but rather reasons very much like those motivating the choice to enter other professions."[34] Sex workers in Miami, according to Kurtz and colleagues, refer to themselves as and prefer the terms "sex worker" and "working woman" to prostituted women. Similarly, research in Washington found that sex workers and women working in the adult entertainment industry made choices after evaluating benefits and drawbacks of various forms of work and factors like job flexibility, financial rewards, and work environment.[35] Women in Barton's research also explained their decision to work as dancers and strippers as a thoughtful evaluation of alternative options. Unlike nine-to-five jobs, dancing and stripping afford women more free time because the work schedule is so flexible, but most importantly the pay is better than other available work, and this is especially important for women with little promise for professional careers. Another Canadian project found of escorts and sex workers that their choices to enter these occupations outweighed benefits of alternatives. These fields provided more flexibility in schedules, social entertainment, and popularity within social networks, while alternative low-paying jobs, for example, at McDonald's would constrain their independence, sense of worth, and income. For these reasons, sex workers and escorts refused to take on alternative options of low-paid, impoverished work.[36]

The paths to shoplifting and sex work for women in my study were paved by early life trauma and further clarified with adolescent and young adult experiences. Both groups would seek companionship on the streets further reinforcing their reliance on drugs. Sex work specialists usually ran from their homes. Shoplifters were more likely to stay at home until later ages in the predominately working- and middle-class neighborhoods in which they lived. While they bought or used their drugs in similar settings as women from impoverished areas, middle-class expectations and culture continued to condition their lives to some extent. Shoplifters were much less likely to drop out of school, perhaps a product of their middle-class ties but no doubt a function of the lesser traumas they suffered earlier on. Not running away, not dropping out of school, and working in conventional occupations from time to time protected them in many ways from the pulls to sex work so evident in the lives of women raised in the drug-infested, poor environments who did become part of the urban street culture as runaways and dropouts. Sex workers were more likely than were shoplifters to have suffered additional traumas in adolescence—particularly violence on the streets and the dilemma of trading sex for housing brought on by their runaway status. Lower class culture seems also to have conditioned the choices of sex workers, particularly those who were runaways. These women were aware of the commercial sex industry in their own neighborhoods as girls; they knew it was an option open to them. Living the fast life, especially as runaways and dropouts, they knew their sexuality could earn them money they needed. Their decision to work in the commercial sex industry was an important step in their specialization in street sex work.

The crime preferences of the women in my study were conditioned by the social circumstances in which they lived—social class and culture, as well as abuse early in life—but also by the important decisions they made in adolescence and young adulthood. Once addictions became most important in their lives, the women made thoughtful decisions to live through crime—relinquishing employment and hustling money through other crimes when presented with opportunities, but most especially maintaining specializations as shoplifters and sex workers. Women in my study are survivors of child abuse and neglect, certainly drug addiction, even homelessness and violence on the streets, and they survived many years *through* crime, but they did not *survive* crime. For them, sex work and shoplifting are voluntary occupational choices. In the next chapter, I explore how the women in this study are able to make the jobs of shoplifting and sex work profitable and reliable specializations as participants in the urban drug culture.

4. *Making Crime Specialization Work in the Urban Drug Culture*

Shoplifting's my crime, that's my crime. —Carmela

In this chapter, I explain how women interviewed for this study maintained specializations as shoplifters or sex workers. Well integrated into the urban drug culture, all of the women were addicted to drugs. In addition to paying for food, housing, and other necessities, the women had their addictions to feed. Over the course of these addictions, they engaged in various crimes such as sex work in strip clubs, shoplifting, other forms of theft, and occasional drug selling, before establishing their specializations and relinquishing employment for criminal careers. Any line of work that the women might settle into had to produce a lucrative, reliable, and efficient source of income. While sex work's capacity to produce such cash flows has attracted scholarly attention, this chapter offers fresh data, which suggest that shoplifting is a viable a source of income. Shoplifting requires less time and may produce more income than sex work. However, as I show in this chapter, the pull to sex work is strong, and success as a shoplifter places more demands on women than success as a sex worker. As a result, fewer women in the study maintained themselves by shoplifting (32 percent); most gravitated toward sex work specialization (68 percent).

Neighborhoods where the women resided and engaged in their drug use are among the most economically deprived and socially disordered urban areas of Philadelphia and Camden. They harbor drug cultures where the drug trade (i.e., drug packaging, distribution, and sales) and drug use, which are pervasive, organize economic and social life. Bernadette told me: "In all the areas there's drugs everywhere. There's drugs on every corner. There's different people that got houses, they got people running drug houses, running crack houses, shooting galleries, there's crime everywhere." While this illicit economy operates around the drug trade, it also involves other forms of criminal behavior committed by individuals and businesses alike. Drug users commit crimes to earn money for their drug addictions, while others rent out indoor locations where drug users feel safe, operate illegal hotels for transient housing and sex work, and purchase shoplifted merchandise for resale profit. The attitudes and behaviors within the drug culture characterize a social life not only tolerant of deviance, but also in many ways expectant of crime.

As the women in this study explained why they chose to specialize in shoplifting and sex work and how they worked their crimes, it became clear that crime specialization depends not only on the women's active efforts, but also on neighborhood resources. Specifically, women's ability to make crime specialization work for them in their urban drug cultures is conditioned by their access to crime, their personal knowledge and resourcefulness, and what I refer to as *accommodating systems.* Access to crime refers to basic demand for illicit goods and services (sex work and shoplifted goods). Personal knowledge and resourcefulness concerns the skills women acquire as sex workers or shoplifters and their ability to acquire status and exploit their reputations for gain. Accommodating systems (e.g., hack drivers willing to transport shoplifters, rooming houses, speakeasies) comprise neighborhood structures that enable women to maintain criminal specialties in either sex work or shoplifting by facilitating the crimes. These factors—access, personal knowledge and resourcefulness, and accommodating systems—are fundamentally important for successful specialties in shoplifting and in sex work, but in different respects for each crime.

How Shoplifting Is Financially Profitable

Opportunities for shoplifting are limited in Philadelphia and Camden neighborhoods where the women in this study lived and used drugs. Such neighborhoods have local corner stores, bodegas, or "mom and pop" stores, but they lack the larger, well-stocked establishments that are most suitable for profitable shoplifting. Tracy explains why she never shoplifted in her neighborhood: "We didn't shoplift there because they didn't have much stores over there, not like they got over in [New] Jersey." As a result, profitable shoplifting requires women to travel outside of the neighborhoods to suburban shopping malls or downtown department stores. Veronica explains: "I would always go in a suburban section. I would go away from my home. We didn't have very many stores, so I would travel." Areas with shopping malls and large department stores such as Macy's, Target, Wal-Mart, and J. C. Penny, auto parts stores, pharmacies such as CVS, and home goods stores such as Home Depot are the best locations for shoplifting. Esther comments: "That was shoplifters' heaven, where all malls is, shoplifter's heaven. I'm serious."

Francine's picture of shoplifting sheds light on the money that shoplifting brings:

> *And the money? Sometimes you can steal enough where you don't have to go out every day. You could be cool for a whole week if you have a good day.* [What is a good day?] *For me a good day is two hundred because I only shop a bag at a time, maybe two or three bags a day. You boost [shoplift] enough for your drugs, something to eat, who you owed, the dope man [drug dealer], and the drivers [individuals hired for transportation to and from stores for shoplifting].*

The women rarely have their own vehicles for travel, but they avoid using public transportation. Waiting for a bus wastes time when a woman plans to go to several different locations during a single shoplifting event. Efficient use of time is even more important when shoplifting's goal is quick cash to buy drugs. Riding on a bus limits what a woman can carry, reducing her productivity. The bus also makes women more vulnerable to apprehension, making public transportation a bad idea for shoplifters, whose freedom from apprehension depends on staying out of sight and earshot. Sandy learned this directly: "When I caught the bus, I had to crouch on the bus several times. The guy that finally arrested me said the reason he arrested me was 'cause he heard me talking on the bus, talking about something I got for somebody. . . . It's easier in a car."

Hacks or Drivers

Gypsy cabs or unlicensed taxi services that offer low-cost car service in urban neighborhoods are the principle mode of transportation for shoplifters. Called "hacks" or "drivers" by the women in this study, these entrepreneurs drive neighborhood residents for legitimate purposes, such as trips to the grocery store or medical appointments, but they also help transport drug users to dealers and take shoplifters to their targets and return them to their neighborhoods. Carmela explains the hacks' function, the competition among them, and the profits they earn in her neighborhood:

[Would you shoplift at places that you could get to walking?] *No, I would get rides.* [From whom?] *Hacks. I would probably right now say they call me the queen of shoplifting. Everyone calls me the queen. I got hacks that I could call and they'd take me out right now. I've seen three people, three hacks arguing with each other because they wanted to take me out, and I went with the fourth one!* [Who are hacks?] *There's hacks down on the street; anyone on the street will take you 'cause they're getting half. They're hacking for drugs [driving to support their own drug addictions], so instead of getting five dollars and take someone across town, they're taking you to shoplift, they're gonna make a hundred or more. They'll bring you wherever you wanted to go. Most of my drivers are good friends of mine now.*

Shoplifters generally pay hacks half the profits when the shoplifters sell or, as they describe it, "cash in" or "cash out" their goods. From the hack's vantage point, earnings associated with driving for shoplifters are greater than those associated with transporting people within their neighborhoods or simply taking residents across town. Esther says: "Can't drive a lick, don't drive nowhere. I get a driver, so I say to my driver, you drive me to Pep Boys, you get paid good, and they always do it."

Francine has drivers who will take her as far as New York City, about a two-hundred-mile round trip: "You get a good driver who don't mind drivin'. You have to take care of your driver. He'll take you to New York if you have to. Ya know, well not many people go to New York, but they go across the bridge to different places [in New Jersey]. [*What would you pay the driver?*] Half. Say, I make fifty, the driver gets fifty."

Driving shoplifters may be more time-consuming than shuttling residents running errands or making simple cross-town trips because shoplifters travel farther, but the greater return on shoplifting travel reinforces hackers' involvement as accessories to shoplifting, especially when they too are drug users. Candee's comments illustrate this point:

Say I take a hack and we go and then cash in and then I want to look for another place [to shoplift]. Sometimes the hack gets sick [from a need for drugs], so I just go to make a quick hundred. I go in [the store], run out, cash in, have everything you want. We got the gas, we got the tolls, and we get some drugs so we're both not sick no more. Then we go get the next stores. [So you went this morning. How much did you net?] *Three hundred, my drivers made one fifty each.*

Customers and the Demand for Goods

Demand for below-retail-priced goods is pervasive in distressed neighborhoods harboring drug cultures.[1] This makes shoplifting outside of the neighborhood profitable within the neighborhood. Alice explains this illicit economy and the opportunities it creates: "There's an economy out there that wants the product. And if one person can do that product, I took it like selling Avon. It's just like running a sale in the department store."

Shoplifters can earn money by returning stolen goods to the store without a receipt, but doing this is inefficient, risky, and limits earning capacity. Women who seek steady incomes must avoid this approach; they must sell their products. While demand for shoplifted goods clearly exists in the urban drug culture, it is not as obvious and noticeable as drug use, drug selling, and sex work. Buyers for shoplifted goods require cultivation. Often through word of mouth, but generally through directed effort, the women who specialize in shoplifting have recognized demand and established themselves as reliable suppliers of "discount" goods to regular buying customers who are also part of the drug culture. Stable demand facilitates earnings sufficient to sustain shoplifters and their drug needs. When shoplifters cash in, fair market value presumed among them and their customers is half the marked retail price. This is the general rule, unless urgency necessitates a lower price. Tracy's description of two customer groups she developed illustrates these ideas:

[Where would you sell?] *Just in the neighborhood. Strictly in the neighborhood. Usually to drug dealers or meth users; they wanted video games, PS II games, DVDs, [store] gift cards. People had so much faith in us as a group we had people who would call as they're driving by. . . . We went to corner stores.* [How would you know to go there?] *You start going to different stores. You hear about it from other people, and then you always throw that little question in, you know, "You need baby formula?" After a while, you start knowing people who grow an interest in certain things, like store owners, like the mom and pop stores they want baby formula, Enfamil and Similac. I used to steal it at six and eight [dollars] a can, the big ones cost like fifteen [dollars]. Usually I take a couple dollars off for mom and pop [the local corner stores] . . . so it would be half whatever it costs.*

Shoplifters must develop rapport and trust with their customers. Veronica explains how her relationship with customers evolved. It is standard that shoplifters obtain written lists of merchandise, or "orders," requested by customers, particularly local stores. For shoplifters such as herself, shoplifting is a business venture. She recounts:

I had clients. That's what they were; my clients were storeowners that I had in the neighborhoods, little grocery stores. . . . Well they had a tendency to have meat departments in the back of the store and I would sell them shrimp and they might buy ten bags and give me like $80. Well, for them that would be a lot because shrimp, one bag would be $30. Then they want lobster tails. [How did you know to go there?] *Because I lived in the neighborhood myself and how did I find out? I think one day I just walked in. It started with me selling it to maybe one or two people in the stores then one in the Dominican [store]. Then I would place [take] a bigger order, then the order got bigger and bigger.*

For Sandy, status as a reputable and favored shoplifter leads to constant demand for her goods, which guarantees sale. This enables her to select among customers who will give her the best return for her effort. While she sells to individuals, she prefers local shops. Proprietors of local shops are the shoplifters' most common customers, and the women rely heavily on their continued demand. Sandy takes orders from customers but can shoplift effectively without orders because she knows that whenever she has goods, they will sell. She explains:

[How many customers do you have, would you say?] *The individuals, twenty-two to twenty-five people, I guess, but mostly stores in Cramer hill and most of the stores in North Camden.* [Certain stores?] *Every store you go into, all these little corner stores. I even have one corner store in Cramer Hill that sells my quilts right on the shelves! He buys 'em off me for a certain amount and then sells them in the stores for a certain amount. . . . For instance, bodegas, they'll ask me, like, if they want a queen size or king size [comforter or sheet set] or a certain type of pattern that they want. They even get the books [store catalogs] and show me in the book! . . . and then I steal it, go back, and just walk into the store, give them the quilt, they give me the cash, and I walk out. If I know that these people want a certain amount of sheets and I know I'm the only person going in Strawbridge's and Macy's and grabbin' 'em, then I know the price I can ask. Sometimes I just go and grab what I can grab and then take it to a store and see if they like it or not. And then there's times where people ask me, they want this to match that or this quilt and those sets of curtains, this six-hundred-dollar Ralph Lauren or Tommy Hill sheet set with the quilt to match, and then I'll do that. . . . Whenever I have something, I'm guaranteed to sell it. The point is where I want to go to sell it, because I know which person is going to give me the most and which person is going to give me the least, as a last resort and first priority.*

According to Carmela, most mom and pop stores in one section of her neighborhood are buying customers: "[I sell in] stores all over Camden, I have stores in East, North, and Polock Town . . . I would say North Camden is the biggest. I could go to any store in North Camden."

Other types of businesses that serve neighborhood residents are another source of customers. These include auto repair shops, hair salons, and bars or speakeasies (unlicensed bars in private residences that sell inexpensive homemade liquor at all hours). Shoplifters are able to sell goods quickly and at greater quantities to patrons within these settings than they are on the streets and to customers spread throughout the neighborhood. Eileen explains:

I'd take things I thought I could get rid of. Like, I used to go in a place and I would steal cordless phones 'cause I knew that I could get rid of those easy. You know things that people would actually need. [How would you get rid of these things?] *I used to go into a hair salon and people would buy 'em. 'Cause I would go to the hair salon and I would see people [other shoplifters] coming and selling clothes and things like that, and they would make a lot of money so, I gave me a bright idea, oh, I could do the same thing . . . and it worked.*

Francine prefers to work with customers in local bars and speakeasies. As a rule, she takes orders from customers before she shoplifts but feels confident that whatever she shoplifts will sell. Her use of these establishments in the neighborhood enables her to meet her drug needs efficiently:

It was never a problem selling stuff. [Would you take orders in advance or would you just have an idea that people would buy?] *Well sometimes, they say, "Can you get me a pair of Dockers?" and you know when you can, and you say "Yeah, I can get you a pair. How many pairs you want? What size are you?" You take orders and then you go where you usually go and make money and it's mostly bars. I'd go to speakeasies. Speakeasies are everywhere. . . . I'd get the money, then I'd get me a shot of corn liquor, and then I'd stop and get me two bags of coke, and go to the gallery [Shooting Gallery, a drug-use location] and mix my stuff up.*

Veronica sells to both individuals in the community and local stores. Selling to drug dealers supplements her earnings. Stockpiling goods is effective for quick sale, immediate access to money for many of the shoplifters. Veronica says: "Well I know that the dealers like certain things. This one had orders for ties, big things of ties; people like that stuff. . . . When I needed money I just have to go down my basement; then I would start saying, 'Oh, who needs this and that?' When you get around, you can get a good deal."

Eileen also sells to drug dealers who place orders for different types of goods they need at different times: "They would put in orders. They say, 'Well, if you could get me this, then you'll get this [amount of money]'; you know, you'd have a certain amount of time to get it for them."

Esther avoids drug dealers and sells to neighborhood businesses from whom she is most likely to obtain a financial payoff worth the risk of apprehension and punishment posed by her offending. She reasons that by virtue of their status as addicted women, dealers may exploit female shoplifters, assuming they are desperate and willing to accept an unfair price for their goods. She explains to whom she would normally sell car batteries and why she avoids drug dealers:

Take 'em and go sell 'em to the garage for half price, with warranty. I'm serious! Never sell 'em to a dope dealer because they feel as though that you so bad off to do it. You got a ninety-eight-dollar battery and they telling you ten dollars. No sir, you go right directly to, you know, to somebody who knows the worth of it, and they give you your proper price. [Does that mean that you were not that bad off with the drugs?] *No, that means, I was horrible! That means I was hard off, boy. But you know, come on, you just done committed a felony, and I don't play with that. . . . Enough of 'em [batteries] it would be grand larceny.*

Not all of the shoplifters share Esther's point of view. Especially once a woman has developed experience and status, a businesslike relationship with drug dealers can be quite lucrative, as Carmela has found. Her supply of merchandise to dealers also helps to sustain the drug culture and its illicit economy. She comments: "I was selling them walkie-talkies over in North Camden to all the drug dealers. I was getting like forty dollars for a set for that."

Nonetheless, a hierarchy of preferred customers described by the women places local bodegas, corner stores or mom and pop stores, and other establishments over drug dealers, drug users, and other individuals within the neighborhood. The reason for this is simple: Stores are the most reliable and stable buyers. Especially those in the business of selling retail merchandise in an impoverished area require a consistent supply of merchandise at reasonable cost.

"Taking Care of Business"

The women who shoplift characterize their involvement in shoplifting as a profession. They resemble those commonly described as "professional shoplifters" in shoplifter classification schemes in their motivation for financial gain,[2] but here I refer to professionalism as work ethic. Shoplifting is work. Tracy explains: "Every day, it was a job, a full-time job, every day. We did it over and over and over. We wouldn't get high until we cashed out everything."

Veronica comments: "I considered myself a professional. I didn't even have to be high at one point just to go ahead and do it. I would think that it was a job. On a day alone, I could make like three hundred dollars. You're talking about three hours of work."

For Carmela, shoplifting is important work not only for her own earnings, but for helping to keep her customers in business. She distributes "products" to stores serving low-income residents. Doing this makes her feel respectable and important:

I can actually say I'm really doing good at it. I don't have to look for people to sell to. I have too many people that buy my products. . . . Even though I do this strictly for my survival, I could say I am a professional. I think it helps a lot of people out, when I sell my products to the stores, and it depends on what kind, but you're sellin' for less. 'Cause in a way, I don't think anyone should pay the price you have to pay; I really don't. You're helping these people out that don't have the money to feed their kids because formula [food for infants] is not cheap, and I do my part to feed the innocent. It's a shame, but a lot of kids go hungry. That's the way I think it's helping and what I'm doin' is not degrading me.

Shoplifting work requires not only a solid customer base, but also knowledge of acceptable selling prices and skill at negotiation. Sandy says:

I've been doing it all my life. I'm a professional. [What do you mean?] *It would take me two hours to make what I would make in forty hours [of working a traditional job]. So it is an easier way to support a habit and everything else. It pays for wherever I stay at, for food and transportation, clothing, everything. There's times where I'll do it specifically just for the money for drugs, but then there's times I have to pay the bills or I owe a debt. I've even shoplifted to give money to other people, 'cause I know I can go back to the stores. . . . I make a good sum of money shoplifting. I've learned how to negotiate. I speak a little bit of Spanish so it's good that. If I start like at one [hundred] fifty, they'll talk me down to probably to one [hundred] twenty. And I learned that through the years of saying, "OK, well, I want fifty dollars for this sets of sheets," and I end up walking out with thirty [dollars], because not realizing they're playing the bargaining game that I didn't know how to play, you know.*

The shoplifters' interactions with their customers are similar to what one might imagine of a merchandise supplier in the general sense. Their occupational choice requires the women to cultivate customers, market products, take orders, and collect profits. Esther explains:

I'd go and make the sales first. I'd say. "Listen, this is what I got; put your order in; when you gonna have the money?" So I could just collect the money. You know I would definitely have a sample. I'd have the sample out to show 'em because you're taking care of business. I had a rapport with some businesses. . . . Oh man, a good day would be something like over five hundred dollars [of income], and I was giving away more than what I was smoking. I made a real job of this crime.

These business tasks (cultivating customers, marketing products, etc.) widen the customer base and directly affect profitmaking, keeping the women committed to the offense. Their directed efforts most certainly help sustain the illicit economy within the neighborhood drug culture.

Sandy's comments illustrate the perception of shoplifting as an occupation, an essential position within the underground economy:

I'm just, it's all, let's just say it's all part of the leveler. Like, I sound like the top, I'm the top man I should say. I sell it to them and then they sell it. The stores sell. I have some people that use 'em. I mean, I have a small quantity of people that actually use 'em for personal use. Maybe four or five people. Most people resell what I sell 'em. I have a lot of men that buy 'em [comforter and sheet sets that she shoplifts] for their wives and a lot of women that buy 'em in bulk to resell 'em. A lot of people pack 'em up and send to Puerto Rico, Santa Domingo; they send 'em back to their families. I have a lot of men that send 'em back to their country and sell 'em for double what they're worth over here.

Some shoplifters have developed specialties within shoplifting, which means they steal only particular types of goods, as is true for Sandy's exclusive dealing in expensive linens and bedding. A shoplifter's perception of risk for arrest sometimes determines her specialty. For example, some shoplifters prefer to shoplift food items in bulk, rather than expensive merchandise from department stores, because they perceive a lower likelihood of detection and arrest for stealing food items in busy supermarkets. Sandy is a specialist who shoplifts only those bedding and linen products she can openly carry out of a department store, reasoning that the large amount of money she stands to gain makes the risk worth the effort. Through her access to customers in the neighborhood where she buys heroin, Sandy has maintained a consistent income through her shoplifting specialty. In supplying these goods, her competition is limited and she is able to maintain a stable market for the sale of her goods. She explains her specialty within shoplifting:

I go to the stores by the merchandise they have, actually, because the quilts that I get are what the people ask for and they're expensive ones. I couldn't go into a Kmart compared to going in a Strawbridge's. It goes to the point where the person asks me for, they want this certain type of quilt, so then I'll go in Strawbridge's, grab that quilt, and walk back out. And there and Macy's are the only place I really know where the quilts are at and where they're not alarmed. . . . And I go where the price is on them [merchandise]; I mean, some stores don't have the price of them, which makes it harder for me 'cause I'll have a six hundred dollar item and people don't realize it six hundred dollars. So certain stores I'll go into just because they have a price tag on them so I can explain exactly what I'm selling it for. . . . I've only taken, like, comforters and sheet sets. And that's all I've ever been known to do because it's, it seems easier, simpler for me to do, to walk out of the store with two giant comforters, than it would for me to, like, grab pants or pills and, you know, conceal them somewhere and then have to walk out of the store. That's what I've been doin', takin' a comforter, which is, I walk out of the store with two, you know, large, like comforter bed in bag sets, which are, like, some are six hundred, eight hundred dollars apiece. The quilts and sheets that I get are what the people ask for, and they're expensive ones.

Most shoplifters are generalists, as I have documented among other, primarily minority and female populations.[3] Generalists provide an assortment of shoplifted goods for sale to their customers. Whether specialists or generalists, the women spoke of having a solid and stable market for the sale of their merchandise. Esther is a generalist. She describes the goods most profitable for her:

Clothing or shoes, no, not that much, not often at all. There's not that much money in that. Dove soap and stuff like that, cosmetics, cologne, makeup, stuff like that, personals. . . . I had a thing for Dove soap. I would go get the ten-packs. . . . I was stealing something like, um, three hundred dollars worth of meat from Pathmark. . . . Small equipment like radios and phones, household and sporting goods like knives, appliance, and cleaners, and large equipment and house items like TVs, machinery, furniture, bikes, often. I was selling tools, cherry pickers. I was selling the large and small.

Veronica also provides a variety of goods to her customers. She relies most heavily on food sold to local stores but shoplifts virtually anything customers will buy: "I started out with sheet sets, then clothes and food. I've taken safes out of a store, big safes out of Home Depot. My favorite was TVs, the kind with the VCRs. I started from taking Scott's, big products, like Tide detergent, Downy, anything of that nature people need, anything people will buy."

Candee does not sell food, but does supply the range of items a person might need for the home: "Like appliances, toasters and coffeemakers. . . . Sometimes I would go into the Home Depot and steal little items like batteries, stuff like that or, mainly batteries. Batteries people would buy from me, ya know. . . . We used to steal baby formula, and we used to sell that too. That was something else too. Ya know, canned baby formula."

Eileen's customers know to request only small items she can conceal. She explains: "I would get a list of things, like makeup and Yankee candles, things like that, go to Kohl's or CVS and then sell it to my friends or stores here."

Carmela is also a shoplifting generalist with just over two years of experience in the crime, having learned through interactions with other shoplifters that local bodegas seek particular items. What she shoplifts depends entirely on her customers' needs and buying habits. Drug dealers require goods useful in their work (cell phones, walkie-talkies), individuals request food, and local stores need hygiene products and infant formula, for example. Demand for some items, such as over-the-counter medications, is stable, while demand for other items changes. Here she describes personal items she sells to stores:

> *I'd just go in, and, like, the owner of the store was over there. He would give you a list of stuff to buy so then you know.* [What kind of store? An established chain, like CVS stores?] *No. Mom and pop stores, bodegas. They tell you, "What I need, and this is what I buy, and this is how much I pay." I've sold shampoo, deodorant; like, I got some people on one side of Camden that want nothing but Pantene products. They'll get it cheaper from me. I got one that likes Dove products. I got North Camden, they want the formula, like forty, fifty cans of that and the diapers, aspirins, all different types of medication, Crest Strips, they'll actually take anything. . . . I do top dollar . . . like three, four hundred dollars a shot. Like I said, I could sell anything now.*

Within their own attitudes and practices of professionalism, the women have status and reputation among customers, other shoplifters, and other members of the urban drug culture. This helps them to maintain their lucrative earnings. For Francine, experience and status are also emotionally meaningful to her. She explains:

> *I get quality stuff. Now, I wouldn't consider myself a pork chop; ya know, they called greasy because you be stealing cheap shit, greasy, pork chop because they're stealing real cheap shit. Ya know, going in the dollar store. I'm a good booster. . . . I'm good at it. It was never a problem selling stuff. When you're a good booster and you come within that circle and they say, "You know Francine, don't you?" And they say, "Yeah, I know that's a bad bitch, boy. She'll steal your ass off." That's something to be proud of. If you a good booster and their driver know you good and the dope man know you good, you can get the stuff [drugs] before you go out [to shoplift] and just pay for it when you get back; that's if you have a good reputation.*

Sandy comments similarly on the importance of status and reputation she gained through her hard work:

> *I think everybody knows who I am. The attention I get from people, wanting to be around me. Because that's how people know who I am. I mean if I was just a regular dope fiend off the street buying drugs, people wouldn't pay any attention. But a lot of people stop me. . . . People literally stop me on the street and ask if I have anything or what I'm getting in. They call me; they know I'm a good booster.* [How does that make you feel?] *It makes me feel that they need me. . . . Like, I'll have people that call me on my cell all day. I mean, I even have county officers in the jail and sheriff's officers that I go for . . . and, as a matter of fact, when I got arrested in Camden, they were joking about it. They're sleeping on the sheets that I got arrested for. Sleeping on the sheet that I sold 'em!*

Women are able to use shoplifting as an alternative to sex work for generating incomes in the urban drug culture. A woman's ability to operate a successful shoplifting business is constrained by the economic characteristics of her social location (lack of retail establishments) but at the same time supported by the deviance and crime of others (hack drivers and those who purchase stolen property) within the social location in which the urban drug culture exists. To recognize and cultivate the systems supporting shoplifting in that environment requires significant effort, and doing this makes shoplifting profitable over the long term. A woman's ability to make shoplifting work requires a willingness to step outside of gender roles, to resist the pulls toward sex work inherent in the urban drug culture. When she is able to do this, the money she earns from shoplifting can support her addiction and other basic needs. The factors important for understanding how shoplifting can be profitable are equally as important for understanding how sex work can be profitable, but these factors work differently for the two crimes; sex work is much simpler, as access to the crime is direct and accomodating systems facilitating the offense are ubiquitous within the urban drug culture.

How Sex Work Is Financially Profitable

Opportunities for sex workers are ubiquitous in neighborhoods where the women live and use drugs. As their stories demonstrate and prior research has established, strong demand for sex work makes possible convenient and direct access to financial earnings through this line of work. This creates a powerful incentive for women with drug addictions living in impoverished areas to define themselves as sex workers. Sailie established herself as a sex worker because of this:

Toward the end of my addiction, I prostituted more than I stole. Then I shoplifted only when I was hungry. I'd go to the supermarket with a dollar, buy a loaf of bread, steal a pack of chicken and a bag of rice, and that was dinner. I shoplifted less because it was easier to be on a corner and make money. I could do it all night. I couldn't steal in a store all night. . . . It was easier to prostitute. It was quicker money . . . guys would proposition me so I figured if I could make money with them one time, I could go out on the corner and make money all night. And that's what I did. I would make money all night, and then I'd spend all day getting high, and then start all over again in the evening. I did it every day, every single day. I was offered it, and I found out I was good at it and I could do it. That's why I stuck with the prostitution.

Street sex work provides "fast money," as the women explain. Direct access to money satisfies the need to buy drugs, and productivity of time and energy is essential because many times the addicted women are desperate to obtain the drugs as quickly as possible. Shay puts it simply: "Prostitution you just be a minute or two and you got money like that." Street sex work requires less time, effort, and travel than does sex work in the boundaries of strip clubs and other such establishments. Need for direct access to money for drugs and the strong demand for sex work within the neighborhood drug culture makes sex work a powerfully seductive alternative to shoplifting. Zeleste describes her decision to specialize in street sex work:

One night I was out there and I'd seen this girl by the name of Fir. I was getting high with her. We smoked a couple of hits together, and it was real late. I don't have any more money on me, and she was like, "What are we going to do? We got to get some more." I'm like, "Well, I don't know," and she's like, "Wait here and I'll be right back." I didn't even know what she was doing; she was like, "Wait here and don't ask questions, just wait here." I'm waiting on this corner, and then all of a sudden she pulls up by me and this guy is letting her out of the car. All I remember, she walked up to the corner, I never seen anybody make money like that on the street. She walked to the corner and was back in ten minutes with fifty bucks. I said, "How did you do that?" She said it was easy; she said, "They pick you right up. You do what you got to do and now you got your money and you're cool." I was like, "I want to do that." She was like, "Oh you never did that before?" I was like no, ya know, escorting, you know. I was like, "I'm not doing that street thing. Oh no, you get killed like that."

Zeleste continues:

Oh, but we were out that same night, her and I were out there doing it. Oh, wow, this is easy, now I can have some money, get what I have to get and get home. . . . [When you did it the first time, you were standing there and somebody pulls up in a car?] *I never stood. I walked. I just started walking. I got pulled over, my heart was pounding, I was like, oh my God, oh my God; I was so nervous 'cause it was so much different than the escort. You're getting in someone's car, but you really want to go get that hit, ya know, you did, you just overcame all that. . . . Of course and then I started doing this a lot because it was easier than having a check on, ya know, to go downtown, go in a hotel calling, you know what I mean? When you wanna cop [want to purchase drugs], I could just run up to the corner, do what I got to do, and I'm done. The money with the escorting was the way to go, but this was the easy way out when you put yourself in a position when you had no drugs left, no money, especially if you were put out there late and you needed to get some money quick.*

As most women in the urban drug culture who are in crime seem to use sex work for income, sex work is perceived as normal, acceptable, even expected. Cheryl clarifies this:

You become desensitized to it because everybody else is doing it. The guys are doing it, the girls are doing it. [Why not shoplifting like you and your boyfriend had done?] *For me, it was just too much of a hassle, 'cause you got to steal it, and then you have to go somewhere to sell it, then you have to get the money and then go get the drugs . . . and it's just why do all that, when I don't even have to leave the corner? The drugs are there. It's all in the neighborhood. With boosting [shoplifting], you have to travel. Prostitution is more degrading and all that, but it's more convenient.*

Because it is so normal in her neighborhood, Shay never initially viewed her behavior as prostitution. Her customers were men she had known throughout her life, men associated with her father and grandfather. Most of the sex workers recount similarly how they never fully defined their involvement as prostitution because "it was with people I knew." Shay recalls:

I always heard the girls in the neighborhood making quick money down on 7th Street. When I was there I saw what it was all about. The girls tell you who to be with, you know, come across this one and he got the money. They'll direct you where to go or who to be with. . . . At first I didn't think it was prostituting because the men that would go around there I knew, so I thought it was okay because I knew them, ya know what I'm saying? [Men from the neighborhood?] *Yeah, I mean we're talking about men that were friends with my grandfather, men that were friends with my father, so I'm like, well, it's okay because they know my family. . . . People who do drugs all run in the same circle. Everybody I knew was down there . . . little did I know I was all caught up with that lifestyle. It was fast money.*

Eva says: "You can find tricks anywhere, it could be your next-door neighbor, the person you least expect it, will proposition you, older men. Even if you're not looking for, it would come at you."

It is easy for sex workers to build a clientele. Customers are everywhere. Going into a local bar within the neighborhood is enough to gain access to sex work. Estelle explains:

My thing was mainly bars. I used to go to this bar and I just go in there and get with a few of the men in there. [How did it all start?] *You know, just go there to the bar because I lived in that area.* [What was your point to go in there?] *To have a drink. . . . I didn't approach them; I would go in there and sit, you know.* [Men would come to you?] *Yeah, well, you know, start a conversation. . . . I didn't do it like the first day. I was going there from time to time, and I got more and more familiar with them, and, you know, we would go in the back and I would get with one or two of them, and then that was that.* [How would this transpire?] *They offered me to come and be like a waitress and just perpetrate and, like, serve different men. . . . I would have a certain time. Maybe on like Monday mornings and I would take maybe three or four of them on a one-on-one basis back in the bathroom area. . . . There was an Italian club also, and they would call me on Sunday and I would go down there and take a few of them.* [Did you ever have to go searching for a trick?] *Not really, most of the times was, like, already arranged.*

Women have simple access to customers by walking a street in their neighborhoods. La Toya describes how exceptionally easy it is to attract male customers:

We'd go anywhere in the neighborhood. We just be walking down the street and just picking up whoever. Then we were just so lazy we just wanted to walk around the block. [And it was pretty easy to find a date?] *And it was pretty easy to do. You just walking down the street. Wear a little halter top and a pair of tight jeans with some thongs, you're doing something. Sure enough you will be picked up. You got to show a little bit of meat. You go to show the thongs. You have to have your thongs sticking out of your pants. There's always somebody out there.* [Always a supply of men?] *Yep. Always somebody out there.*

Just a woman's presence on a street is enough to be solicited by men looking for sex. Estelle's comments illustrate this passive access to sex work earnings: "Sometimes, I would be just taking a stroll and they approach [me] on the street in their cars. [You were out there to prostitute?] *No. I was just walking, just walking down the street."*

Loretta also comments on the strong demand for sex work and the simplicity of attracting customers on the streets: [*Did you have to search or wait for men, or did they come to you?*] "They be there. Like walking to the store, like the corner store, the Chinese store to go get yourself something to eat, go get a pack of gum. It's just that simple, go get a pack of cigarettes. It's that simple."

Regular Johns and Neighborhood Tricks

Routine arrangements with regular sex work customers facilitate steady and stable earnings. Regular customers and preferred johns among them reside outside of the neighborhoods. They travel into the area for sex, bringing into the women's lives and the illicit economy within the urban drug culture an external source of continued revenue. Women have developed regular customers using their own resourcefulness (i.e., skills and knowledge) and their reputation among men. Reputation has cash value, as Harriet reveals:

This one guy that worked for the gas company used to come see me every Thursday and Friday. He would come see me every Thursday and give me ten dollars, and we do what we gonna do, and he said, "I'll see you Friday, and I'll leave you twenty-five [dollars]." He said, "I'll always give you more because I don't see how people can cheat you because what you do to a person, you can't put a price on it." They told me that's how good I was, that I couldn't put a price on it. He kept his word. So every check, every Friday when he got paid he would come see me before he went home.

Sailie's comments further illustrate the importance of personal resourcefulness and earned reputation for generating stable and reliable customers and profitable earnings:

Actually, I was good at what I did. I had a reputation in my neighborhood and be known to be good at certain things, and I liked it when people said, "I heard you do this good, I heard you do that good." I took it as a compliment. Ya know, I made a lot of money prostituting because I was good at what I did. [What would you get a night?] *I got from anywhere, being out from midnight to five A.M., I could bring home about two hundred dollars. For five hours of work, it's not bad, and on the weekends, like Friday and Saturday nights were even better.*

However, it would be wrong to reduce the relationships with regular customers to simple transactions. Many women developed strong ties to regular johns on whom they depended for material and emotional support. This is especially important for understanding why the women remained engaged in sex work. Harriet explains:

After a lot of things that was done to me as a child, abuse and all, I never really let a man get into my heart; I never let him get close to me when we did business. . . . Out of maybe like fifty guys that I dealt with, there's only two of them that was here in my heart. I give them the utmost respect, ya know; I turned down a lot of clients when they was around, ya know. I wouldn't do a lot of things because they was around 'cause that's how much I cared about them. . . . They gave me more respect than any of the boyfriends I ever had. They treated me like a woman and they did do things; they taught me what romance was; they taught me what love was.

Shay has Larry, who came to her as a trick and whom she later "married":

It was in the wee hours of the morning. He was starting to go to work. There's a coffee shop we have down in South Philly, and he always knew my grandfather so he knew who I was and he knew I had an addiction and he had said to me if I ever wanted to change my life, he said, "I know where you live." . . . Then, I met up with him again and I looked like a bum, dirty clothes and I was just dirty. He said come on with me. I used his shower, he fed me. He went out and bought clean clothes, and I left for about a week and he came looking again and he's like, "This ain't no way to live; you're going shit or get off the pot." He said, "I seen you grow up"; one thing led to another, and I winded up marrying him. He pretty much raised me, I think, considering that I came from a broken home, he raised me. He raised me mentally wise, maturity, and just he raised me. . . . I've been trickin even in my marriage, about eight years. He's got his own plumbing business, so honestly when I looked at him, it was like, wow, I hit the lottery. I always hear girls talking about it, but I never thought this is how it comes about.

Some of the sex worker–customer relationships provide the women a sense of worthiness and protection, often mitigating their degraded status as street prostitutes and their anxiety about victimization. Zeleste enjoys enduring relationships with long-term customers:

He was my very first date [customer] . . . he would pick me up, would date me, would pick me up, would date me, would see me out there and pick me up and take me out to eat, give me money, buy me my stuff. . . . He is not about drugs, but he really wanted a relationship because he really likes me, and I now have two kids with him. . . . I ended up a couple of time getting arrested, and I got bailed out by my lawyer friend, and he's also another significant person in my life. I met him as a date. He has a wife of many years, and they're a marriage of convenience. He's my very best friend.

Men who live in the neighborhood, "neighborhood tricks," are a "last resort." Shirelle reasons:

The guys in the neighborhood, I would just go to their houses. They're like, how can I say this, I would basically be looking for somebody riding around in a car [a man presumed to be from outside the neighborhood], and if I couldn't get with somebody in a car, then as a last resort, I would go visit in the neighborhood houses, you know, to the neighborhood trick. Because my thing is they're always gonna be there. [Why would you be looking for someone from outside the neighborhood? Would the men who come through in the cars give better money or something?] *They could. But, it's just that the guys that in our neighborhood, you kinda like, after getting to know them a little, you kind of get to know their schedule. You kind of get to know where they work at, you know, and it sticks in your head when they get paid and just about, round about, how much money they're gonna give you. It's like they're always gonna be there because they live in the neighborhood. But most of the time you're waiting for somebody that's not from the neighborhood; you know your customers.*

Neighborhood tricks are undesirable customers because they are the client base of street-corner prostitutes. Women in this study distinguished themselves as having regular johns, preferred customers from outside the neighborhood who are more businesslike and respectable. The women avoided doing business with neighborhood tricks because this would situate them among the lowest ranking prostitutes in the sex work hierarchy. Lauren explains:

My clients always had businesses, or they had credentials that was good. I didn't have to mess with the neighborhood guys; I didn't mess with the dope dealers. I wouldn't trick with the dope dealers and stuff because I didn't carry myself [that way]. I stayed clean; I wasn't a dirty person, ya know. I ate; I went to the churches and get my clothes. I would go to the churches, to community centers. That's where I would go eat at.

The women in my study who have acquired regular customers and who rely exclusively on their sex work business rank themselves above street-corner prostitutes, who appear to them as the most destitute, willing to take any pay for their service. According to Edwina, respectable sex workers resist pressure to cheapen the value of their work.

Sure, I ran into a plenty of people, tricks that was like, "Sho, why should I pay you this when I can go get it for five dollars, three dollars?" I'd say, "Well, go ahead and get it; if you chose to get it from somebody that's dirty and nasty and funky, go ahead. But, you ain't gonna have that way with me." . . . I don't mess with Tom, Dick and Harry. I stayed clean, they stayed clean because most of my clients were married and after a lot of my clients met me, they didn't trick with nobody else, see I had special kind, I didn't trick with just any and every body just for money. I had special people that I would trick with because first of all it's a different approach. I would go by the way they talk and the way they carry themselves before I would go with a man because a lot of them were like, "Come on, baby, I need my dick sucked," and I was like, "So do I," ya know? I carried myself like that. They weren't going to disrespect me like that. I always stayed nice. I got my hair done, I kept my nails done. Even though I smoked crack I still kept up my appearance. See you got better clients, you got respectable gentlemen; you didn't get no hoodlums, no niggers walking around all stinkin and all raggy ass.

This pressure to cheapen the value of sex work is a very real threat, especially when a woman is desperate for the drug. Not only is the money a sex worker stands to earn through her work reduced and consequently her ability to purchase the drugs she needs to feel well, but also her reputation and self-perception are at risk. Because of this threat imposed mainly by drug users and other neighborhood men living as part of this urban drug culture, the sex workers must continue to maintain the current customer base of men outside of the neighborhood. Sex workers who fail to maintain business are at risk of falling into the ranks of the truly desperate street-corner prostitutes. La Toya's remarks illustrate perceptions of the truly desperate street-corner sex workers: "You're going to get used and used because the drugs are going to drag you into the floors. I mean you're going to start off dating for fifty dollars; then sooner or later you're dating for five [dollars]. You know men going to get tired of it; they start disrespecting you."

Ronni elaborates on the devaluation of work for street-corner prostitutes[4] and explains how walking a street rather than working a corner helps her avoid pressure to cheapen her work:

I'm not going to say I had control of the drugs, but there were things about myself; first of all, I can get a date and charge you fifty dollars for a blow job, fifty! Yeah, do I look like a cheap ho? I ain't look like a crack head with my head all bad, looking all sick. . . . I'm not going to stand on the corner; I feel like I'm too good to stand on the corner. I would walk the road.

At some time or another, a handful of the women in my study have felt so desperate for the drug (when released from hospital, for example) that they have taken very little money for their services. To their benefit, however, sex workers in the neighborhoods of Philadelphia and Camden have no shortage of willing customers who will pay for the services of a "clean" and "respectable" sex worker. To maintain a cost-effective business, the women explain, they know to avoid standing on corners waiting to be "picked up," and instead they walk, they rely heavily on routine arrangements with their regulars, and they work hard to maintain their appearances. Even if the women are desperate for drugs, customers are out there who will pay a "respectable" price for "respectable" sex workers.

Rooming Houses, Bars, Speakeasies, and Crack Houses

Sex workers rely on an array of neighborhood establishments to conduct their business. Speakeasies are located in homes or apartments and provide a local supply of alcohol (usually homemade), gambling, and entertainment around the clock. Speakeasies appear to be quite commonplace within these poor urban settings, and like local bars, they accommodate prostitution: Sex workers are invited in by owners to service the paying clients inside and collect their money. Because the prostitutes' presence brings in more men, speakeasies make an easy profit. Hence, sex workers are not required to give up any percentage of their income to the owners. Loretta describes the appeal of speakeasies in the neighborhood:

'Cause they be open after the bar. The bar be closed, and you could go there any time of the night. If the bar was closed, you could go there. The bar ain't open first thing in the morning, so you can go there. You want a drink five o'clock in the morning, you just go there and knock on the door. . . . And they charge less [for alcohol]. They let you in. Some people go so much that they gave them credit.

Women often spend hours at the speakeasies serving drinks, drinking and using drugs themselves, and cooking while they prostitute with the men inside. In addition to payment for their sex work, women earn money through tips. Nikki explains:

The man across the street, he had a speakeasy . . . they was playin games for five hundred dollars apiece. . . . I was servin' the people with drinks and stuff . . . liquor and the beers and whatever. . . . Sometimes I would cook, fried chicken and greens and all that, macaroni and cheese. . . . Sometimes I left there, I was drunk. . . . I was making like two hundred dollars for helpin' them serve and all that.

"Crack houses," "head houses," and "shooting galleries" provide somewhere to buy and use drugs and to carry out sex work. Some are abandoned homes taken up by drug dealers or users, but the ones most commonly used by sex workers are functional residences. "Rooming houses" or "hotels" are private residences offering rooms for rent by the hour or day at very low rates, where men and women reside transitorily, engage in drug use (but not drug purchasing), and most commonly, it appears, conduct sex work.

Shirelle clarifies the differences between a crack house and a rooming house and how each facilitates sex work. Here she describes a crack house and how lease payment for use of the house transpires between a sex worker, her customer, and the crack house's proprietor:

There's this one crack house though that I really like and everything in there worked, everything. He has a nice, nice ass house. I go over there and I pay him a couple dollars, and I take a shower or bath and sit there and get high. We might have sex [trick for money or payment for the room] ever now and then. . . . You bring somebody to his house, they give you twenty dollars for the room for like two hours. He [the date] pays you or let's say he gives you fifty dollars for [to buy] some drugs. He tells you to keep ten of the fifty. That's thirty dollars right there automatically. [So the person running the crack house supplies the drugs or just a place to use drugs and trick?] *People come and sell the drugs. They [crack house proprietors] supply the place. He get money from people that come in and sell. They get money or drugs from people that come in and rent rooms [for sex work]. They get money from people that just want to come in, sit down, and get high. Man, it's a lot of money in a crack house. There's a lot of them and there's some good money up in that.*

Contrary to stereotypes, not all crack houses are dangerous.[5] Some sex workers in this study have relied on them for housing and for sex work. Rooming houses, it appears from the accounts of women in this study, are usually designed for sex work transactions, and their use by sex workers and their customers is quite commonplace. When a sex worker meets a customer in a local bar, she can take the short walk to a rooming house, rent a room, engage in sex, be paid, and return to the bar. Shirelle describes a rooming house:

There's this guy named Sam, and he has a rooming house. He rents his rooms for five dollars, and you can stay as long as two hours, and he's very particular about the people that he lets in his house. So for me when I go over there, that's like a safe environment. You won't hear like knocking on the door, "You gotta light, you gotta match, you gotta cigarette? I'm going to the store, do you need something?" There's none of that. The whole time you're there, say you check in at two, if you're checking in a two o'clock, he writes it down. . . . You know you can sit there and do all the drugs you want. You can run in and out as long as you're respectable. He don't have anybody coming in his house selling drugs, 'cause that's drawing too much attention to a cop. I used to like going over his house. Five dollars for two hours, shit. . . . You would have to come as a couple. It would have to be a guy and a girl; you can't, I couldn't just go there myself and be like, "Here, five dollars, I want the room." It was only for couples and basically it was for tricking. He didn't care what you did when you were in the room. You know, he knew that you was gonna get high. He didn't care about that. [Would you still call it a crack house if it is used just for tricking?] *No. It was a room. We call the place, you need a room? That's all we call it when somebody says, I would get rooms.* [You're not really talking about a hotel; you're talking about peoples' houses?] *Yeah.*

Many sex workers live in rooming houses where they also engage in sex work. In addition to paying daily rent, they give the owner of the rooming house an additional fee for using the room to service customers. Ronni finds that living in a rooming house makes for a convenient sex worker–customer meeting place and increases the efficiency of her work:

I would stay in the house but I had tricks to come see me. If I met you and I thought was all right, I gave you my cell number. You call me on the cell phone. . . . Anybody that dealt with me knows to pay me up front. You pay me my one hundred dollars and you gave me ten dollars for house. If you don't do nothin' with me in an hour, you're blown. . . . I got somebody else.

These other people out there waiting for me. I be in the other room; I go outside. I might just go stand on the porch.

Living and working out of a rooming house makes sex work much easer than having to go outside in undesirable conditions to meet customers, as Sailie has found:

Like on a rainy day, I wasn't goin' out. I ain't gone out in no rain. On a rainy day, or if the police was hot, hot, hot, like too many police outside or too much police traffic or it seemed like narcs [drug enforcement police] out there or it seemed like bikes out there, I ain't gone out. I just had to make a couple phone calls . . . whatcha doin' . . . and they [dates] would come to my room I rented. . . . Then I had my johns that also got high. See, some people say a bad night is a night with a few tricks, a good night is a night with one trick. [Because he has drugs?] *Uh-huh, and so I get high too.*

Harriet elaborates how rooming houses provide women a safe and comfortable location to operate their sex work business:

I started to live in a house. I had to pay him ten dollars a day to stay, so that's when I was able to get off the corner. I gave him ten dollars a day; plus I would bring some of my clients there that would give him money to do my stuff, to do my little thing. . . . After a while they just started coming there; I didn't have to stand on the corner anymore. So they automatically knew where I was at and seeing that it was a nice place, we had hot and cold running water, ya know, the kitchen you could go cook and eat, and they played card games so it was a house that I would say you run a business from. You know that was one of my benefits I reaped. [It was crack house?] *It was not actually a crack house; it was a house, but it was where people could come and get high that they used to play cards on the weekend and everybody in the room would gamble and play cards, but it wasn't abandoned like. He had wall-to-wall carpeting in his house, and I had my own room, my own TV, everything. I could wash up, take a bath, and all that.* [And he would rent rooms out for extra money?] *Right, so it was like a hotel, but it was a house and he had like four or five rooms in his house. He would rent rooms.* [Did you also get your drugs there?] *Well, the drugs I had to go around the corner. And see, I did that for maybe like ten years, ya know, and then I got to the point where all I had to is call and they delivered my drugs like it was a pizza.*

Shoplifting Work and Sex Work

Within the urban drug cultures of Camden and Philadelphia lives a prosperous illicit economy. Ruggiero and South call the illicit economy a "bazaar" offering every consumable and service for need, pleasure, and diversion.[6] The illicit economy in Camden and Philadelphia drug neighborhoods carries many types of work and workers organized by a division of labor. Some workers distribute drugs off the streets, some on the street, some package drugs, some engage in robbery, shoplifting, and other forms of theft, some are messengers and errand workers, drivers, renters of safe houses, sellers of paraphernalia for drug users, or drug-selling lookouts, others are sex workers, pimps, and hustlers of all varieties. A person's capital (skills, learned knowledge, mastery of tools, aspiration, leadership, place in social relationships, teaching ability, task management) shapes where she or he fits into this division of labor within the illicit economy, options for work, and potential for prosperity.[7] The stronger a person's capital befitting an urban drug culture, the more likely it is that the person will rank high in the division of labor with prestige, having access to powerful, high-paying occupations, perhaps managing a large drug distribution organization. Those with weak capital are likely to fall toward the bottom of the labor force, adopting a minor, risky, stigmatized, low-paying job or no work at all.

Age and race factor into this division of labor, according to research. Set in a high crime slum of Chicago's west side, a study on older aged (fifty to sixty-eight years) male heroin users with long addictions found that capital changes with aging and this in turn affects work opportunities and work prosperity. Earlier in their lives, the men would finance their addictions through shoplifting, robbery, dealing, and running errands. As the grew older, they could no longer keep up with the physical demands of their early work and were reduced instead to low-paying work (drug baggers, errand boys, and lookouts) or begging for money and handouts.[8] In the matter of racial marginality, a study of the heroin market in San Antonio found that African Americans had very limited success in drug-selling networks, but not Whites and not Mexican Americans.[9] The heroin market in San Antonio is a lucrative business for Mexican Americans especially, no doubt a function of that group's majority in the demographic makeup of the city.

Just as scholars in the study of legal work recognize gender as a status factor shaping job opportunities and prosperity, criminologists and sociologists in the study of crime see sexism alive in the illicit economy. Arguably, the hegemony of males in illicit economies such as urban drug cultures mirrors status, standing, and work in the legal economy, where women are the group marginalized and men enjoy higher standings, respect, and earnings. In his classic study of work and the division of labor, Caplow noted how women are recruited into jobs that are of lower status than male jobs and that require them to be passive and dependent (for example, on men or on machines to get work done).[10] Stereotypically perceived as competent, assertive, and independent, men have an open door to jobs of greater status and independence from management by women. This is patriarchy in the workplace. Hierarchical status and work structures translate into power differentials whereby men as a group have more power in organizations. Contemporary scholars like Walby continue to see gender segregation as a dominant force in the division of labor within organizations even today as women's involvement in higher status positions within public and private industry has increased.[11] Notwithstanding women's movement into upper level jobs, women as a group in the workplace still take a back seat to men, serving more managed and peripheral roles, for example, and receiving less pay for similar work.

In the world of crime, sexism exists too. Men are stereotypically leaders with a desired capital like personal strength and drive, aggressiveness, objectivity, the ability to work independently and cooperate with others, to spawn growth, and so on. To compete with sexism, women then rely primarily on their strong capital, sexuality. Research supports this perspective. Men dominate lucrative drug-dealing and -selling markets, and while women may be able to engage in drug selling and other "male" crimes, their involvement is normally in limited capacity or confined to marginal roles.[12] Steffensmeier refers to this gendering in the illegal world where women situate at the lower levels of labor in least desired jobs as "institutionalized sexism."[13]

Based on interviews with men in theft crimes, Steffensmeier and Terry found that men objected to collaborating with women in crime because women lacked a certain capital sought by thieves, like trust and willingness to take on risk, those masculine traits perceived by thieves themselves to be essential for success. They did involve women only when necessary to make their own work more profitable.[14] From a three-year ethnographic study of forty-five women drug users in New York, Maher and Daly found that none of the women owned or ran drug-selling businesses, but many took on work related to selling.[15] Many purchased drugs for others or steered new drug users in the neighborhood to the sellers in return for a few dollars. Some ran shooting galleries where users could enjoy their high; others sold needles and related drug paraphernalia. Only seven women (1.5 percent) sold drugs for dealers, but only temporarily. Like other researchers, Maher and Daly attribute women's involvement in selling to the temporal opportunistic needs of male sellers; in times of strong police presence or when regular sellers become jailed, drug sellers allow women to take on the risky role of street dealing, but only as long as necessary. Like other researchers, Maher and Daly imply that women's limited involvement in drug selling is a product of male exclusion, male power in the drug economy. One project with somewhat different results is research conducted on women drug sellers at Bushwick in Brooklyn and Washington Heights in Manhattan.[16] Most of the women studied did sell drugs at some point in their street lives as part of a larger organizational structure (84 percent) and they enjoyed good incomes. Those women were able to carve a niche for themselves in the male-dominated crack and cocaine markets, but it seems a larger socioeconomic movement—that is, the crack epidemic in the 1980s—that increased the demand for street dealers (and not real transformations in gender status and hierarchy) created this opportunity for women and they seized it. The authors also noted that drug selling enabled women to avoid lower tiered street hustles, like shoplifting and sex work.

In the urban drug culture, women do involve themselves in various forms of theft, including shoplifting, but their status as women, their subordinate position within the division of labor consigns them primarily to sex work, a dangerous, highly stigmatized occupation even in that illicit economy.[17] True, sex work in urban centers is highly gendered: The Uniform Crime Report for 2005 shows that in the nation's cities women made up 67 percent of all prostitution arrests. Across the country, the total number of men arrested for prostitution was 14,615 compared to 27,026 women.[18] Maher reports that for drug-addicted, criminally active women in a New York neighborhood where crack selling and use is pervasive, "sexwork [*sic*] was the only income-generating activity consistently available to women drug users in Bushwick" (1997, p. 130). As the process of sexism in the urban drug culture perpetuates itself, continued demand makes sex work the most conveniently accessible means to earn incomes and sustain drug-use needs. Indeed, most women in my study are sex workers entering this life over many years of sexism and patriarchal pressures; sex work is a constant, easily accessible occupation for women. Notwithstanding the powerful effects of a troubled life on the capital a drug-abusing woman possesses, women living as part of the urban drug culture can also make shoplifting profitable and develop a strong capital in skill, drive, and work style accompanied by structural and social accommodating systems in these areas. My study seems to be the first in its focus on women shoplifters in the urban drug culture and contrasts with the normative description of shoplifting as a low-skilled, undesirable job at a bottom of the labor market. Rather, my research shows that shoplifters are workers who self-select the job not because they were blocked from other illegal work they desired, not because they were pushed down to the work, but for the fit of the work to their needs, and they are skilled at managing every aspect of their profession, resulting in very good profits.

Crime specialization for income is work, and this work embodies the same basic structures of legal work but without moralizing. In her 1978 book, Miller explains how crime work parallels legal work.[19]

> *A fundamental assumption of this approach to deviance is that deviant workers are primarily engaged in activities that yield monetary rewards that can be used to sustain their lifestyles. They are like all other workers in modern society who are also concerned with making a living. It may be true that there are other rewards and motivations associated with deviant work, but that does not make deviant work uniquely different from other types. Non-deviant persons also work for a variety of reasons. Work in modern society is, however, primarily an economic activity, whether the work roles is popularly conceptualized as professional, non-professional, or deviant. Thus, although deviant workers differ from others with respect to the stigma that is attached to their work and themselves, the negative public image of these persons only complicates their work lives—it does not make their work categorically different from that of others.*

Peter Letkemann was a pioneer in the study of criminal behavior within the rubric of the sociology of occupations and work.[20] According to the Letkemann's research, crime work specialization is "a line," the crime equivalent to specialization in ordinary, noncriminal occupations. Conceptualizing crime as work rather than simply as deviance, Letkemann demonstrated that criminal specialization is occupational and carries with it many of the same technical and organizational dimensions of work in the conventional sense. An occupational perspective on criminal specialization can account for why a shoplifter sells to corner stores rather than peddling goods on the streets. In the framework of crime specialization as occupational, my analysis indicates that a shoplifter's concern with stability in demand, efficiency in sales, and fair exchange rates can make sense of her behavior. Without focus on the technical and organizational aspects of crime, according to Letkemann these explanatory factors remain hidden or misunderstood.

As different occupations require different sets of skills, so do criminal occupations. Klockers's life history of Vincent Swaggi is a classic example of crime as work.[21] Swaggi was a fence (a dealer in stolen goods) who sold his merchandise out of a neighborhood store (upward of 80 percent of his business came from the sale of stolen goods.) Tracing Swaggi's career development from a youthful hustler to a professional fence, Klockers was able to illustrate how this crime requires skills and techniques very much in line with those found in regular store owners, most especially secondhand shops. Like store owners, for example, the fence negotiates purchase of goods for his inventory, warehouses goods for stock, keeps a register or catalog of stock, offers assorted goods for customers with different needs, and sets a competitive but profitable retail price. A more recent life history of a fence, by Steffensmeier, further illustrates how crimes require particular skill.[22] Sam Goodman was the subject of study and described his experience over years of work as a fence, an intermediary between thieves and customers in the business of selling illegal goods. According to his account, the successful business of fencing requires social skills to interact with customers, thieves, and other fences, technical skills to select goods and negotiate his buying and selling price, and organizational skills to fool police, recognize market fluctuations in demand, and maintain profits and success over the long term.

McCarthy and Hagan's research on young drug sellers is another example of research on crime as work. That research took a different approach, concentrating on how different forms of capital (human, social, and personal) known to increase success in conventional occupations apply to financial success in drug selling.[23] Human capital is essentially a person's marketable skills for a particular work setting, built from education and instruction, which over time increase a person's productivity and financial returns. Social capital refers to power and influence gleaned from social networks. A person engaged in strong connections to other individuals and groups with requisite power and influence on drug selling can develop a valuable social capital as a resource for her own success in the trade. Personal capital concerns special traits of an individual that contribute to economic success, like a desire for wealth, a willingness to take on risks, and a willingness to cooperate with others. Results of multivariate analyses revealed indeed that a person's capital also corresponds to occupational success in the illegal sector. Youth with human capital and strong social and personal capital were the most financially successful at specializing in drug selling; they had a drive for success, accepted risk in the marketplace, collaborated with other drug sellers, and learned from others in important drug-selling networks.

Conceptualizing crime as work, my research also shows that the occupations of shoplifting and sex work embody habit and ethic, training, skill, proficiency, conflict resolution, planning, and risk management (which I elaborate on in the following chapter). Shoplifting is a particularly skilled occupation. Similar to new employees in conventional work, shoplifters learn by instruction, by example, and often through rounds of on-the-job training with increasingly advanced tasks and responsibility until each is ready to work alone. Over the career, shoplifters continue to learn and hone their skills; like legal workers, they compete in the marketplace, carry through mundane day-to-day tasks, cope with uncertainty, negotiate setbacks, develop innovative styles for greater efficiency, and employ tactics to maintain profit in the longer term. A shoplifter with a drug addiction must have strong capital to enter into this occupation, and to remain prosperous she must continue to increase her capital by embracing a strong work ethic and commitment to business. While there are many studies that have explored sex work, the focus has usually been to characterize the lives of women before involvement or to illustrate risk they face on the streets. There has been little interest in exploring the crime as work, particularly how sex workers take care of business and attain success. My study shows how the work compares to shoplifting in its routinization, customer relations, and use of strategies to attain success. Shoplifters learn how to maintain business and increase profits, for example, by specializing in particular merchandise for their most stable buyers. Sex workers use skills to maintain stability and profits too.

Techniques sex workers use to make their work prosperous in their work is to target on customers they know and trust. Another is to conduct work in urban drug cultures not in outside areas. According to Rosenbaum's research of sex workers in San Francisco, drug addicted street sex workers conducting business in places where drugs and sex work thrive (like urban drug cultures) compared to other neighborhoods have only a supply of the least desirable—slum dwellers and other drug users:[24] "In addition to neglecting her appearance, the addicted-prostitute begins to work neighborhoods where her connection resides; in this way, she is never geographically too far from a fix. In these neighborhoods, however, only the low-paying johns will solicit her."

To the contrary, my research shows that women strategically select urban drug cultures to make more efficient both their drug use and sex work. These neighborhoods offer a dual source of supply for the sex worker, men on the inside and the best customers who come in from the outside. Neighborhood men are a constant supply used when outsiders are unavailable to the sex worker. Women learn from others and by experience to gear work to men from outside the neighborhood not just because working- and middle-class outsiders can pay better, but because these outsiders are also qualitatively more desirable: Outsiders are more respectful, reliable, and businesslike.

Another technique of sex workers is to make customers come to them, to pick them up on the street at a particular location and time, or to call on them indoors at apartments and neighborhood establishments like rooming houses. A Canadian found similarly that experienced sex workers invited regular customers to their apartments or homes. Some even placed ads in local papers for their services. This approach enabled them to better control working conditions and demand higher rates than on street sex work.[25] Some neighborhood establishments are geared to sex work, others to drugs, and some a mix of the two. Maher and her colleagues distinguish between freakhouses and the traditional shooting gallery or crack house.[26] The former are male-run homes or apartments that offer sex workers a place to wash, eat, and rest in exchange for drugs and sex. More than that, freakhouses operate like brothels in a sense, where customers pay an entrance fee to access women for sex. The more drug-focused establishments that allow sex work are apartments or houses commonly known as crack houses or shooting galleries. The primary service offered to neighborhood users is a relatively secure place to use drugs for a short time in return for money or drugs to the owner. Sex workers might also rent a room to carry out their sex work, but the business focus in these houses is to provide a setting for drug use.

Workers in crime distinguish themselves from their colleagues in a sort of hierarchy of prestige based upon factors like skill, income, and management of work. Polsky studied pool hustlers who rig billiard games for income.[27] While pool hustling, like shoplifting and sex work, may occupy a higher or lower status than other crime work, the social worlds within a criminal occupation are hierarchical as well. Pool hustlers who win at games with other pool hustlers enjoy a high status, according to Polsky's research. Winners are outstanding players, intense and fierce in the eyes of colleagues. The loser of these contests is the lowest form of hustler, one without privilege who lacks what it takes even to be regarded as a hustler. Status and ranking within a crime are also evident in Letkemann's research.[28] In the crime of bank robbery, Letkemann's subjects described how the most skilled professionals held in admiration look down upon the lowliest workers, the one-time bank robbers, the inept, blundering "note pushers" who have no right to be called bank robbers at all. Maher described a split among sex workers in Brooklyn who defined status in relation to other sex workers.[29] Women on the job for years (before the 1980s surge of crack into the area) identified as "professional hookers" and referred to crack-addicted women with very poor hygiene and young sex workers with contempt, as low-level desperates with disgraceful hygiene who bring down the price of sex work.

My research also shows that street sex work has its own status hierarchy. Occupying the bottom of the hierarchy are street-corner workers (who stand on corners actively soliciting for any customer that comes along). In the eyes of women in my study, street-corner sex workers are the most desperate for drugs, do not keep up their appearances, and take very little money for the work. The sex worker who strolls the street meeting up with her own customers and who runs her business by scheduling customers throughout the day ranks higher, earns more money, and is respectable. Continued skill development and management of customers are especially important for sex workers (and shoplifters) to retain a good profit, not only in the face of competition from their lower level counterparts, but also after setbacks like incarceration. Shoplifters rank in a hierarchy of occupational prestige too. Professional shoplifters (engaged for income) are at the top and all others below. Among professionals, shoplifters who manage all of the work, who can get high resale prices, keep reliable customers, expand their customer base, and stay out of jail, enjoy high status. Top-tiered shoplifters apprentice newcomers. Younger, less experienced shoplifters with few business customers earn lower profits and situate lower in this hierarchy.

As I have explained in previous chapters, family dysfunction (alcoholism, drug abuse, violence, trauma, and child abuse) and social milieu (neighborhood deterioration, high crime, and drug infestation, social networks) contributed to the troubles faced by women in this study and their involvement in drugs and crime. I analyzed in this chapter how urban drug cultures in cities like Camden and Philadelphia neighborhoods made possible their lives in crime. This pathway model of women's drug abuse and criminality can even be viewed a step back, through broader, macro-level factors like economic and social movements that contribute to family dysfunction and neighborhood milieu. The state of a neighborhood, for example, is not only conditioned by residents, outsiders, crime, housing, family structure, and so on, but also by events that have occurred outside of the neighborhood and in the past. The same can be said of the state of the family. The idea is that families and neighborhoods are not closed systems isolated from changes about them. They are open systems. Open systems are built, according the words of geographer Doreen Massey, "by layer upon layer of interconnections with the world beyond."[30]

Research by DeKeseredy and his colleagues took such an approach, connecting woman abuse in Canada's public housing and in the rural United States to broad social and structural forces, including transformations in America's economy, exclusion of the working class from fruitful labor, and masculinity.[31] According to their report, the shift in America from an agricultural-based economy threatened the hegemonic masculinity of rural males. When rural men worked in farming and factories, in coal mines and sawmills, they exemplified the ideal patriarchal family. They were the primary breadwinners in masculine occupations and the heads of households. As the nation entered the information age, their jobs began to disappear and so did the dynamics of family structure, threatening the patriarchal structure and hegemony of rural men. Rural men rely heavily on peer networks, which through heavy drinking and other behaviors serve to express masculinity. Sexual assault of their spouses or former spouses is one mechanism through which men re-create and reinforce masculinity and avoid losing status among their peers.

Scholars in political science, geography, economics, business, human ecology, urban planning, and sociology have written extensively on how economic and labor shifts in post-World War II America contributed to the development of neighborhoods I refer to as urban drug cultures and the corresponding troubles faced by individuals and families in those neighborhoods.[32] Debates aside, this body of scholarship describes how expansion of manufacturing jobs (producing goods and services) during the period of World War II coupled with a phasing out of agricultural labor led to massive migration to industrial cities in the North. At the same time, racial discrimination in the housing market created obstacles for African Americans, who were low-paid workers, to live in the periphery of industrial centers, consigning them to inner-city poor neighborhoods. As industry shifted away from blue-collar manufacturing in the second half of the twentieth century to an information-based economy marked by technical and professional occupations, industrial giants like Camden and Philadelphia were hard hit. Philadelphia lost 64 percent of its manufacturing jobs, Chicago lost 60 percent, and Detroit lost 51 percent between 1967 and 1987.[33] Further, restructuring has had the most devastating consequences for urban communities that are minority, increasing the level of social and economic exclusion (joblessness and poverty). Workers in better economic and social positions with skills to compete in the new marketplace, namely, Whites who occupied the higher paid positions before, tended to migrate with the new industry outside of cities to suburbs and rural areas, leaving minority communities even more isolated. According to Rose, neighborhoods that I refer to as urban drug cultures were formed primarily during the period of in-migration of poor African Americans to cities for manufacturing work. When jobs left their cities, so did the better economically and socially positioned Whites, but African Americans remained and their ghettos became further isolated from the outside economic and social world.[34] Even as America competes in the information age at a global level, earlier effects on minority neighborhoods, like poverty and joblessness, persist.

Kodras's research on Detroit is an example of how decline in manufacturing jobs created hardships for minority individuals and poor neighborhoods.[35] By the middle 1960s, the auto industry employed more than half the labor force in Detroit, but things changed as the industry there followed the larger global reorganization of auto making, closing factories, moving to automated production, and shifting work overseas. Through the 1970s, more than 70 percent of workers in Detroit lost their jobs and the poverty rate increased, most dramatically for African Americans. The impact of this restructuring on African Americans and corresponding racial discrimination in both the labor market and the housing market "had a catastrophic effect, because blacks were strongly concentrated in the lower tiers of heavy manufacturing, the segment hardest hit during deindustrialization."[36] African American workers in Detroit's auto industry held the lowest paying jobs and were the first to go, as the auto industry began its decline. Their low wages and discrimination in the housing market meant African American workers lived primarily in the poorest urban neighborhoods, cut off from new jobs opening in the suburbs and consequently from hopes of prosperity. Poverty set in for those generations and the next. All of this was a recipe for the development and persistence of ghetto neighborhoods, segregated economically and socially, perfect settings for urban drug cultures. Since then, Detroit's revitalization efforts have failed African Americans too, according to Kodras, as the new industry is high-tech and corporate, still far out of reach for the inner-city poor who are still structurally, economically, and spatially isolated.

In the case of Philadelphia, Anderson's ethnographic research in the 1970s and 1980s described how industry shifts as well as race and class movements created the urban African American ghetto neighborhoods I refer to as urban drug cultures.[37] His research focused on areas between the University of Pennsylvania and Drexel University and includes the neighborhood called Black Bottom, where many women in my study were raised. When industry moved into Philadelphia in the early 1990s, so did working-class immigrants settling into housing built for them, for their class, housing very distinct in structure and size from the estates in the surrounding affluent areas. Row homes and duplexes there are very similar to Camden's tree-lined Fairview Village built in the same period for the newly arrived working class at Camden's shipyard. The advance of transportation systems brought with it new residents in search of work, particularly poor African Americans from the southern states displaced by agricultural advances. Affluent Whites began to move farther out of the city because of this invading lower class, according to Anderson. Just as the affluent Whites had resisted the invasion from the working class, so did the working-class Whites, who pushed African Americans into that once affluent space, now transformed into multiple-family dwellings. After the 1950s, with industry shifts from factory to corporation and emerging gentrification of African American neighborhoods for Whites, African American neighborhoods became more distinctly separated, deteriorating rapidly into low-income, high-crime spaces with a rising population of the low-skilled and unemployed and a decaying quality of life. Between 1940 and 1980, the proportion Black in Philadelphia grew 25 percent, but increased in these neighborhoods Anderson dubs Northon by 52 percent. During the same period, the rate of educational attainment grew in the city by 35 percent, compared to 23 percent in Northon. By 1980, 11 percent of city residents had achieved a college education and 54 percent were employed, compared to just 3 percent and 37 percent of Northon residents. Largely unskilled, youth experiencing this reality see their opportunity of a good life in the conventional world limited, but realize they can compete in an illicit economy. Over time, a street culture becomes a powerful force, calling youth loosely tied to conventional society "loudly and insistently."[38] The social context of persistent poverty, according to Anderson, joblessness and exclusion, is a fertile ground for the drug culture. Like their postindustrial neighbor of Camden across the Delaware River, the Philadelphia Black neighborhoods became an urban drug culture or, in the words of Anderson, an "urban jungle" beset by illiteracy, poverty, joblessness, high infant mortality, welfare female-headed households, violence, drugs, addicts, and wandering homeless.[39]

The point is that just as female criminality flows from family dysfunction and the way of life in a neighborhood drug culture, family and neighborhood life do not exist in isolation. Neighborhoods develop and transform by forces acting upon them as well as the behavior of individuals inside. In the same way, external forces like economic change, violence, drugs, and criminality in neighborhoods affect family life, as does the behavior of individuals within the home. Families and neighborhoods are both agents and results of change, and so are female offenders who despite troubled lives make crime work for them. In a broad sense, female criminality is in reality a product of layer upon layer of connection to the world.

Accounts from women in this study suggest that while street sex work is a preferred income-generating crime for female drug abusers, it is not any more profitable than shoplifting. Both shoplifters and sex workers explained how their criminal specialization over all other means provides them the most reliable, consistent, and lucrative source of financial earnings to support themselves and their addictions. Dependable, daily access to cash was their primary objective. Earnings through shoplifting and sex work are a function of access to crime, demand for goods and services, and neighborhood systems accommodating the offenses, in addition to individual expertise, competence, and status.

The demand for sex work implicit in the neighborhood drug culture and normalized by men and women alike makes for simple and direct access to income obtained through this crime. This makes financial earnings through sex work convenient. Sex work is more convenient than shoplifting because it requires less travel and fewer transactions. Shoplifters must travel to a retail establishment, engage in the theft there, then return to the neighborhood to sell the merchandise for profit before satisfying their drug needs. Sex workers gain access to the crime with little effort directly within their neighborhoods, on the streets and in bars. As their stories illustrate, sex workers tend to become more thoughtful and proactive as they gain experience and knowledge, relying heavily on regular paying customers and manipulating resources existing within the neighborhood drug culture that facilitate and sustain their offending, their earnings, and therefore their commitment to the crime. The direct and uncomplicated access to financial earnings through sex work, demand for sex work, and neighborhood resources supporting sex work operate in tandem directly within the neighborhood. This is why so many female drug users choose street sex work as their specialization and why these women abandon other forms of sex work and shoplifting.

Notwithstanding the powerful forces within the urban drug culture pulling female drug abusers into sex work and keeping them there, shoplifting can be prosperous for women. Shoplifters have to be much more autonomous and resourceful than sex workers, seeking out systems accommodating their offense. Access to the crime is limited by social location and, therefore, indirect, requiring travel and significant effort on the women's part to maintain profitable earnings. Demand for shoplifted goods is much less obvious than demand for sex work, requiring the women to cultivate systems within the neighborhood that will facilitate and support their offending. It appears that the shorter duration of overall time involved in generating earnings compared with sex work balances the travel and related expense necessary for shoplifting. As the women explained, sex work might involve eight hours of work for supporting a daily drug habit, while shoplifting might involve half that time, and as profits are usually sufficient in a shoplifting event, the crime is worth the extra effort it involves. With experience and reputation, shoplifting specialists were able to maintain good financial earnings, even higher earnings than sex workers were. Unlike sex workers, all of the women who specialize in shoplifting perceive their involvement in the crime foremost as a profession and a respectable, integral part of the illicit economy. Their offending experience, competence, and reputation are no more developed than those of sex workers are, but unlike sex workers, their offense is not sexualized or gendered. Perhaps this freedom from gendered organization in her work helps to define for the female shoplifter a sense of conventionality to larger society helping her to commit to this work.

Both shoplifters and sex workers feel confident that their specialization will continue to earn them the money they need to survive life addicted to drugs. Through their own efforts, the shoplifters and the sex workers have benefited from the illicit economy within the urban drug culture, and they have been fundamental actors supporting it. To maintain a successful specialization, shoplifters and sex workers must manage arrest and other risks imposed by their crime to earn the money they need. The next chapter takes a close look at how shoplifters and sex workers perceive risks imposed by their crimes and how they work to manage these risks in the stores and on the street.

5. *Risk Management Strategies for Shoplifters and Sex Workers*

You're risking freedom, whether you're going to get killed or you're going to go to jail. —Ronni

To maintain a criminal specialization in shoplifting and sex work requires a woman to acknowledge, accept, and manage the risks she faces in her crime. The shoplifters and sex workers I interviewed speak knowledgeably of the potential harms and personal costs of their behavior. At some point in their criminal careers, all of these women have been apprehended, arrested, and had criminal sanctions imposed; being detected and arrested is thought of as an inevitable part of the work. To be sure, the women do not see this as a rite of passage to be proud of but instead an inevitable consequence of their frequent and continued involvement in crime. As the women discussed their experiences with arrest it became quite clear that neither group—shoplifters nor sex workers—is deterred by arrest. They do not report feeling guilt or shame imposed by these consequences and are not concerned about losing the respect of others or future prospects (because they are already "cast outs"). Remember, they are drug addicts who will be "sick" without taking drugs every day. As long as they are drug addicted, they said, life in crime is inevitable. Only incapacitation will hurt them.

For shoplifters, steering clear of incapacitation means they need to worry about apprehension by store security, deal with limits imposed by retailers who ban them from stores, and avoid incarceration. Shoplifting specialists must accept that each time they enter into the crime they face apprehension, a "fifty-fifty chance," many of them reasoned. With each new conviction, shoplifters face the possibility of harsher penalties, much more so than do sex workers. For sex workers, apprehension could also cause them trouble, but violence on the streets can kill them. To survive this life in crime and to make crime work over the long term, shoplifters and sex workers must and do manage their business, including the dangers inherent to their work, which is the subject of this chapter. Finding ways to escape apprehension and incapacitation is of paramount importance and is seen in every aspect of their criminal involvement—in the decisions they make in their commission of the crime and when in trouble with the law.

In the first part of this chapter, I sketch out risks inherent in shoplifting and sex work and the most common ways shoplifters and sex workers carry out their crimes to reduce and manage these risks. While the two crimes necessitate different skills, both groups commonly rely on mindfulness and intuition, a sixth sense to warn them when danger is imminent. They have learned how to respond to this sixth sense. Each group's members put to work other strategies unique to their particular crime that they have learned are necessary to manage work and to be successful. Furthermore, shoplifters and sex workers know the criminal justice system is inefficient. In the second part of this chapter, I briefly illustrate how decisions made by shoplifters, sex workers, and formal players in the criminal justice system help shoplifters and sex workers maintain criminal careers.

Confronting the Dangers of Shoplifting

Each time a woman shoplifts, she puts herself in a dangerous position. If she is apprehended, not only is her freedom at stake, but she also most likely will be without the drugs her body craves. Sandy describes the last time she shoplifted:

The last time I shoplifted was yesterday. I guess I got the idea in the morning when I knew that I needed money, and I used my roommate's truck. I entertain the thought probably for like two hours before I go, make sure I figure what store I want to go to, or what I want to take, or where I'm going to take it to sell it. I think, like, every level when I do it. I knew the stores didn't open till ten o'clock, so I went to the mall, like, ten of ten before the doors even opened. I thought about what I was gonna do; I knew I wanted to go in and grab two quilts because I know I needed money for a couple of days. When I go into the stores it's already preplanned.

I'm thinking, like, a fifty-fifty chance of going to jail when I walk into that store, and I know that. It's a fear that I don't enjoy because I sweat and I shake and, but it's, like, I know I have to do it. Some people say there's an enjoyment in it. I find no enjoyment in it at all. And, I went into the store, I'd say as soon as they opened up. I walked upstairs, I looked around at the quilts, talk to the ladies, I took two quilts and went down the escalator. I looked around while I'm in there and make sure nobody's paying any attention to me. I went in there dressed appropriately, make it look like I belong, you know, 'cause I'm into Macy's and Strawbridge's, J. C. Penney's, make it look appropriate like I'm shopping in there.

Then, I'd say my fear lasts for a good half hour afterwards I walk out of the store, because I'm still shaking and sweating and it's hard for me to drive because I'm scared; even though I know it's the fear, I still continue to take myself in there. . . . I put it in the trunk or whatever, and I usually bring to, either Cramer Hill or North Camden to the service stores that ask me for the quilts.

Sandy, like all of the other women who specialize in shoplifting to support themselves, knows her freedom is at stake well before she enters a retail store to shoplift. She must prepare, not only practically for the business of her crime, but also emotionally to carry it through. Shoplifters relax their nerves prior to entering into the crime and employ various practical techniques during the crime that involve their deliberate interaction with employees, but rarely their use of special tools. Shoplifters never fully commit to the crime until they step past the store's threshold with the merchandise. Intuition tells them when to call it off. To go into a store, load up, and to "get over," or succeed, requires planning; the shoplifter must determine what merchandise to steal, where and how to steal it, and how she will dispose of the goods for cash before she rewards herself with drugs. What her customer wants and how soon helps a shoplifter decide which stores to select. Practicality determines how she commits the crime, that is, the particular style used to take and carry away merchandise. This sort of planning is a continuous, cyclical process with adjustments made along the way. Each new successful outcome, each close call, and each unsuccessful outcome (resulting in apprehension or poor monetary return for effort) provide additional information for the shoplifter (feedback on her performance) that she uses to adjust and readjust her overall strategy to succeed in the long term.

"You Have to Condition Your Mind"

The shoplifting specialists I interviewed typically shoplift daily, sorting out their shoplifting agenda before setting out to commit the crime. As part of this preparation, each shoplifter must ready herself emotionally. She can only commit to the crime once she keeps in check her fear of detection, and she must present to others an appearance of normalcy (being edgy and looking worried is not normal). Lee explains how the plan to shoplift works, the importance of overcoming fear, and how drugs fit into the picture:

Well, going in you have an order, somebody requested something so you go to a particular store, you go get what it is that they want, and of course, you're contemplating on the money that you're going to get and deciding already what you're going to buy, what you're going to do with it. You know what I mean. Not too often do you think about getting caught. Okay, you go in, I'm going to do this, but I'll be glad when it's over; but you don't go in and say if I get caught, I'm going to jail, blah, blah, blah, you don't really cover all that. Plus, you have to condition your mind to go in the store; you can't go in there thinking stupid you know. If you go in there thinking you're going to get caught, then you're going to get caught. You go in there thinking I'm gonna get this or I got to; well, not so much I gotta get it because desperation will get you caught too. If you go in there desperate, like if you're sick on dope you shouldn't go, because that makes you desperate. The object is to get well [use heroin] before you go. . . . You don't think about goin' to jail when you go in; you just think about getting over. That's the main objective, to get over. . . . My heart skips a beat . . . but that leaves, it has to go, ya know, that initial entrance into the store. Almost like goin' to war, ya know; this is it, this is like a do-or-die situation. Just like going on stage, pull yourself together, man. . . . Now, the whole ride back we'll talk about different spots, you know the malls, so and so and so and so just to make plans for the next day. They got some plus stores, they got a plus store in there. I gotta go there tomorrow. Oh, and so and so is selling, like, we scope out; we go alone and that's our main conversation coming back until we start selling our stuff and getting our money.

All of the women in my study use drugs before they shoplift. Being just high enough on drugs reduces their trepidation and invokes a willingness to accept the risk of apprehension. Alice's explanation illustrates this reasoning:

That's the only time I could really do it. I couldn't do it unless I was high; I couldn't. I'm scared to death to go in a store and steal anything, put my hands on anything that doesn't belong to me, unless I'm in another state of mind. On drugs I guess, you know how you're not thinking rationally. I'm not thinking about the consequences at the time. It gives you a little more heart. I know I should be thinking about, "I could get arrested" but I'm not. . . . Normally, when I'm under the influence of drugs or alcohol, nah, I'm not afraid of anything. . . . A lot of times if I'm sober, I really, really think, think hard about it. I mean, like, even if I have it and I really see that I can get away with it, I'm just so scared I don't have the courage anymore 'cause I'm actually a coward if I'm not using drugs. . . . So sometimes afterwards, especially when I'm high, when I come down and I'm like, "Oh my God, I stole all this stuff. What if I woulda got caught?"

Drugs calm the nerves and endow shoplifters with a subliminal strength, confidence, and courage in the face of danger. Sober, Shawn, like most others, considers the consequences of her actions. High, she ignores them. Lee said simply, "When I'm high, I just don't give a fuck," meaning she is simply no longer too afraid to risk apprehension. Nannie reasons similarly that her willingness to accept the dangers of detection can only come when she is high on drugs:

Drugs is what gives me the balls to go in there. If I'm not using, I don't have the balls to go into the store. If I'm not high or if I'm sick, I don't have the balls to go into the store and walk out with something. If I'm not using I get paranoid; I'm scareder. When I'm using dope [heroin], I do like two or three bags and I'm relaxed enough that I think it's OK. I'm not that scared; but a lot of times I should be more on my toes than I am.

Being under the influence of drugs can have drawbacks too. With their minds dulled, shoplifters can be less intuitive to cues that they are in danger of detection and, as Veronica's comments illustrate, potentially more willing to act irrationally in order to get away. "I know one incident: The Merion police was on a bike and this guy ran out of the store and he was telling him that I don't think she paid for this, and when the police officer came, I was gonna run over him. I wanted to run him down [with the car] because I didn't want to get caught."

"You Can Move Faster Alone"

In addition to using drugs as part of their overall strategy, the women typically engage in the crime without the help of others. Doing this, they explain, helps to present to other shoppers and store personnel an impression that they are just another shopper. Shoplifting as part of a group is risky because a group tends to draw attention and, most importantly, working in a group requires trust, something not easily developed or maintained in the drug culture. Lee says:

I was always alone, never had no one to go with me. I didn't trust anyone. I always felt like when you move, you can move faster alone. They wasn't dressed properly and they wasn't up to par, and I needed that. I needed that look. I didn't want that attention. I didn't like to take anyone. I always went alone.

A shoplifter working alone is responsible for her own behavior and can better manage the scene, but she also maintains an edge in the market for stolen goods. Sandy allowed others to shoplift with her in the beginning of her shoplifting career but never again; those individuals learned her techniques and began to compete with her by stealing similar products and moving in on her customers.

If I know I'm the only one doin' it, then I know I have control over the situation, and I don't go into a store with anybody else because what I do a lot of people don't do. Once they see from me what I do, and how simple it is, a lot of people will try to start doin' it and try to go to my customers and make it hard for me. Like if I sell something for a hundred and fifty dollars, they'll come and sell for maybe half that, and it would make it too hard for me to try to come in and resell something. I don't go to the stores with anybody because of that fact. I don't show anybody what I do or tell 'em.

Individuality and autonomy generally are preferred over group shoplifting. The exception is Tracy, who has always shoplifted as part of a group of drug users with whom she lives. For her, this method is easy and convenient because she reaps rewards even when she plays a marginal role. She works various aspects of the crime when it is her time in a rotation—being the lookout, diverting security, driving the car, acquiring the merchandise, and walking out of the store. Successful group shoplifting requires each group member to prepare, trust the others, and communicate effectively during the commission of the crime. For example, never should all members of the group be close to one another in a store because this would draw too much attention. Tracy rationalizes her choice to shoplift as part of a group (it is convenient), describes how the group readies itself and minimizes risk (cleaning themselves and getting high, maintaining distance), and explains a method used to shoplift and dispose of merchandise for income in Home Depot.

There's four people, a couple of guys and a couple of girls. It was convenient. I mean, I didn't have to do that much work. We all worked together. I mean, sometimes we sat around and did nothing; other days I had to go and do the dirty work and then the partnership, it was just easier to do it that way. . . . Usually what we would try to do is wake up, but we wouldn't go when we would be sick as a dog, because that would draw attention to us if we were in a store like walking around holding our stomach. You really wanted to get a shower but not look too nice, 'cause then all the guys would be staring at you. . . . really don't want to draw attention to yourself. . . . So we would find out what stores we were going to hit and what we were going to steal, like, just say we were going to Kmart, we would steal a whole bunch of valances and things that are small like that. They don't give you cash, you would return them and get a gift card, and you would sell them to some of the people in the parking lot. Toys "R" Us, where else, Home Depot we would take circuit breakers and smoke detectors. We'd get empty boxes, just a box like that and it would be empty, and you walk like we're going to return something and grab the real thing like an air compressor or something, stick it in the cart, say we want to return it and walk out. Back in 2003, it was easy to get away with it. Now, you can't do this. You can steal a circuit breaker and stuff like that, but you have to have a driver's license to return it. [Would you all go in the store?] *No, because if we all went in the store, you look suspicious. You try and stay as far away as possible, because you don't want to draw attention to ourselves. One of us would go in, take something, walk to the car, and another person would go right back in and return it for a gift card and then try to sell it to someone in the parking lot or in the store.*

Francine learned how to shoplift as a member of an organized group. Over time she assumed various roles. At first she was the "stemmer," the lookout inside the store watching for employees and distracting them when necessary. As a rookie, she followed instruction.

They tell you what to do, ya know; like your first, second, third time, they tell you what to do. They say, "When you go in there, walk straight to the skirt section. There's a lady over there; watch that bitch, don't let her know." Ya know, stuff like that. . . . When you're the stemmer your job is to get her attention. "Excuse me, can you help me?" You know, get her to turn her back or something. . . . Everybody has a job. If you doing alarms right it's good to have somebody to like cough or talk real loud or something to distract the sound of the alarm poppin'. Then you got the alarms that have the ink. . . . Another job that I had is I had carried a bag out. One [person] popped the alarm, one would bag it, and the other one would carry it out. That way it broke down almost evenly. Because the one that carried the bag out the store should be getting the most [money] . . . because that's the one that's gonna get the case unless they got it on camera and they see all three of you working together, but when you walk out that door with that bag in your hand and they got you, you got that bag.

Mentors teach new shoplifters how to act, what to watch for, and how to get out. All of the women in my study shoplifted with at least one other person (usually as part of a pair) at the start of their specializations before setting out alone to learn shoplifting techniques. On the rare occasion a shoplifting specialist might allow another person or group to join her, she selects fellow drug users in need of drugs and money but never family members. Involving family is morally wrong, as Esther explains: "No, that's home; I never interfere. Listen, that was *my* bad, the drugs was my bad, my family ain't got nothing to do with it. Do you understand what I'm saying? It would be on me, not the peeps. This is you; you don't involve your family 'cause you twisted. You know what I mean? At least I got common sense enough that, you know, keep those kind of morals."

Francine once made the mistake of shoplifting while her niece and nephew waited outside the store. Involving them put their safety in jeopardy, and now the children know she is a thief:

The last time that I got caught for shoplifting and that was in 2001. I hadn't been in this store for months, and I had gotten cocky with myself that when I walked in and I came and looked like it was going to be a piece of cake, I got one of his shopping bags and went on in the back and loaded it up. . . . The guy stood up and said, "Could I see your bag?" So I looked at him and I said, "Here, take this here," and he said, "No, I'm calling the cops." So I'm thinking about my niece and nephew. I said, "Just take this here and let me go." He said, "No." I said, "Look, my niece and nephew are here; they have no idea that their aunt is around here doing this dumb shit." They took the shopping bags I had and called one of the managers and told him I had stuff in there; it only came to eighty dollars. I never ever got caught and tried to get away or fought back if I got caught. I got caught; that's it. But this is one time I felt as if I had to try and get out of there so I can get out to my niece and nephew. I was saying to myself, as soon as that door opens, I'm going out. Now, the man was standing guard like a bulldog. So this lady came in, and I was runnin' out the door, I was runnin'. He caught me on the back of my shirt. I felt so stupid, that was that, waiting for the police. I said, "If you're not gonna let me go, let me make a phone call so I can call somebody to go get them." So I called my sister; I said, "You're not going to believe this, but I done got busted; the children are sitting outside playing. Can you get them?" She went and got them so that was off my mind. I went to jail . . . I was totally embarrassed. It didn't bother me that much before if I called home and said, "I'm locked up," ya know, but my morals changed. Those kids, ya know, they know that I'm a thief.

"You Have to Follow Your Instinct"

Though the women prepare themselves emotionally to begin their crime, the women never fully commit to it until they step past the boundary of the store's entrance or exit with merchandise. To know when to proceed and when to call off the crime requires constant awareness. The shoplifter's eyes scan the setting; she watches for employees, security, other shoppers, and cameras. From the moment she steps into the store until she is safely driving away she must also use her sixth sense. A shoplifter must feel or perceive that the crime is progressing in her favor to carry it out. A gut feeling that something is wrong—that is, a shoplifter's intuition and her own experience that apprehension is imminent—is a cue not to be ignored. Candee talks about the importance of mindfulness while shoplifting.

You know many people say they don't shoplift because they are afraid of getting caught and because they make better money doing something else. I am afraid of getting caught. But that leaves, it has to go, that initial entrance into the store, this is it. If you go in there thinking you're gonna get caught, then you're gonna get caught. When you get in there, sometimes you don't do it. Sometimes I get a feeling; it's just something that tells you not to do it. And you don't.

Tracy refers to this awareness of imminent detection as instinct: "The thing is that you just know when you're gonna get caught. It's something that you feel. It's something you have to follow your instinct."

Alice calls the feeling a vibe:

If I got nervous. Or, sometimes, I just, I think if, um, that the guard in the store thinks that they're making eye contact with you, I'll stop. Like, some people around here say, like, they get a rush if they can steal something and they know that the guard was watching. I'm really scared of stuff like that. I don't get a rush like that. . . . I guess it's more so just having a feeling that it's ok. Like sometimes, some things you have a bad vibe.

For Carmela and others, cues can manifest physically. "If you're gonna get caught, you're gonna get caught, like if you grab it and run or if you just walk out with it. . . . I don't want to be in jail, but I'm not worried about going to jail. I don't know why I get those feelings too; if somebody's on me, my stomach will start turning and I'll just walk out of the store."

Shoplifters must be aware of and responsive to the emotional or physical cue, the feeling that the situation is just not right, that risks are now too great. Shoplifters pay a price when they disregard cues. Lee says:

While I'm in the store I just try to focus on getting what I need and then walk out, and keep my eyes open the entire time. . . . There's times when I'll stop at the door because my fear is so much and I'm scared that someone's going to grab me from behind. My instinct would tell me; like my instinct told me the other day in the store not to walk out with anything, and I listen because as soon as I was standing at the door, two security guards walked past me and one went outside with his walkie-talkie looking for me. Then you realize why it was—he was talking on his walkie-talkie waiting for me to walk out with something. So my instinct told me not to shoplift, so I didn't walk out and I won't go in that store anymore now, because I know they're waiting for me to come back. . . . The times I did get arrested, it's like I knew they were watching me and I still did it anyway; like my instinct told me not to walk out with anything and I knew that one person was paying attention to me, keeping an eye on me, I still walked out anyway.

Getting Out without Getting Caught: Shoplifting Methods

The particular shoplifting method the women use is yet another opportunity to manage risk of apprehension. They draw on the same resources honest shoppers use to carry merchandise out of retail stores—shopping bags, shopping carts, and items visible in hand—and seldomly deviate from these methods. The women avoid the "grab and run" approach and rarely use special equipment such as tools to gather tethered or secured merchandise or bags made to override detectors at store exits (often referred to as "booster boxes," or "tag bags" in Texas), because these methods increase apprehension risk and reduce future opportunities. Francine refers to "grab and run" as "throwing rocks at the penitentiary." This, she says, is not a prudent approach; it is asking for trouble: "You got the ones that don't take prudence. They just run in the store, grab a handful like you got brodies. . . . Brodies mean you're being bold about it, you don't care; like say you stand up there and you're right in front of the owner. That's a brody. Just come in and grab a handful of stuff and walk out. You're throwing rocks at the penitentiary."

Nannie sometimes used a tool intended for store personnel to remove security tags on merchandise at purchase. She explains how this tool works:

I used to take them alarms apart and stuff like that. You know those things they have on there, they're silver. Well, it's like when you take them apart they're blue dye or something come on you. I had gloves like, and I had a thing like those people do in the store; they put it under that . . . I had tooken it from another store. A lot of people in the department stores be leaving their counters so I took that. . . I took the thing [alarm] off [the merchandise]. It was so funny you take it off and click it and throw it in the trash. . . . So I was, like, since I had that thing, once you clip that [alarm], you got it. You know what I'm saying? So that means that once I walk through the metal detector, right, that it wasn't going to go off because I did what the people would do, clip it off.

Carrying such a tool and exposing it inside a retail store is chancy, as Esther said: "Yeah, yeah, you need a pair of tweezers and all that deal, clippers and stuff like that to do that. I'm not going through that. It would be my luck I'd clip the wrong thing."

Retailers usually know what products are popular with shoplifters at the moment and use preventive measures to secure them. One measure is to use a metal stamp or strip (similar to what one might find on a library book) that triggers an alarm when passed through sensors at the entrance or exit if it has not been desensitized at the register. When a shoplifter targets such products (meats and beauty products, for example), she can usually very easily wrap the metal sensor with aluminum foil (or simply tear it off when she can locate it precisely). This works best in grocery stores where foil is available for the taking. The foil acts as a barrier between the security device and the detection mechanism at the entrance or exit. Such security measures are simple and easily overcome by shoplifting specialists. Rose explains how easy it is: "So now, almost every store has these cords lined with foil, like, foil inside. . . . I walk into a CVS or something and pick something like Crest strips [which has a shoplifting detection device on it]. I found a new way though, if you take foil and wrap it around [the item] or like if there's something with foil and you walk out, all the security devices won't go off."

Shoplifters acquire merchandise in the store the same way ordinary consumers shop. While a shoplifter might prefer one method, concealing items in a retailer's bag, for example, she can adapt to change and must in order to succeed at the crime over the long term. The quantity and type of merchandise as well as the retailer selected for shoplifting help a shoplifter select the best method to use. For example, shoplifters do not conceal large, bulky, or heavy items that are not always bagged when purchased. They simply exit the store with these items in hand or in carts, as would shoppers who have paid for these goods, less a sales receipt. Sandy shoplifts bedding products from large department stores that offer no shopping carts to shoppers. When she targets comforters (which are too large to fit in bags), she simply carries these items out without concealing them. Taking two, one in each arm, will earn her enough money for that day, at the very least. She explains that this method—walking out of a store with large items not bagged—seems ordinary to store employees and other shoppers, not suspicious.

It seems easier, simpler for me to walk out of the store with two giant comforters than it would for me to, like, grab pants or pills and, you know, con-

ceal them somewhere and then have to walk out of the store. That's what I've been doin', takin' a comforter, which is, I walk out of the store with two, you know, large, like, comforter bed-in-bag sets, which are, like, some are six hundred to eight hundred dollars apiece. I wouldn't put them in a bag because usually there wasn't one that would fit, and I was under the assumption that most people, the majority of people, wouldn't assume that somebody would walk out with something like that [without paying for it].

Sandy also needs a supply of small, expensive bedding products for her customers and knows walking out of a store with these items open and in hand is out of the ordinary, suspicious looking. When a shoplifter is targeting items normally placed in a retailer's bag when purchased, she has several options. She may hide the merchandise in her clothing, but doing this means she could never talk her way out of the theft as being a sincere mistake. A less risky approach, one used most commonly by the women in this study, is to conceal items in a shopping bag, such as one taken from that store in the past, taken that day from behind a register in the store, or taken from another store. The bag is concealed upon entry, then filled, and the shoplifter exits with the bag visibly in hand. Sandy likes to take bags from one retailer to use at a different store. Once inside the targeted store, she opens the bag and fills it with the products she needs and then walks out of the store, impressing to others around her (most especially store security) that she is an ordinary mall shopper who has browsed inside the store with purchases from another store. Sandy explains how she does this and why she conceals this bag upon entry.

If I want sheets, I usually go to the opposite store. Like, I'll go to Macy's and get a bag at Macy's, go into Strawbridge's. I would just take the bag. I look around for a register there's nobody standing at, take the bag, stick it inside my purse or underneath my jacket—it counts on what I'm wearing—go into the opposite store, and open up the bag, quietly because they're loud bags, and put four or five sets of sheets in there, and walk out. Because the object is that if I'm inside of Strawbridge's and I have a Macy's bag, you [security] have to be sure that I didn't have that bag when I came in. So, you can't stop me unless you're guaranteed that I didn't have that bag and that I loaded something in there. I don't really know if that's true; I think it's just common sense. Because if I didn't purchase anything inside of that store, and you saw me come in the store with that bag and you saw me walking out with a bag, well, that's fine; you're gonna stop me and arrest me. But, if you seen me walking out with a bag, but you don't know what happened when I came in, you're not too sure to stop me. You don't know if I really stole anything or not.

To make entering into the crime worthwhile, shoplifters must acquire enough merchandise each time that will earn them money for drugs that day and perhaps the next several days. The appeal of shoplifting in stores such as Macy's is quality of merchandise and the financial value it brings to shoplifters and their customers, but the downside is the limited resources available to shoplifters to carry away merchandise. They can only carry so much with two hands, so when they do shoplift in stores such as Macy's or Lord and Taylor that do not provide carts to shoppers, they will need to shoplift a small amount of higher priced merchandise or shoplift multiple times in a day. For this reason, many of the women in this study rely heavily on retailers that do provide carts to shoppers, retailers such as Kmart, Wal-Mart, Home Depot, and grocery stores. When they began their shoplifting specialization, the women stole few items, often in hand or in hand-held baskets, but later had to change. Carmela explains why shoplifting using small hand-held baskets is a bad idea for the professional:

With baskets or putting stuff in your pants it's not enough money. I'd be doing that all day. I would be doing that from sunrise to sunset. You're not gonna get that much [money]. . . . Somebody comes in [to "cash out" with a customer] with a little basket filled up with stuff; I'm coming in with shopping carts full of stuff. I do top dollar. Somebody comes in with a [hand] cart four dollars, eight dollars. I make hundreds. . . . A professional would take everything in that cart off the counter or shelf and the amount of money you're taking don't compare.

As a rule, the women who shoplift in stores with shopping carts never bag items within the cart prior to exit. Veronica sometimes does and explains how:

I would bag it up myself sometimes when I was in an aisle. [Wouldn't it be strange to be in an aisle and see the person pass you with bags?] *Some people like myself, I would always pretend I was going to the bathroom. By then my cart was filled up with everything I needed so I would go to the bath-*

room and you could do it [bag the merchandise] in the bathroom real quick. Then I would go and have a receipt in my hand to make it look good.

Candee is another shoplifter who hides food in grocery store bags but does so directly in the aisles. Her reasoning is simple: the store is busy at the right time and the security lax. This method, however, allows her to take away only so much.

First I find a bag person, right? I send somebody in there; I say, "Go in there and tell 'em your grandmother dropped her bags and they'll snatch around ten or fifteen bags, right? They come out with the bags. I tuck the bags neatly away. I get a shopping cart and go shopping. Just shop, shop, shop, shop, shop. I fill the cart up, then I take the meats, take them security devices off, like sometimes they have like little triangle stamps that when you go through [the exit] it beeps, bom, bom, bom. So I just snatch it off, just rip it off and put them in the bags, put the bags on the side of the cart. Go up in the line. [Didn't you think that bagging the meats in the aisles would draw attention to you?] *The store is full. You got to know what time to do this, and then they hire drunks as security guards. The Pathmark they really hire lousy security. They'll help you out with the shit. Wait, wait, hold up. I get to the [checkout] counter and start unloading. I have somebody with me. You know I might take a girlfriend and say, "Come on, go with me, come make some money." This is how easy this was. I say, "You keep on loading [items on the counter at the register for checkout]." I take the bags, pick 'em up. I say, "I'm going to go get the car keys." And take the bags I have and walk out of the store. She can leave anytime.* [So, she's left there at the counter with the goods being rung up while you leave with the expensive meats. What does she do then?] *"Oops, I forgot my wallet." You know what I mean? Something like that.*

Bagging merchandise in a store's aisles or in the restroom and walking about with merchandise already bagged seems too risky according to most of the women, and reasonably so. It is out of the ordinary. It is also unnecessary. The preferred approach is to make the food or merchandise they target work for them. Carmela's description of how she shoplifts in grocery stores illustrates the method used by most of the women in this research. She will hide products to be sold (which are usually small) within the inner part of the cart with large, bulky items normally not bagged at all, such as paper towel or toilet paper rolls and cases of water or soda, lining the outer part of the cart. She explains:

Yeah, like I take carts of stuff out; the house is full of food. . . . Formula, diapers, aspirins, all different types of medication, Crest strips; they'll [customers] actually take anything. . . . Right, so my cart is full with a little bit of everything . . . my cart is probably like three, four hundred dollars a cart a shot. . . . I line around the sides with, like, bulk products, and I throw everything in the middle and then I'll put a big thing of paper towels on top or something on top or a case of water. They don't see what's in the middle, right, they just see me walking out with all bulk products.

Because shoplifting is their business, the women take much more of a particular product than would a regular customer. As mentioned previously, retailers know what products are popular with shoplifters and secure them in different ways, such as with sensors that set off door alarms. Taking products off shelves, removing sensors, and placing them into carts is the riskiest part of shoplifting these items. Shoplifters have to be aware of cameras, other shoppers, and, most especially, store personnel. Carmela explains how to respond when an employee comes near:

When you're actually putting it in, like I got a majority of the stuff, then I put the baby formula. I want like forty, fifty cans of that, so you put forty, fifty cans in the middle; that's the biggest risk, if somebody working walks by while I'm putting all those cans in the middle, I'm trying to play it off. Like one store, it's cereal, so I have the cereal boxes lined up on the cart as I'm filling the cans on the other side in there. This way if a worker comes, I knock the cereal boxes over and they hide all the food.

Veronica explains shoplifting a television, visible and in a shopping cart. The correct exit to use is the one without security. Like the other shoplifting specialists she is flexible, using different methods when appropriate to the retailer and the type of merchandise. Looking like any other shopper is key.

It was a TV. I put it in the cart; I just look around and make sure there were no security guard around and took it in the cart as if I was shopping. . . . I looked so honest, I guess. . . . You would find out which door was safe, like they didn't have anyone there, they didn't have the machine that goes over the device, or if there was, I would just walk around it and go to the next exit, usually most exits in lawn and garden they don't have them. . . . I didn't always use carts 'cause not all stores have carts; like Macy's, they had bags. I'd have a bag with the store's name on it, and I did that. Yes. I would have them folded up in my pocketbook. . . . I looked so honest. They didn't know, they didn't look at me. They didn't know. They didn't look at my appearance. . . . They would never think that I would do anything like that. No, they would never think so they wouldn't watch me.

Act Like a Regular Shopper

A good booster, a professional shoplifter, knows how to "get over" and get out of the store. Employees of stores must see the shoplifter as nothing other than a typical shopper, sometimes a picky shopper. To trick employees, the women deliberately interact with employees and even law enforcement at stores while they commit the crime. Sneaking and hiding increase a shoplifter's vulnerability to apprehension. To act as a normal shopper means asking for assistance with merchandise, browsing, saying hello. Doing this does not expose their crime but decreases their sense of vulnerability. Dressed appropriately for the particular retailer, the women play the role of shopper. To employees at Strawbridge's, Sandy appears to be a regular shopper. She has developed a kind of personal acquaintance with the women employed in the bedding and bath section of the store. Because a normal shopper asks questions and interacts, so does Sandy:

I think of the way of being dressed, the way I act. I'll talk to certain people, I don't act shy, like, I don't hide from anyone in the store. I go right up and look at the merchandise. I'll talk to the lady who works there . . . about new patterns they have, what's on sale, or whatever, and as soon as she turns her back, walk out with it. There at Strawbridge's in Cherry Hill, we was on a personal basis, she used to talk to me every time I came in there, not realizing I was stealing. She would just talk to me . . . about her family and my family and as soon as she turned around, I'd walk out of the store. I'm acting like I am shopping, and that I have money to purchase what's there, and I really don't.

The women know the "art" to the crime: dressing, acting, manipulating employees, and rotating between stores. Dressed for shopping at

Pep Boys auto parts store and pretending to be a mechanic, Esther even demands help from employees while she commits the crime.

I used to take and dress myself up as a garage worker: I put a pair of overall on like I worked in a garage. I'd take some grease and put on my face. Can't drive a lick, don't drive nowhere, I get a driver. . . . Well, didn't I take my behind, I had one keys in this hand, and I tear the yellow pages out and fold it up and clench it between my teeth and go, see that's a diversion cause that's what color the receipts are for one, right? And the keys, like I'm driving, you know what I mean? And I got a couple dollars in my hand to make it look like I got some money. And I go to Pep Boys looking very, very, very angry. Very angry. I walk over to the batteries, flip the ninety-eight dollar battery, the tops off, take the other one . . . and put one in each hand and walk out of Pep Boys store, turn around, and sometimes on a feisty day, I would turn around and look as if to say I wish one of you all would say something to me. Wait, hold up, and on a feisty day I would say [to an employee], "Come here, you; come help me here. Don't you see I'm an older woman? Come help me with this to my car." I'm serious, but see I got skilled with this. What you have to do, 'cause you got cameras on you; they might not be aware, but they got cameras on your ass. When it come around, the first of the month, somebody looking for you. Somebody's looking for you so you know this and that and you just . . . you lapse in between months, because, you know what I mean, they gonna forget them tapes, you understand what I mean? They got a new set of tapes . . . I got skilled. There's an art to it.

With her grocery cart lined on top and sides with bulk products to conceal the other goods inside, Carmela heads through the store exit only "as long as there are no workers around" who witness her slip past cashiers. When watchful eyes are on her, Carmela readjusts her tactic by talking her way past employees out of the store. This method works for most other shoplifting specialists I talked to. Carmela elaborates on this method, which she used the morning we spoke for the first time:

I walked through customer service with the damn cart, talk to them, and then walk out. [What did you talk to them about?] *Job applications and sometimes I even fill them out but not with my real name or nothing, bullshit names, bullshit address, everything. . . . I went through the [checkout] line because I didn't see no other way out, and I went to the cashier and said, "I have to cash my check to pay for this stuff." They said, "We can't do that [here at the register]." I said, "I need to talk to customer service then . . . my kids need to eat," and so I went up to customer service and I got there, I said, "I need a super card thing," and that was a whole other bullshit story when I got there. So the cashiers looking over me now, I'm standing there for a while so then they don't even pay attention to me no more. They figured I paid for it because they seen me walking up from a cashier. They go about their work; I talk to them for about five minutes and walk out with the cart. I see a security person sitting down, and I'll be talking to them with the cart right in front me.* [And nobody ever said, "Let me see a receipt"?] *No. They see me come out of the check-in aisle; I already paid for it that's why I'm here [at the exit]. . . . Every worker is there, everyone sees me. It's not that risky. I mean, if you were a worker, would you say something to someone who walked out with a cart of groceries? I wouldn't think that in a million years. I never got caught with the shopping carts.*

I have my mind on everything. I have my eyes in my mind on everything, on the speaker, when you call someone from customer service, anything and everything, ya know. You have to be aware of everything; you can't be sloppy. You can't just go in there and be sloppy. If you want to get it done right, you have to know what you're doing; you have to keep an eye on what you're doing. . . . I act like a regular shopper, look to the sales, ask questions like "What do I do with the coupon? Can I get a rain check?" [Why do you do that?] *Just to make it look good. They keep their eye off of me because they think I'm a regular shopper just looking for a bargain. . . . I actually had a young kid [store employee] bring four carts out to my car. Yeah, I've got guys on the street that are husky and wouldn't think of doin' nothing like this. I would like to be a fly on a wall one day watching myself.*

Working the Streets

I know what to do and what to say. It's my profession as far as prostituting. I know how to walk the streets. I was familiar with the drug dealers, I know where the [drug] houses are and I know who is there, I know what street to go down, what avenues not to go down. —Bernadette

Each day and every night while working the streets, sex workers have on their mind not just the drugs they need, but also the police and violence that could find them at any moment. While shoplifters are most concerned about apprehension, sex workers usually experience arrest as a temporary setback, sometimes even a welcomed rest. For them, the key to surviving life in crime is to elude predators who can kill them. Sex workers are also at risk for violence when they're not working at the hands of other drug users and intimate partners. For protection, they might carry weapons, screen potential dates, look for cues that warn of imminent danger, and try to control where the sex work transaction will occur. Women in my study rank victimization as the most important risk they face in their work, but they also concern themselves with arrest, a subject studied much less often. Here, I voice the perceptions and experiences of sex work specialists about dangers they face in their work, including violence, and lay out how skills and strategies such as watchfulness, intuition, relying heavily on trusted customers, and performing sexual transactions indoors are key to handling risks of apprehension and violence. Strangers represent the greatest risk; sex workers do not know if they are police who will arrest them or men who will hurt them.

"Rule Number 1: Don't Get in the Car with No Cop"

Undercover police, "vice cops" or "narcs," patrol the streets of Camden, North Philadelphia, and other neighborhoods where the drug culture thrives. Sex workers know that each time they make a transaction with a new customer their freedom is at stake, especially when they are carrying drugs because this usually earns them a night in jail. All of the women specializing in this crime have made the mistake of getting into a car with an undercover police officer posing as a sex work customer. I asked Tanisha for advice on how to avoid arrest. She relays this from her own mistake:

Rule number 1, don't get in the car with no cop. If you're tricking you got to make sure it ain't no narcotic. . . . Vice cops they too slick nowadays. They too slick. That's what got me locked up, a vice cop. He looked young, he looked hip. He said, "Yo, what's up? You're looking all good." I mean you get near the car. He says, "You need a ride?" No, what he said was, "Do you need a ride?" I said, "Yes," and I got in the car, and he said, "Your piece is real pretty." He said, "Why you out here?" Usually the dates don't ask you nothing like that, so it should have dawned on me then, but I'm so loaded and so full of drugs it didn't even dawn on me, you know, what are you doing out here. You know why you out here doing this, all pretty, and

I'm looking at him, like, but it ain't really dawning on me . . . so he's like, "Where do you want to go? I got a couple of hours; I got like forty-five dollars." So I said, "Pull over right here." Like that, but I never gave him a price, but you don't have to nowadays, all you do is got to be in the car. So when we pulled over and I got out the car and I went to go walk in the hotel, he was getting out of the car but he had a phone. So he shut his door and then he opened the back door and grabbed the phone, and I walked up the steps and said, "What are you doing?" He like, "Nothing; I just want to cut my phone off. So when he flipped it, the cops in the undercover know that was behind him that he got one, so he sent them a chirp. He chirped them. So all I know it when I got in there, and I had a bag of crack on me, and I dumped it in the trashcan because I knew I said, "This is a cop." I said, "It didn't dawn on me before, but this is a cop," and sure enough I see the room was full of cops, and I got busted. When I went to go turn around, he said, "Don't move." I said, "Oh my God."

The advice not to get into a car with police sounds simple, but accurately determining whether or not a man is a police officer is not always easy. "They dress like regular people in regular clothes," Tanisha continued, and they drive cars that fit the neighborhoods. As participants and observers of police work in the neighborhoods where they work, the women know they cannot make assumptions about rules police follow and how police act. One rule: If a trick is not willing to expose himself when asked, he is probably police, according to Ronni.

On the street, I can kind of, my vibes tell me whether or not you're a cop or not and there were certain things I could make you do or say. One of the rules for police officers is you're not supposed to show your body parts. They are the ones that are new because you can tell the newer ones. I'm going tell you what they do. You say, "Let me see your dick." They say, "Let's wait till we get to where we're going." "All right, let me out. When you get to where you're going, pull your dick out yourself; don't pull it out for me. If you can't pull it out right here for me, I think you're a cop. Show me your dick before I even get in the car."

However, assuming police must behave in a particular way or follow rules is risky. Ronni continues:

Police officers and even though they don't follow the rules, believe me, police officers do not follow rules. One of the rules is you're not supposed to show your body parts. They show their body parts. You're not supposed to fondle the person, the person, the provider, me, but they fondle me. They'll fondle my tits. They'll even have me give them a blow job and say you're arrested and arrest you, ya know, they'll arrest you. But you can tell the newer ones. They follow the rules.

Several of the sex workers in my study talked of unethical encounters they had with police, such as criminal coercion into sex (about 5 percent) and paid sex work transactions with police (10 percent). Bernadette told me police were among her frequent, paying customers, the "biggest tricks in Philadelphia." She describes her experiences with police on the streets and illustrates why a sex worker should never make assumptions of how police should and should not act:

See a lot of them trick with you then lock you up, so it's not always true, it's not always true just like I said; I had cops I tricked with and I had another cop I used to buy drugs for his girlfriend, ya know what I'm saying. I used to trick with this one cop and his wife, ya know. . . . Ya know and a lot of them, a lot of cops used to see me. I had one cop, I was in the car giving this guy a blow job and he was going to lock me up because he told me I was too good. He said, "You need to get a house. You don't need to be out here on the street. You need to get a house to do your work," 'cause I gave this man a blow job. The next thing you know I lift my head up and I see these men clapping, three or four police officers, standing there clapping, and I said, "Oh God, I'm going to go to jail," and they just clapping and they said "Girl, you worked him out!" For about a half hour I worked on him, and he said, "I'm not going to lock you up this time, but get your house because you're too good to be out here making this kind of money."

The best way to evade arrest is to avoid police all together. To remain free, sex workers must be street smart. They have to be attentive to their surroundings, watch and listen, and remember when and where police are and regularly show themselves. Nikki elaborates:

It's the way you carry yourself, how you observe your neighborhood; you have to know about your neighborhood, what's going on with the neighborhood. You have to know the times to be in the street, the times not to be in the street. I know the times when they do their sting operations not to be around, ya know, and then you also have to know your clients on how they talk to you because I got in the car a couple of times with a couple police officers, most people say, "You want a trick?" or this, that, and the other. They come, "You want a date?" They're more polite, more conservative about it, and you know they're cops. See it's just the type of person, your character. . . . I used to tell them, "Cop, get out of my face," and a lot of them be like, "How did you know?" . . . Because I've been around cops. Some of them looked like it, but some it's hard for you to tell, but if you've been around a lot of undercover cops a lot, you learn. I learned these things. I know who Starsky and Hutch is. . . . They never really bothered the neighborhood people as long as they wasn't doing no shooting or standing around doing no killing. As far as standing on the corner, they see them [sex workers] all the time; they're peanuts to him.

Though they will try to avoid contact with police, in many cases sex workers can go about their work avoiding arrest most of the time, according to the women I interviewed. Patricia has just two prostitution charges in her eight years on the street: a good track record, she told me. Her experience is characteristic of sex workers generally, many of whom have been out on the streets for many years with few arrests. The women report that police know who is and who is not a prostitute, and they usually enforce the law informally, sometimes telling sex workers to move or to get off the street. Patricia elaborates: "They knew what the women were doing out there because if you're from that area you know certain corners; they know. They would come up to me and show me five [dollars] and say, 'Have you seen this person?' Ya know, 'Have you seen this person? Do you have any drugs on you?' Ya know, things like that, and then just 'Get off the corner.'"

Many sex workers say they can sense when a situation is just not right, much in the same way shoplifters do. Sensing danger, a sex worker must trust this feeling. Lauren says, "You got to go with your instinct," but weariness at nights and craving for the drugs can cloud judgment and get her arrested. Arrest is a setback for sex workers but usually a temporary one and "not a big deal" because they are normally back on the streets within hours. So the women take arrests in stride. In reality, according to the women, the chances of arrest for prostitution appear to be quite low in the neighborhoods they work. The constant supply of sex work customers, the availability of rooming houses and other locations where women take sex work customers, and other, more serious challenges of policing in urban drug cultures are the reasons for this. Eva comments:

I could go in a neighborhood and just date the whole neighborhood. It was like, the law was never involved. . . . It depends on where you are, but the neighborhood, you walking around and the cops are walking around, but they don't know. They think you know these people; they don't think you're going to trick this man somewhere unless you stop a car, and very seldom I stopped a car, it was always walking.

The best ways to avoid police are to use busy indoor locations such as rooms and apartments for sex work, and to rely on existing customers. Edwina, like most of the sex workers, feels safest indoors. Her regular customers know how to contact her and where she is. They go to her. Her only real worry about apprehension occurs when she wants to meet a potential new customer, which she does on the streets: "I used to be on the corners, you know, and then I brought it down and then I just stopped doing the corners. I started just having people call me and come by my house. So, to me, it was, it wasn't a too much of a bad risk. Especially, beings that I was having them come to see me. Dates came right there to me. The money came right to the mailbox."

"You Got to Set Your Ground Rules"

According to extant literature, violent victimization is the greatest danger for street-level prostitutes, who are assaulted, raped, robbed, and killed on and off the job. While sex workers may face intimidation by police who force them into sex (rape them) and may be abused by husbands and boyfriends, the violence they encounter most of the time is in their work at the hand of customers, managers such as pimps, and other drug users hustling to survive on the streets. Violence against sex workers in Camden and Philadelphia is perpetrated primarily by new "tricks." Their constant need for drugs and their complacency with this crime keep street sex workers in the midst of danger. All of the women in my research have been "ripped off" by customers who strong-arm them for sex without pay, and most are victims of rape and beatings. In her two years on the streets, Cheryl has escaped much of this violence, but she knows how quickly her luck can run out. Despite the convenience of sex work, the ease of access to the crime, and the demand for the work, she knows this crime choice can get her killed.

I never had anybody really hurt me or anything like that. I know girls out there, they've been beaten. I've been doing this four or five years, and I just thank God that I've been fortunate enough that is hasn't happened to me. Like I've been ripped off, sure, but I've never had somebody put their hands on me. Like if you shoplift, you're not gonna die. A lot of the girls get raped on the street continually. The biggest thing to worry about is your life, just your life.

During her ten years on the streets, Renita has battled violent men. She has to because it is "part of the job." Sitting safely with me in a room off the streets, protected from that violence, her words communicate only so much of what she went through emotionally and physically. "I had a gun up to my head a couple of times. I had a knife up to my neck one time. I have been raped another time, beaten up and raped and stuff like that. Getting hurt, getting beat up, ya know, it's part of the job." For the rape and robbery sex workers experience at the hands of customers, La Toya blames a culture of violence in the urban drug world, a sensible explanation.

It's sad to say that there's a lot of people taking it more less than buying it. There's a lot of girls out there getting raped. A lot of guys out there feel as though if your life is violent enough for you then why should I respect you? Why should I let you live? . . . I mean I have gotten into a car with a guy that put a knife to my boob and told me to suck his dick, and it's just like that, I mean it's just like to where it's though they feel as though you not worth nothin'. . . . There's a lot of females that make it bad because a lot of them burning them on their wallet, taking their stuff or, you know, so when they get somebody that ain't gonna do that they feel as though they need to take you. They shouldn't have to pay for it.

Sex workers in my study said they are most vulnerable to violence when they take strangers to hidden-away places and when customers decide the location for sex work. Jarena made the mistake of choosing an abandoned house. The customer, a desperate drug user, knew that was her place to get high, and he sought her out again and again, not for sex, but for her money and her drugs.

Actually after I started getting robbed, raped and robbed and all that stuff, I started hiding my money in the inside pants. That's when I started getting smart and I was twenty-five, and three times in one week I got beat in the head. The first time I got beat the same guy, because he wanted me to do what he wanted me to do. We was in an abandoned house. . . . He appeared to be angry; he grabbed my hand, and when I got up to try to run out of the house, that's when he grabbed the broom handle, that's when I had the wooden broom handle [for protection] and he started beating me on my head and I'm trying to protect my head. That was the first time. I ran right around the corner, my grandmother lived right around the corner at the time and I was all bloody at this point. I went around there and my uncle was there; he smoked too. I went in my grandmother's room and you know and I'm asking him, "Could you give me a lighter?" and he's looking at me bleeding and he's telling me that I'm bleeding and he's calling the cops and I'm trying to smoke crack and he just snapped the pipe out of my mouth and he just took off, my uncle, and he ran to the corner and when I ran to the corner that's where the cops were. That's the first time I had a seizure. I went to the hospital and I had to get stitches all over my head, you know, two here, three here, four here, and three days later I'm back in the same house again, with all those stitches in my head, here he comes with a two-by-four asking me for money and crack, and I try to get out again and that's when he beat me again in my head and there was nobody around and I was unconscious. A lady had passed and she saw me laying there in blood again, and then she called the cops. . . . I guess like after a few days after that, I was back in the same spot again and here he comes again; this time there was people in there and he singled me out again. All three times, he got nothing, absolutely nothing, but this time he got arrested. This time I had a bandage around my head from the first two times when he beat me in my head, and I had dents in my head back here from before and he beat me in my head. He hit me twice and he started kicking me. I went into a seizure and the next thing I knew I was in Temple Hospital, and I am still having seizures till today. I have over a hundred stitches inside of me. I was twenty-five then and I'm thirty-nine now, and I still have seizures from the head trauma.

Avoiding being alone in dark alleys, abandoned houses, and other such hidden-away places is one way to reduce the likelihood of victimization. Another is to carry protection, usually a stick or metal object found on the streets. The best approach, according to the women in this study, is to rely as much as possible on regular customers who can be trusted, because these men want business to continue as usual. If a woman must interact with strangers, she has to be mindful and be in charge every moment. She must take control because passivity can get her killed. She must be wise, look for signs and signals that danger is imminent, and be ready to react when instinct tells her she is losing control. When a sex worker allows for any negotiation about what she will sell, where, and for how much money, she is losing control and increasing risk. This the sex workers learn from experience. Edwina had worked early on in Camden under the management of a pimp named Wendy. He set her hours, arranged her dates, and earned most of the money. He was violent too. The best thing a sex worker can do to protect against violence, according to Edwina, is to control the work, every aspect of the work.

After I got out of having a pimp I decided to do things my way. So it was better for me to keep my own money and prostitute myself, ya know; it's better that way. Because when a prostitute has a pimp, she ain't never gonna have things her way, she ain't never gonna have any money. She might have a few dollars, but why have a pimp when you can do it yourself. I live like that today. I don't have no main man. . . . Wendy slapped me around but the girls that I was living with he used to beat them with hangers, and you could barely rest; we had to bring in two or three hundred dollars a night. We couldn't come home unless we had two or three hundred dollars. I got out of it one day. I took myself out of it. I just started doing in on my own again; if I want to sell myself, I want to do it on my time, like I was saying. You're not going to tell me I have to out on the street around the clock and, you know, I got to eat. You tell me when to eat and what to wear, I'm doing it my way. It's my way or the highway. . . . I was the type of woman even though I sold myself it was, you have a limit to it, you have a time limit on it, and if you don't get yourself satisfied I ain't got nothing to do with that. It's time to go. I wasn't having it their way. I picked out the limit. Women got to always let things happen her way. Don't let it go their way, because letting it go their way can get you killed. When I was on the street and you didn't seem right, I would just back off. There's been a few times when I was in tricks' cars, I used to do stunt jumps, have to jump out while their car is still running. I always kept my hand on the door in case I had to jump out the car, do a stunt jump. . . . There's been a few times when I was in tricks' cars, I had one put a razor to my throat. He had brought me up, brought me somewhere before I knew anything about Germantown, brought me out here in the wilderness, some part of Germantown where there ain't nothing but trees, and this was at night. He wanted his money back. That taught me something. That taught me never go nowhere with them. Always let them, you always make the place. Never, you let nobody tell you where they gonna take you. You have to set down your ground rules, not let them tell you what to do because if you do you're going to be a slave, and like I said, that can lead to your death or them slapping you around, doing whatever they want to do. You got to set your ground rules. I still do that today. If you don't, the consequences could be fatal. I live like that today. . . . I always prayed to God before I made any moves, before I tricked with anybody, before I went out of the house. I always asked God to watch over me, and bless me and keep me safe.

Rarely can sex workers look to others for protection; managing their business means managing violence. About 5 percent of the women in my study worked under the management of a pimp, but even pimps cannot protect a woman from danger,[1] Claudia told me, because "once you get in the car, he's gone. Even if he had a car and he could follow me, you never know who you're getting in the car with." Controlling the situation is up to the sex worker herself. Being direct about what services she will provide, where, and for how much money is the first key to survive violence. The second: be ready to run or, better yet, to fight. Harriet has been working the streets of North Philadelphia for twenty years. She taught other sex workers to watch the eyes, watch the hands, and be ready to fight.

On the streets the police used to call me "the madam" because I used to teach the girls how to protect themselves because I got raped once until one of the guys that tried to rape me I beat him with a two-by-four, and I stabbed him four times. All I would do, see I used to stand, there's like a bridge and they have poles there and I used to keep all my weapons behind the poles. I used to keep pipes and sticks and everything. I used to go up on the bridge. I used to ride down on the dirt. I used to have me a stick buried down in there. So if they act like nuts, then I turn around and be a nut. I got raped a couple times and a couple times a guy tried to shoot me, ya know, so I had to learn to protect myself. One time, a cop came up and a nigger was down there with his pants down and I was beating him with the stick and I was beating him because he pulled a knife out on me 'cause he was taking his money back. I was like, "Nigger, I'm gonna kill you; you're crazy. I worked too hard." You know and he's pushing my head, pushing my head, and I'm down there in the dirt on the bridge on my knees and then he gonna pull a knife out on me talking about taking it back and he shoved his dick in my throat, oh no you're not, so I learned to fight.

Every time the girls would get in trouble, they would call me. I taught them how to protect themselves. I used to tell them, "Your eyes don't lie; you watch the eyes and the hands and the bulges in their pocket because if their hands move, if they keep their hands in their pockets, there's something wrong. Ya know, if they do have their hands out of their pockets, you look for the bulges in their pockets and they always keep one hand in their pocket. I said, "Their eyes don't lie"; I say wherever their eyes move, then that's where they have that they're doing something. Ya know, because I used to always tell them if you're going to in an alleyway on the corner or up on the bridge with somebody, you always make sure that their hands is free, you can see their hands at all times, 'cause they keep their hands in their pockets, they got something in their pocket and they're up to something. Ya know and I used to tell them, ya know, "The eyes don't lie." I say, "When they're about to strike, their eyes are moving to make sure they can grab what they want, and that's what you watch for; you watch for their eyes." Ya know, and I told them and when nighttime fall, if they can't go where you want them to go, leave them alone because obviously they're up to something, and a couple of girls, they stripped a couple of girls had run down the street butt naked, ya know, they pulled knives out on them, took their money, stripping their clothes out in the wintertime, ya know, and they's running down the street hollering my name, hollering my name, and I would just come out from nowhere, and then that would just freak them out because I would come out from nowhere, and I kept me a nice two-by-four with tape around it and I would use that, so I did that for maybe like five years. Ya know and then I got tired because I didn't extort from the girls.

Dealing with the System

Detection is the first threat to survival in crime, then arrest, conviction, and incapacitation. Detection does not necessarily lead to apprehension or arrest, and arrest does not always lead to conviction and incapacitation because, in part, the formal players in the process—police, prosecutors, judges, and store personnel in the case of shoplifters—have discretion whether and how to invoke the criminal justice process. In the case of shoplifting, for example, retailers differ in their policies for handing shoplifters. Some retailers (such as big-box stores like OfficeMax) have no store security stationed in stores or do not prosecute shoplifters found with merchandise of low value, while others actively pursue shoplifters. In typical cases when shoplifters are detected, security or store personnel apprehend shoplifters once they exit the store and detain them (usually in a special room), handcuff them, and check them for merchandise. Apprehended once as she stepped through the exit of a clothing store at Cherry Hill Mall in New Jersey, Eileen remembers what happened next:

They said, "Excuse me, Miss, I have to ask you a question," and I looked and I said, "Oh shit." I was like, "Well, I'm gone back to jail again." I was like, "I did it to myself"; I would have to face the consequences, I'm like, "You's a dumb motherfucker; you know you ain't supposed to be doing that shit." . . . Then they said, "Where are the jeans that you have on?" I said, "I don't have any jeans on," and then they took me down the basement and they put me in the room so the males couldn't see. Then they had a female and she made me strip, but I was like, "I don't got to strip." I just lifted my jacket up, and I had them on my waist.

When merchandise is found on the person or property of the suspected shoplifter, it is recovered and the shoplifter is interrogated and deposed for future court dates when necessary. This includes a documentation of merchandise the suspect attempted to acquire; personal information about her, including previous instances of shoplifting at the retailer; and a set of photographs of her for store security records. Depending on a range of factors, including the type, amount, and value of merchandise a shoplifter attempts to take, the shoplifter's demeanor during the detention process, and her past involvement with security personnel at the store, security may issue a warning to the shoplifter not to return to the store for a period of time (i.e., ban them from the store). This may be an informal process, but it often involves a civil injunction. Sandy explains:

The judge tells me when I get arrested that I'm not supposed to come back in the store or back in the mall, one or the other. [Well, how would they know if you came back?] *Because, the cameras or security would pick me up. It's trespassing. There's a camera usually, and they have like a photo row, I guess you could say, of certain people that you're suppose to pay attention to and aren't suppose to be in the store. . . . If I was in there shoplifting and I get arrested for shoplifting, then later on down the line they realize, well, she's been arrested for shoplifting here before, and she's trespassing on top of it.*

Law prohibits Sandy from stepping foot into Macy's and Strawbridge's stores, and while she still does, risk is always on her mind. Even when she might never have shoplifted in a particular Macy's in the Philadelphia area, going into that store is risky, as she explains, because store security often rotate between stores.

The places that I go to are limited now. I'm banned from just about every store in every mall. My face is pretty much done everywhere. And then, the other day when that security guard walked out. That let me know that's one more store I'm not allowed into. Stores I've been arrested for, already once I wait like a year or two and go back and started doin' it again. So I think the risks are getting higher. Suppose I go in Strawbridge's in Cherry Hill . . . something I didn't know until a couple years ago, the security guards switch off. They could go work in Deptford one day or they could go work in Morristown one day. They alternate. So suppose I think I can go to Macy's in Deptford and think everything's okay, not realizing that that one day it's a guy from Cherry Hill's working, and he's the guy that's arrested me before.

Security may also detain shoplifters until police arrive to take the shoplifter into custody (law enforcement is sometimes stationed at retail stores in some locales, particularly in high-crime areas). Warned but not prosecuted criminally for attempting to shoplift, Lee was banned from a store in a Philadelphia shopping mall and she complied with this order: "The first time I got caught, they took my name and everything and they said, 'Well, we don't want you in the store no more,' so they [banned] me just from that store. I didn't take my chances; I never went back out to the mall."

Police also have discretion when in contact with shoplifters. Their decision to arrest is guided by legal (number of previous encounters with police; type, amount, and value of merchandise; outstanding arrest warrants) and extralegal factors (shoplifter's attitude and demeanor, retailer's willingness to become involved in a criminal case against the suspected shoplifter). Police may do nothing and release the shoplifter. They may issue a written citation or ticket at the scene and release the defendant from custody if the offense is a minor one (a disorderly person's offense). The citation is similar to a parking or traffic ticket or summons and requires the suspected shoplifter, now a criminal defendant, to pay a fine to the county court of jurisdiction if he or she admits guilt to the crime or to appear at a scheduled hearing on the case if he or she is not willing to admit guilt. Eileen was issued a citation in place of being arrested, in part, as she explains, because this was her first offense, she cooperated with store security, and the merchandise she attempted to acquire was of low financial value:

That was like my first shoplifting, so the man said that the reason they let me go and not sent me to jail was because I didn't refuse after they grabbed me; I didn't say, well, "Get off of me, you're hurting me, you raping me," you know, all kinds of stuff. I was just like, okay, so I'll follow you down the steps, and I didn't like run away and all that how they do. I just did whatever they told me, so I went along with what they said. Well, I just got fines and I had to do community service. They didn't want to press charges because it was only one pair of jeans, and I gave them back. It ain't like they caught me and I was on the outside and I threw them and they were dirty or whatever and stuff like that.

When shoplifters and sex workers are detained and arrested, their court processing varies considerably. In some cases, courts dismiss charges against them, for example, in the case of shoplifting when retailers decide not to pursue cases or when police who make the initial arrest or issue the citation at the retail store are not present at court proceedings to provide testimony. Courts may subsume shoplifting or prostitution charges within other offenses, for example, when a woman stands before a court with other charges that may carry stiffer penalties than the shoplifting or sex work charge. Typical of criminal case processing in this country generally, the shoplifting and prostitution cases against the women in this study have almost always been resolved before trial—dismissed or reduced through a plea agreement requiring them to admit guilt to the court in exchange for a less punitive sentence than might otherwise be imposed. Punishments given at sentencing upon conviction vary. Prostitutes may spend a few days or months in jail or may be ordered community supervision by probation; most often they are ordered to pay a fine stipulated in a citation they receive from police on the scene. Shoplifters can receive similar sanctions, but for them criminal statutes require progressively more punitive sanctions with each new conviction. Most troubling for shoplifters are risks to their liberty imposed by repeat or habitual offender statutes (known familiarly as "three strikes and you're out") in Pennsylvania, New Jersey, and most other states. This means that convicted shoplifters charged anew face more serious charges and in-

carceration when convicted. Even when the value of merchandise she shoplifts would normally be a misdemeanor charge, repeat offender laws make them felonies. "Strike" laws require mandatory incarceration. Esther is concerned about this risk now more than ever before.

I was arrested for shoplifting around ten times. It didn't matter; I got used to it. Got probation twice, jail once; they dismissed the other cases 'cause they was misdemeanors, they wasted no time with that. But now I think about it [the risks] all the time. Three strikes you're out is the latest thing now . . . when they came out with this three strikes you out and it's a felony now.

Rose says:

We talked about getting caught and arrested; you go to jail. That right there is the pits because there goes your freedom and everything else, and every day that you're in jail, you have to wonder what's going to happen to you, especially if it's your third or fourth time going to jail for the same thing. You don't know what's going to happen. If you lose, you lose a lot, but that's the price you have to pay.

With each new apprehension, arrest, and conviction, Sandy has received progressively more punitive sanctions required by New Jersey statutes. Still, like all of the other specialists, Sandy knows that these penalties are inevitable and compared to the frequency and duration of her involvement, a marginal setback to her shoplifting business.

I've been arrested, ah, for shoplifting so far, eight times mostly felony charges. The first two times I got caught I got a warning. The first time I got arrested I got slapped on the hand . . . they just gave me a court date, I went to court, they gave me a fine, it was done and over with. I guess I was almost twenty. I was released, and I was scared enough I didn't go back in the stores for a while. Then gradually, you tend to go back every day. Like, I would take, like, four sets of sheets and sell them for fifty dollars apiece and go, "Well, this is a couple hundred dollars. This'll last me for a few days. I won't have to go back to the stores." Then I'd be back to doin' it on a gradual daily basis, again. . . . The second time I got slapped on the hand, but the third time, I thought I was going home and I wasn't; they gave me six months in jail for it, 'cause it [sanction] goes with the amount of the comforters I took—they were over two thousand dollars. So, the amount of money [value of merchandise] and the store security requested that I get the maximum, I guess, because I was in the store several times and they finally picked me up. I guess that was their way to get back at me. It was after I came out the six months, I didn't do any drugs for a while, but then I started shoplifting again to support my habit. . . . The fourth time I got arrested, I was in jail for, like, thirty days waiting on a court date, so they gave me time served. The fifth and sixth time . . . I got sentenced six months for both of them, but they ran 'em together [gave her concurrent sentences to serve]. I did two and half months and came out on parole [probation]. The seventh time I got arrested was the last end of last year. I got arrested in September and I stayed in jail till December, and they added more time onto my probation for it. . . . Then, the last offense they indicted me by grand jury, so, I still have one pending case open. The reason they've been charging me with felonies is because the amount of the merchandise and the times I've been arrested and convicted. This charge now, I'm lookin' at three years in prison, but my probation officer will help me out with that. And, I'm banned from a lot, like, a lot of malls, I'm not allowed to go inside. They're very angry; a lot of stores are very angry with me 'cause of the times I have got away with, compared with the times I, you know, they had me on camera and they're really cracking down on it. So the only reason I've been doin' it for such a long period of time, I mean, is the times I have got caught are nothing compared to the times I've gotten away with it. So, I can't really complain about the times I got caught because there've been times I went inside one store every day for months and then, finally, they arrested me.

While Sandy has had charges dropped, she has never absconded from court. She has always faced the consequences of her crime. The others rarely complied with court orders. They know the system is inefficient, and they benefit from this inefficiency. Candee says:

The first time I didn't have much stuff; they [police] gave me a citation. All right now, I got busted again shoplifting. Once again, they let me go with a citation. Now next, here we go, I get locked up again, but this time it was over the amount that they give citations for so I end up at 8th and Race and this is when I get fingerprinted, and I have a bench warrant. Now, one bench warrant, they let you go, it used to be. Right, so when I go in front of the magistrate that morning, I had one bench warrant, they let me go. I get busted again, they let me go again. Busted again. Now I got two bench warrants, this means I can't get out. I have to go to jail and go to court. So

I go to jail, and I stayed in jail for this time eight, nine months. Lucky for me, I had those two open cases and then the case I had just gotten [the final arrest she refers to here], and they threw them all out so I go home.

The reality of criminal justice is that in many large jurisdictions such as Philadelphia and Camden, shoplifters can fall through the cracks of the system and not be held accountable for their crimes, sometimes for months or even years. Because the criminal justice process involves various actors and different agencies stressed by workload pressures and limited resources, the criminal justice process is not seamless, coordinated, and efficient, as the casual observer may assume. For example, as part of their work, police are responsible for taking into custody offenders with active arrest warrants, but they must prioritize their efforts in this regard in order to get work done efficiently. As a result, shoplifters (as well as sex workers and other minor offenders) are inevitably low priority, and police more often discover that a shoplifter or sex worker has an active arrest warrant when she is arrested on an unrelated charge (usually drug possession), rather than actively pursuing shoplifters or sex workers with arrest warrants. Additionally, even when arrested and charged for a new offense, shoplifters and sex workers often can escape accountability for a previous failure to comply with court orders. For example, courts may fail to discover the existence of outstanding warrants even when processing a suspect for a new crime, especially when women use aliases, and courts may dismiss previous violations or subsume them into the new charge. Tracy remembers her experience:

If you miss court so many times, eventually the vendors do not show up and it [the charge] would have been done away with, but I pulled up [absconded] too many times [for subsequent shoplifting arrests]. They sent me to jail, and they gave me ten thousand dollar bail. The way to get out was to take a deal, so they gave me eighteen months probation. There was only one I was convicted of because the others [shoplifting charges] I just disappeared [and the court subsumed these previous charges into that current offense].

Shoplifters and sex workers alike know how the criminal justice system works and benefit from its failures. Like store security, police, and other players in the system, shoplifters and sex workers make decisions that affect their movement through the criminal justice process. One decision is to ignore the requirements set forth in the offense citation. Another is to abscond from scheduled court dates and sentencing when the court finds the defendant guilty. Others involve failing to pay fines ordered, perform community service, or report to probation or other court-ordered community supervision. As a result, the women are out on the streets with warrants for their arrest. While these decisions place them at even greater risk for punitive penalties when police and the courts catch up with them and create even more anxiety and uncertainty for them in their work with each new apprehension, shoplifters and sex workers do what they must to maintain their freedom.

Using Risk Management Strategies to Maintain Criminal Careers

Shoplifters and sex workers possess technical and perceptual skills that help them manage risk and get work done safely and efficiently. Just as conventional occupations require these skills, so do criminal occupations. Shoplifters and sex workers, like police and accountants, must be able to sort out and complete tasks, manage their time, deal with stress, plan for contingencies, and so on. As different legal occupations require particular skill sets, so do criminal occupations. Technical skills are those actions in the start to finish of work. Women in my study who sell sex rely on technical skill in their work when they meet customers, negotiate service and price, make the transaction, and part ways. For example, Quenelle describes how she learned a particular sex skill:

They called me the blowjobologist. I taught myself with a cucumber, all different size shape cucumbers you know, because all men's penises are not the same length, shape, width, or what. So you have to start from the small and the main thing is working your jaw muscles, it's all about your jaw muscles so your teeth don't touch them because if you have teeth pressing there, you're going to pull his skin. So then, I started after that, I started on something more tender like a banana or something like that. . . . I would learn. I would practice. I used to watch tapes and stuff.

The skill is not the sex act alone, but involves the entire event from beginning to end. The technical skills of shoplifters involve getting to a store, making entry, covering the scene, acquiring goods, getting out, and making a sale.

While a routine method of getting a day's work done might characterize a particular line of work, there is rarely a universal style for workers to accomplish tasks, as my findings show on shoplifting. Furthermore, as technologies advance in the world around, so must workers in any occupation, and they learn necessary skills through experimentation, experience, and learning from others. Advances in store security make shoplifting more difficult today than twenty years ago. Now shoplifters must be attentive to surreptitiously placed security tags on merchandise and security monitors throughout stores. Sex workers must know that police do not always drive in marked cars but can be afoot, dressed to blend into the urban drug culture, and act as drug sellers and sex work customers, so they too must advance in their knowledge and skill to maintain business.

While workers in crime and in legal occupations possess a range of skill for the work, they put to use only those skills necessary to complete a task, rather than display the full skill set all the time. For example, house painters know to repair damaged surfaces before painting and they generally start from the top of a house and work the painting downward, but how they make repairs and whether they make use of scaffolding will depend on the situation at hand and on personal style. The point is that workers such as house painters possesses requisite skills for getting work done but do not apply every skill all the time. This idea that criminal offenders draw from a solid skill base comes from the work of Letkemann in 1973. Letkemann learned from safe crackers of many ways to open a safe, but the technique used depends on the situation at hand. When constrained by time and in close proximity to the public, the prudent safe cracker might opt for mechanical instruments to open the safe discretely, rather than blowing with explosives. The same idea pertains to shoplifters and sex workers, who draw from a repertoire of technical and perceptual skills only those particular skills needed for a given situation, no more and no less. When a shoplifter recognizes the store exit is clear she may exit unseen, but if she notices a store employee at the exit then she might decide to put to work her skill at dialogue to present normalcy and get past security as a regular shopper. It would be unnecessary and foolish of her to call upon a store employee when she is passing the store's threshold when the coast is clear. During hot police presence a sex worker will stay off the streets and conduct work at indoor locations available to her because exercising police evasion skill on the street is needless and risky.

Planning is an essential skill in crime just as in legal work. Letkemann, for example, found that men engaged in organized forms of theft planned their crimes by dividing required tasks among members based partially on skill level. My study also shows that shoplifting requires planning, whether the crime is an individual venture or in a group context. Shoplifters review orders prior to commission of the crime, select stores based on these orders, time constraints, and other factors, and prepare emotionally to overcome worry before they enter into the crime. In the rare instance when shoplifters engage in crime as a group, a precrime conference among members clarifies particular roles necessary to pull off the crime and assigns workers to roles (driver, lookout, diverter, the taker, the seller). A novice shoplifter is not likely to be the one handling the exit from a store because her lack of experience can get the entire group apprehended. She might observe the process for some time, then take on a marginal role such as lookout before she is ready to do the risky work. Sex workers plan too. They determine income needed for the day and which customers they will meet, where, and when.

One of the most important skills of shoplifters and sex workers is their ability to interpret cues around that help them determine how to act, what to do, and when to worry. Perceptual skill helps shoplifters and sex workers to work efficiently. Just as workers in conventional occupations interpret symbols and cues, according to Letkemann's classic study of crime as work, workers in crime have an ability to interpret symbols in the world around that affect their work and to use them in ways not intended but for their special interests. For example, consumers in stores use shopping carts as intended, to move throughout a store with merchandise as they shop, to carry the merchandise to the checkout and then out of the store, to make shopping a more pleasant, efficient task. Shoplifters use shopping carts to steal merchandise. To the regular observer, men driving cars through a neighborhood represent the ordinary, and this may even conjure up frustration, especially during rush hour when workers make their way home, but to sex workers, traffic represents potential customers and opportunity to earn money. Shoppers use store employees to help them select merchandise, while shoplifters use employees in ways not intended, for example, to create an appearance of normalcy. Shoplifters and sex workers frequent neighborhood bars not for a glass of something and not to socialize as do others, but to access potential customers for crime.

Perceiving danger, shoplifters and sex workers trigger contingency plans to stay safe. Not unlike workers in conventional jobs, shoplifters and sex workers are prone to occupational hazards and they must be attentive to cues of danger and develop strategies to approach and manage harm. One risk both conventional employees and crime workers face is stress on the job. Stress can originate in the work environment, within the individual, or the interaction between the particular work situation and the individual, according to Michie.[2] It is more likely to unfold when a person lacks control over a particular situation and can manifest physically. For example, shoplifters in my study talked of feeling the greatest stress before they shoplift, particularly at the point of entering stores, and the least stress when the theft is complete and they are traveling away. Sex workers experience the greatest stress when they are face to face with a potentially dangerous situation, for example, when they follow the lead of customers they do not know rather than when they work with regular customers. Workers in conventional occupations, according to Michie, learn from others and through experience to manage stress by practicing awareness to potentially stressful situations and developing action plans.[3]

Stress unfolds for sex workers in their awareness and management of police apprehension, disease, and unwanted pregnancy, but violence is their greatest enemy because it is pervasive.[4] Police harassment, intimidation, ridicule, and forced sex reported by women in my research are also found in other research. In Chicago, for example, sex workers reported that police intimidated them, called them names, and forced them to masturbate.[5] A U.S. Department of Justice report makes the case that police are prone to these sorts of corruption by the illegal and stigmatized nature of the work, especially in areas of high sex work activities. While sex work involves many of the same characteristics of regular occupations, like business management and stress, what distinguishes it from most other criminal work and conventional occupations is the level of violence. The greatest worry of sex workers is violence, and for good reason; with no institutionalized protections for sex workers on the streets, victimization and violence are pervasive. O'Connell Davidson suggests that while workers in other occupations might face violence on the job, particularly those who enter homes alone like plumbers and real estate agents, social convention still protects them most of the time. Social norms in the subculture of the urban drug world are misplaced and sex workers can expect violence, especially when customer conflicts arise.[6] Researchers have established convincingly that women who take sex work to the streets are the most vulnerable (compared to sex workers in other settings) to assault, threats, murder, rape, robbery, and other harms, foremost by customers and then others, including intimate partners and other members of the urban underworld.[7]

A study in the U.S. Midwest reports that 92 percent of female sex workers experienced assaults by customers (slapped, punched, kicked, or hit), 62 percent were victims of robbery by customers, and 62 percent reported rape by customers.[8] A Florida study exposed that over a one-year period, 42 percent of the women had been in a violent confrontation with a customer, 29 percent were robbed of their money by a customer, 25 percent were beaten by a customer, 14 percent were threatened with a weapon, and 13 percent were raped on the job.[9] A San Francisco study showed similar levels of violence against sex workers on the job; 82 percent were physically assaulted, 83 percent had been threatened with a weapon, and 68 percent were raped. Customers perpetrated most of the violence.[10] Rape is commonplace. In her Brooklyn research, Maher reported murders of eight women she studied during her three-year ethnography and extensive injuries to others. Believed to be the victim of date violence, one woman died from a beating. Another was a victim of robbery, thrown from a van by customers who refused to pay after her service, then hit in the face with a blackjack when she tried to retrieve her clothing.[11] Miller and Schwartz reported that 94 percent of street sex workers had experienced some form of sexual assault, and 75 percent had been raped.[12] A Washington, D.C., study revealed 79 percent of male and female sex workers had been threatened with a weapon while at work, 61 percent were physically assaulted, predominately by customers (75 percent), and 44 percent were raped, usually by a customer (60 percent). Women sex workers are the most prone to violence. That study found that 86 percent of the women were physically assaulted and 74 percent were raped, usually by a customer (72 percent) while 28 percent of the men were physically assaulted and just 13 percent were raped and always by someone other than a pimp or customer.[13] In San Francisco, 70 percent of sex workers in research by Silberts and Pines were raped by clients and 78 percent were forced into perverse acts against their will.[14] A Connecticut study of 35 street sex workers reported that 90 percent had been victims of violence from customers, 60 percent were victims of rape on the streets, and 25 percent had a friend murdered on the streets.[15]

A Canadian study of sex worker homicides in British Columbia estimated that the majority of street sex workers murdered were on the streets in their trade; they were women, and murdered usually by strangulation, beating, or stabbing.[16] In another study on the mortality of sex work, Potterat and his colleagues used a combination of data sources including the National Death Index to determine cause of death and associated rates among women sex workers in Colorado between 1967 and 1999. Few women died of natural causes (the average age of death was only thirty-four) while the predominant causes of death were violence and drug use. The murder rate for sex workers was an alarming 229 per 100,000. To put that figure into perspective, the authors note murder rates for the most dangerous workplaces during that period—4 per 100,000 for women working at liquor stores and 29 per 100,000 for male taxi drivers. The authors also note that sex workers were eighteen times more likely to be murdered compared to the average woman of similar age and race.[17]

Sex workers rely on learned strategies to protect themselves against violence. They know through word on the street and direct experience to avoid the most dangerous situations—to give up power over the price, location, and duration of sex work—and take control of negotiations with assertiveness, keep to regular and long-term customers, stay away from known violent customers, and control the sex work destination. Staying off drugs while working and away from young unknown customers can help too.[18] A study by Dalla and colleagues revealed that one sex worker never would date White men driving red trucks because word on the street informed her that these men were the dangerous ones. She relied on information passed between sex workers, a perceptual skill learned from her involvement in the profession.[19] Risk awareness can also develop through humorous recounts of victimization between sex workers, as Sanders learned from her study of sex workers.[20] In some jurisdictions, police even circulate information to sex workers through word of mouth, posters, and leaflets to educate women about how to avoid violent encounters. According to a 2006 U.S. Department of Justice report, police in areas of high sex work traffic pass along information such as "bad date lists" so sex workers keep themselves safe.[21] Neame and Heenan also found that Australia, the United Kingdom, and Canada distribute "bad date" literature, otherwise referred to as "ugly mugs" and "ugly punters."[22] Dangerous dates, according to Williamson and Folaron, are typically young strangers new to the area who may display unusual quietness or act strangely during the date spot negotiation.[23] Intended as a guide for police working in areas of high sex work traffic, the Department of Justice report recommends that police who want to help encourage sex workers to control locations for sex work, avoid secluded, dimly lit, and unfamiliar areas, control negotiations with clients, assertively maintain prices, carry an "attack prevention device," and avoid carrying drugs or excessive cash.[24]

From the point of meeting up with a customer to parting ways, sex workers also rely on their perceptual skills cluing them to danger. Sometimes perception of danger originates as a gut instinct. According to a U.S. Midwest study, instinct is the primary survival strategy of women sex workers. Instinct, like intuition, is, in the words of a sex worker in that research, the gut feeling to "get the hell out as quick as you can."[25] When they do sense danger, sex workers might work to calm the situation through dialogue and renegotiation. Designed to diffuse conflict, dialogue might involve pleading for release using talk about the sex worker's children and their welfare and well-being needs, taking blame and apologizing for the conflict, or pretending to be very mentally ill, according to sex workers in research by Kurtz and colleagues.[26] When strategies like these fail, sex workers rely on other means to protect themselves. Some submit, some run, and some battle. Sex workers know that getting into cars to negotiate price, working with strangers, and allowing the date to decide travel to unfamiliar or desolate locations makes them the most prone to violence, but their ability to act accordingly is sometimes constrained by time and other situational factors like being high or close to police presence. Having contingency plans in place is therefore especially critical for sex workers. According to sex workers in a Miami study, the best way to keep safe is to negotiate outside of a car with customers the transaction before getting in, but that negotiation may be rushed and this means the sex worker may have entered into danger, trapped with a violent date. In this situation the sex worker draws from her skill set that which will help her escape the violence. She might threaten to vomit in the car or get the customer high on drugs.[27] She might surrender to the beating, the rape, or robbery and, as one sex worker in the Midwest study recounted, "give them what they want and pray they don't kill you,"[28] scream for help, jump from the car, or fight with a weapon.[29] The British study, for instance found that every sex worker interviewed carried a weapon such as a knife, razor blades, mace, or butane lighters in the case of an attack.[30] Carrying weapons to resist violence in conjunction with these other preventive measures is common for sex workers, according to these research studies and others.[31]

Carrying forth the importance of agency, of thoughtful decision making in how women carry through their crimes and learn skills for being successful, this chapter has laid out risk management strategies key to maintaining a criminal career. Over their careers, sex workers and shoplifters are actively managing their work and learning skills and strategies for being successful instead of being tossed around by circumstances. An inevitable risk of crime is incapacitation by the criminal justice system, but the shoplifters and sex workers have learned the criminal justice system is inefficient and make its weaknesses work to their advantage, making decisions to disobey court orders and sentences when they are in trouble with the law. Doing this helps them stay in crime for long periods and reap benefits without accountability, at least until the system catches up with them again. The ways in which shoplifters and sex workers manage crime risks from day-to-day is another testament to their thoughtfulness and deliberation.

For sex workers, violent victimization is omnipresent, and this risk seems to balance the upside of a sex work specialization, direct and simple access to earnings in the urban drug culture. Each time they set out in the crime, sex workers put to work strategies to avoid incapacitation by arrest and, more importantly, by physical harm. Strategies include avoiding police and violent men by sticking with existing customers as much as possible; controlling the particulars of each sex work transaction (place, service, fee, length of time) and keeping to these ground rules with all customers; staying away from new customers and out-of-the-way locations; exercising constant mindfulness, most especially of imminent violence on and off the job; and being ready to run or fight in the face of violence.

While a shoplifting specialization requires significantly more proactive work to maintain profit in the urban drug culture than does a sex work specialization, the major benefit to this specialization is the absence of violent victimization. Apprehension, arrest, retailer bans, and incarceration are the greatest dangers shoplifters face, but women do not take these risks lightly, especially with mandatory sentencing in place for the recidivist shoplifter. The women who specialize in this crime put to work a host of strategies during commission of their crimes to manage these risks. Strategies include taking drugs before entering into the crime to overcome the otherwise crippling fear of apprehension; carrying through a self-directed plan normally alone; blending in with shoppers in dress, demeanor, and the use of regular mechanisms to carry away merchandise less a sales receipt; and constant mindfulness coupled with a readiness to call off the crime if necessary.

6. *Out in the Storm*

Throughout this book, using an intersectional analytic framework, I have made constant comparisons between women who specialize in shoplifting and those who specialize in sex work. In doing so I have pointed out similarities but also important differences, some obvious and others nuanced in the etiology of the women's criminal behavior, the ways in which they make their crimes profitable, and how they manage both the business of their crimes and the dangers they face in their work. By disaggregating female offenders, I have learned that women in crime are diverse among themselves. Looking at the particular crimes women commit, it is possible to distinguish female offenders' histories; the multiplicity of trauma, social class background, education, employment, drug use, and work in the adult entertainment industry can distinguish among women who specialize in different crimes. The intersectional framework also exposes social class, race, social location, and neighborhood milieu factors for identifying pathway variations to drugs and crime for these women and for characterizing their crime work. Economic and social capital drawn from once-vital urban industrial centers and replaced with the urban drug economy has created a criminogenic culture in areas of Camden and Philadelphia. These anarchic neighborhoods organized around the illicit drug culture were the childhood playgrounds for most of the women, and where they sought asylum as adolescents has made possible and even encouraged their lives in crime. Bernadette's assessment of such an area in North Philadelphia is illustrative of this sort of environment.

Well, I think it has to do with people in the place. Like in Jersey, in Cherry Hill, people are settled, there are a lot of home women, it's quiet, the neighborhood and the authority, they have control of their neighborhood, they have order, they have certain outline on how to live, how it's supposed to be, and that's mainly because of the neighbors. It's just stricter, it's just, as opposed to a city like North Philadelphia, they don't really give a damn on the street, they don't care; it's like the drugs is running it. There's drugs everywhere. There's drugs on every corner. There's different people that got houses, they got people running drug houses, running crack houses, shooting galleries, there's alcohol on every other corner. The laws are not there, the morals are just different; I don't know, just I don't know. They're different. They're too loose. It's no demand, there's no command, there's no structure in North Philly.

In the same manner, I have shown that women have agency, an ability to make choices. Women are both agents and products of change. Female offenders as a group suffer significant trauma and victimization during childhood and react to these traumas in predictable ways, setting off a course to drug addiction and crime. This finding is consistent with current scholarship. Although limited by addiction and social marginalization, the women are clearly active at shaping their lives in crime. While choices the women made during childhood and early adolescence were clearly reactive in nature, they were thoughtful and businesslike in late adolescence and adulthood, when shoplifters and sex workers alike recognized and used resources within their neighborhood drug economies to support their particular crimes and to develop and sustain a criminal specialization. By conceptualizing crime as more than illegal behavior, this study also shows that shoplifting and sex work are occupational, and in doing this I have been able to make sense of how shoplifters and sex workers act out their crimes, which would otherwise be obscured. Crime specialization helps women sustain their drug addictions and support other basic needs. While gender roles structure the crimes open to women for maintaining an income in neighborhoods where urban drug cultures thrive, women do not see sex work and shoplifting as crimes of last resort. Both shoplifting and sex work specializations can be profitable because of the economic and social structure within these areas. To specialize in a crime for sustained income, women learn how to take advantage of resources within their neighborhood drug cultures—demand for their services and accommodating systems supporting their offense—and they are aware of and try to minimize and manage risks they face in their work by putting to work strategies they have learned. Each crime occupation has its own advantages and drawbacks. The demand for sex work is strong in neighborhoods organized around the drug trade, explaining why most women continue to specialize in this crime even though the crime comes with a high risk of violent victimization. Women know shoplifting requires them to be especially proactive, explaining in part why fewer women choose this path, but a specialization in shoplifting can be more profitable than sex work, with the risk of apprehension and incapacitation being the greatest danger women face.

Findings on Criminal Behavior Etiology

What led the women to crime is drug addiction. Looking at the women as a group, the most significant events leading them down the path to drug addiction and criminal involvement occurred during childhood, with critical turning points during adolescence. The women reflected on childhoods and adolescences marked by cruelty and oppression at the hands of family members within a harsh social and economic structure. Sexual and physical abuse, emotional suffering, neglect, parental abandonment, and socialization into alcohol and drug use in their homes and outside in their neighborhoods precipitated their drug addiction. It was during adolescence, a critical time of psychological maturation and personal growth, that most of the women felt able to make self-directed choices to improve the quality of their lives. Their adolescences was marked by drug and alcohol use, school failure, and flight to the streets, where they learned that shoplifting and sex work could feed their addictions. Now the women see their coming of age as misdirected, but to them then their choices, such as running away from home and living the fast life on the streets, seemed the right things to do and better alternatives to their tortured home lives.

Women who define themselves as shoplifting specialists have had some experiences similar to sex workers but more often relate different experiences, especially in early childhood, involving fewer and less severe traumas and more stable home environments. Further nuanced analysis reveals how shoplifters who have prostituted in the past and those who still use sex work occasionally are more like sex workers as a group than they are like other shoplifters. Sex workers are disproportionately minority women raised in neighborhoods fraught with neighborhood decay, poverty, violence, drugs, and a social culture tolerant of criminal and deviant behavior. For the most part, sex workers' families were broken, dysfunctional, violent, and affected by drugs and poverty. Their usually drug-addicted mothers and fathers were also products of social forces, inequities, racism, and classism. They were surviving too. As girls and teens, the women in my study sought relief in drugs and alcohol in the company of others on the streets and away from school, where they also recognized opportunities to earn money through crime. With some variation, these women took a path to sex work different from the path taken by shoplifters. Women raised in the slums of Camden and Philadelphia know that work as a dancer or stripper in peep shows, go-go bars, and strip clubs can earn them good money, as it did for their sisters before them. In their neighborhoods and among their peers, the pull to sex work is strong, and neighborhood culture sustains this form of work as an attractive proposition to an undereducated, drug-reliant girl. Women raised outside of the inner-city poor have hurt too, but as a group they have experienced the least disruption in their homes and have had more contact and sustained interactions with mainstream society and middle-class conventions. They, more often than sex workers, lived in middle-class homes until their late teenage years, completed their educations, and worked from time to time, but rarely in a commercial sex setting such as a go-go bar. They, too, were out on the streets with drug users in those very same neighborhoods where the sex workers lived, but it seems likely that their exposure to the drug culture and prevalent sex work surrounding it was mitigated by their ties to the middle class early in life. Despite the abuses they had suffered as girls, these mitigating conditions—middle-class upbringing, suffering fewer abuses from parents, graduating high school, and remaining at home until late adolescence—have affected their movement into shoplifting.

Findings on Crime Management

All of the drug-addicted women in the study chose a criminal specialty of either shoplifting or sex work and engaged in that crime in those very neighborhoods organized around the drug trade, where the poorest women and sex workers lived. Crime is work embodying habit, ethic, technique, and skill. What distinguishes these women from other workers is the illegal nature of the work and their single most important motivator, financial prosperity. To specialize in a crime means to engage in shoplifting or sex work exclusively over all forms of work or to rely primarily on that crime for financial earnings. Specialization benefits women because they can develop and maintain stable and reliable paying customers, the most important resource to both crimes. As discussed previously, a woman's childhood and adolescent experiences help to account for her eventual crime specialization. Her personal drive, her recognition by others within the neighborhood, and her manipulation of neighborhood resources facilitating her particular offense do too. Neighborhood drug cultures in Camden and Philadelphia provide many opportunities for women to make shoplifting profitable. The women's particular hustle—shoplifting or sex work—is clearly supported by the hustles of others, the social systems in the neighborhoods that harbor drug cultures in Camden and Philadelphia. Shoplifters take advantage of the demand for their services from corner bodegas that have to keep prices down for the poor residents that patronize their stores, but shoplifters have to work harder to manage their crime business than do sex workers. They must make a devoted effort to travel outside of their neighborhoods to commit their crimes, vie with other shoplifters, and carry out businesslike tasks to develop and retain reliable paying customers.

The women who were raised in these disordered and criminogenic areas—mostly minority women—knew from the time they were girls and teens that sex work was an option open to them. They have seen older generations of women before them prostitute and work at strip clubs, go-go bars, and peep shows. Most chose the fast life of dancing and stripping because it was exciting to dance, and it felt better than working at a low-paying conventional job. This occupational choice sets women on a direct path to prostitution. All of the women who were strippers, escorts, and dancers became sex workers; however, one of these women later beacme a shoplifting specialist, and she is the only shoplifter who had ever worked in the adult entertainment industry (although a few shoplifting specialists occasionally used sex work outside of these commercial settings to supplement their earnings). Working in the commercial sex work environment of strip clubs and go-go bars meant a woman could get the drugs she wanted and earn even more money if she prostituted there, which all of them did. All of them went from sex work inside these settings to part-time sex work on the outside and eventually to full-time sex work on the streets. Sex work in the neighborhood drug culture is ubiquitous, open, and supported by accommodating systems within the neighborhood, such as rooming houses, making earnings through this crime simple and direct—which is why so many women choose this crime. Shoplifters were more likely than sex workers to take conventional employment, but like sex workers, they also supplemented conventional, legal earnings with crime before turning exclusively to the better paying alternative of running a criminal business.

The most important benefit of crime specialization for both shoplifters and sex workers is a continued cash flow, but the downside is danger. As in conventional work, shoplifters and sex workers face stress on the job and other occupational hazards, but their work carries a high risk of incapacitation through imprisonment or injury. Stigma and shame are not dilemmas the women face, because they are already living on the fringes of society within crime. Incapacitation is the most important risk shoplifters and sex workers face. If arrested or physically harmed, a woman may be away from opportunities to earn money through crime and must go without the drugs that she uses to cope with her troubles. Both shoplifters and sex workers manage not only the business of their crime (their customers and their earnings), but also their freedom. Shoplifters are the most susceptible to apprehension, it appears, and to longer terms of incarceration than are sex workers. One of the common strategies they use to overcome their fears and to deceive retailers is simply mindfulness, which sex workers rely on too. Shoplifters generally use drugs before setting out in crime to help them conquer their fear of apprehension, while sex workers do not. Sex workers concern themselves with arrest and are often themselves deceived by police, but they are especially cognizant of violent victimization by men on the streets. They too use common strategies to avoid both police and predators.

General Findings and Areas for Future Research

Findings in this study suggest the need for future scholarship on urban drug cultures, on the intersections between crimes and class, and on shoplifting. This research shows that women who commit the crimes of shoplifting and sex work are both dependent on and essential contributors to an illicit economy and social system within neighborhoods organized around drug sales and use. The accommodating

systems in those areas women use to keep their crimes profitable—that is, the income-generating activities of others such as hack drivers, rooming houses, and corner stores—are no doubt dependent on shoplifting and sex work as well as other crimes. The ways in which crimes in these areas interact to accommodate one another should be an area of future research. In addition, this study shows that shoplifting appears to be a crime of middle-class origins dependent on both lower-class demands and middle-class supplies. Sex work appears to be a crime of lower-class origins dependent on demands and supply in lower-class areas, but as many of the women have suggested, the best sex work customers are men from other neighborhoods, including men from the middle class. These findings suggest two areas for research from a social- and economic-class perspective: study of the etiology of shoplifting and sex work, and study of how supplies and demand for crime occur in the epidemiology of crime. This study has shown that shoplifting matters: The crime is a profitable alternative to sex work for female drug users, drug-addicted shoplifters are professionals in their motivation and method, and an organized illicit economy supports this crime. My research provides a starting point for future research on shoplifting as a specialization for women and men and on the involvement of retailers in the distribution of stolen goods.

Getting Out of the Storm

Where the women who participated my research are today I do not know. I suspect some are back on the streets, especially the youngest among them who are still angry at "the system" for "doing this to them." Tracy is probably one of them. I knew immediately that Tracy was not ready to make a change. Not finished with her first thirty days at New Directions for Women, she absconded, jumping from a second-story window, putting her on the run from the law again. She had taken placement at New Directions as a treatment diversion from jail only, as she explained to me, because she could spend her daytime hours on the streets, so she thought. Tracy was mistaken; a halfway house is not a housing alternative, but rather a phased residential treatment program. During their first thirty days, residents have the fewest freedoms: They remain inside at all times, during which they receive the most intensive forms of treatment and counseling. This requirement Tracy explains, meant she made the wrong choice:

I just feel mad as hell, real mad being in a rotten place like this. I just got to get out of here. I hate this place. Yeah, jail was a picnic compared to this. You get visits in jail. You get phone calls in jail. You get your commissaries in jail. You can drink coffee in jail. I mean in my case, you can smoke plenty of cigarettes in jail. When they lock you in here and they don't let you out all day ever, for a month you can't go out.

Tracy has much to learn and a lot to lose before she can be ready for change. Prathia, aged forty-seven, desperately wants to change:

I was truly tired of getting high, and I didn't know how to do nothing to make it any different. Because every penny I got, I tell you, I ain't had no money to take and go buy me a pair of shoes with, but I bought the cop man a Lexus. I got tired, and I didn't know how to do anything different, so I asked God to do for me what I couldn't do for myself and the only thing I could come up with—go to jail. So, I walked up to probation and I checked myself in. And that's how I got here. I told 'em I was homeless, I was tired, I wanted to change my life. . . . New Directions got me. I don't have a problem with following the program because I want to stay clean and sober. . . . I'm goin' to therapy. And I'm gonna put all these things I just sit and told you, which I ain't told nobody. I'm trying to get all those deep, dark things out of this corner of my body that keeps me sick. . . . I want respect. I want my own self-respect. I want to be able to walk out with my head up high and be proud of myself because I did this for me. I want to change my life; I want to be clean and sober for the rest of my life. I want to live.

Like Prathia, the majority of the women know life is short for a drug-addicted criminal woman on the streets. At some point change is inevitable, whether it is death or sobriety. Edwina told me, "The only thing I haven't did met yet is death, and I'm not tryin' to meet that yet." Francine says, "I just don't want to use no more. I'm tired, ya know, and I'm scared I'm gonna die. If I don't stop, I'm gonna die, and I don't want to die." Prathia, Edwina, Francine, and most others know they have choices, albeit bounded by constraints in their lives. They have been able to make their crimes profitable using their own will, but not without resources available to them (such as the hack drivers and rooming houses). They might have the will to change, but lack the resources to steer a new course in life. Val's comments are insightful:

I've been in and out of jail so many times. The system has never offered me any help at all, but I've been in the system for so many years, I could say I gave the system at least ten years of my life and they never once offered me any help. This is the first time they offered me a program in ten years. It's always do time, do time, do time, and that only makes you bitter and you go out, you do eleven months, you come home, you know you're bitter, you do drugs again, you don't have nowhere to go, no support, you do drugs; that's the only thing you know how to do. What am *I'm going to do coming out of jail? I don't have a home to go to; I don't have no support to call for help that's going to help me. What am I supposed to do? And that's why I've always been, I always said the loneliness, the only thing I have is the drugs. I don't feel like I am alone, or I don't feel like I need nobody. I don't need nobody; I've been doing this by myself and it kept me in the clutch with drugs and you're surrounding everything that comes around with being comfortable with, selling my ass, ya know, or shoplifting. I could have a pocket full of money, but I would go in the store and shoplift. Why? 'Cause I wanted to save my money to buy more drugs and I couldn't spend my money for these things I needed because I wanted to save more money so I could buy more drugs. . . . I was infected with this disease, but I was too ashamed to say I got a problem, I need some help. I use these drugs and I can't stop and my pride, I know you do drugs and you go back and think about it, you know what's wrong with me but then you just do it the next day again, and then I figured it out and at some point in my addiction I just became sick and tired, you know, sick and tired and then you go back to jail, you come back out, and you do the same thing. But you know today right here sitting in this room talking to you I know that I can't; I know there's somebody here to help me now, you know what I mean? . . . I'm forty-three years old, and I'm a blessing. I just want to find a better way to live, you know, and I deserve that. I know today I deserve that. I never hurt nobody.*

Jailing and imprisoning offenders like the women in this study is not the answer; it is nothing more than warehousing the sick and suffering. Drug treatment in local jails is rare and has largely been a failure. Limited resources, offending populations constantly moving in and out, and crowding mean custody is the overriding service of jails in Camden, Philadelphia, and most others across the country. The criminal justice system did not create their problems and the women accept this fact, but they believe the system is yet another force marginalizing them. Sandy told me:

What's wrong with the system is they put people in jail for using drugs because of getting high, not because they even commit crimes, and it's a never-ending cycle. I don't understand where it's gonna end. It doesn't make any sense to me. You've got to help somebody to stop getting high. Instead, if you put somebody in jail, the rest of the world keeps goin' and time, for you, just stops. So, if you're locked up for six months or a year, things in the world change, people live their lives, everything in the world goes on. You come in, you get out the same day you came in, and you don't emotionally or mentally grow at all. Locking people up for being addicted doesn't make any sense to me. I don't understand what the object is. To lock up somebody who gets high for shoplifting doesn't make sense. Lock me up when somebody else killed somebody? It's only hurting people, not helping people.

Lauren says:

Jail's not gonna help. You can keep sending them away, but the problem's still gonna be there. I noticed that even violent crimes now are being caused by drugs. The drugs turned us into different people and keep puttin' people in jail is not helping them. The problem is the drugs. You know, but ninety percent of women now that are going to jail, it's because of drugs. Either selling them, using them, either their spouse is using them and they don't know what to do. It's drugs. Drugs is the problem. You know I've been in and out of jail. I listened to a lot of people talking. Jail is not the answer, and they're trying to take treatment away.

The modern get-tough-on-crime movement of the past twenty years and the relentless use of imprisonment for drug offenders have been a failure in these women's eyes as well as to criminologists. Brought forth by a conservative ideology, policies like mandatory sentences, truth-in-sentencing, and reduced judicial discretion have led to mass imprisonment of drug users, minor offenders, and the most troubled members of our society. Mass imprisonment as a crime reduction strategy has had only marginal effects on crime but has produced unprecedented costs to families, communities, criminal justice systems, and offenders themselves.[1] Just solutions balance the safety needs of communities with the treatment needs of criminal offenders. Sallie offers some ideas for policy solutions:

Ya know, a lot of the girls I would talk to out there while I was prostituting, none of them that I came across wanted to be out there. All of them wanted some kind of help. So I think if the legal system should put more money into helping instead of putting them in jail, putting their money in the programs that are going to help, help the drug addiction and the mental illness instead of financing all this money to build a new jail. They just built a brand-new women's prison [in Philadelphia], but they're cutting drug programs. . . . Yes, I think if I had been offered some type of treatment, I would have taken it, because I think by the time I got arrested for prostitution, I was at a point then when I knew I was in trouble: not trouble with the law, I was in trouble with drugs, and I knew it by then. But, I didn't see a way out. But if they had offered me a treatment program when they first arrested me for prostitution instead of letting me out and I never showed up for a court, I would have taken it.

Alternatives to incarceration like intermediate sanctions and drug courts that divert offenders from jails and prisons to treatment-focused correctional options in community settings are most promising forms of corrections and offender rehabilitation.[2] Key to effective programming in such community-based programs is the provision of treatment and services designed according to an offending population's particular needs—those problems that keep women in trouble with the law.[3] Drug treatment is their greatest need. Mental health treatment is essential. Cheryl says:

There's people that have these kinds of things happening; they really need help. A lot of people are afraid to talk about, like things like rape or whatever, whatever kind of abuse it was like that kind of stuff, like holding it in just screws you up, Yeah, a lot of people hold that stuff in; like especially kids, kids don't trust grown people at all. They're not gonna tell grown people any stuff. A lot of people in jail, almost every time I'm thrown in jail, almost every time people are speaking of their past, they're all like that—I was raped, I was abused, my husband abused me, and all these people need counseling, they need real help.

Quenelle thinks mental health treatment could have made a difference in her life early on: "If I could have got help with the past where I could have stopped getting high, if I had encouragement and more people there that were more positive in my life, I might have chose a different path and then stopped completely."

Patricia's comments illustrate how important counseling can be: "This program worked out really well. It worked out really well, because I found me; I found out who I am again. Not only that, there's issues that lay dormant and I know how to work on them today. I know what I should be doing. . . . I mean, I get depressed, yeah, but I have to turn that into something positive."

For treatment to be effective, it must be accessible. Local governments and agencies must make available services to women and others who are living in these urban drug cultures, not just during correctional supervision but at all times, out in the community. Aftercare is vital. Aftercare is a treatment and supervision phase following the most intensive programming to ease the transition to a crime-free, sober life. Sailie feels safe in the confines of New Directions where she is getting the help she needs, but she knows that once she is again on her own she cannot underestimate her disease—drug addiction:

I put it this way, if I hit the lottery for five million dollars and I was out of this place, I probably go back to using drugs. And I hate to say that, but I'm just being honest. I like to sit here and say that I wouldn't because drugs really took a toll on me, emotionally, physically. But the truth is I like the way drugs made me feel, and at this point in my recovery I still haven't found something to replace that. I still don't have enough self-esteem yet to say that I'm strong enough not to do drugs yet. I don't have a desire to go out and get them today, thank God, and I feel safe here, but I don't underestimate my disease.

The criminal and drug-addicted lives of women in my study and so many others out there in the storm are likely to continue unless Camden and Philadelphia dedicate services and treatments inside jails and halfway houses and on the streets.

In their parting words to me, the women in this study hope for themselves—"to live a quiet, normal life" with emotional peace, sobriety, and meaning and hope for the generations behind them, that no girl should ever have to "walk their paths." How these hopes can come to fruition, they have explained, lies in prevention of child victimization and drug abuse and dedicated treatment for drug addiction and mental suffering. Their answers are the right answers.

Notes

Chapter 1: Introduction (pages 1–26)

1. Shoplifting, also termed "retail theft," is a crime involving theft of goods or merchandise from a store by a consumer. It also consists of altering or removing price labels and security tags and in some jurisdictions, returning stolen merchandise to retailers for credit or cash and undercharging by employees to deprive the retailer the full value of merchandise. In most state penal codes its listing is not a separate offense, but subsumed in the general heading of theft (usually termed "theft" or "larceny") with other theft crimes, such as pickpocketing, purse snatching, theft from coin machines, and theft from motor vehicles.

2. See U.S. Department of Justice, 2005.

3. See Baumer and Rosenbaum, 1984; Kallis and Dinoo, 1985; Ray, 1987.

4. See Hollinger, 2000; Jack L. Hayes International, Inc., 2006.

5. Specialized correctional treatment for shoplifters is limited. Psychological counseling and psychiatric approaches including medication targeting underlying mental health problems were popular methods, especially before the 1980s; see, for example, Edwards and Roundtree, 1982; Gauthier and Pellerin, 1982; Guidry, 1975; Kolman and Wasserman, 1991; MacDevitt and Kedzierzawski, 1990; Ordway, 1962; Russell, 1978; Sarasalo, Bergman, and Toth, 1997; Solomon and Ray, 1984. Contemporary approaches can take the form of classroom-based or home study programs using education and cognitive behavioral components; see Caputo, 1998, 2003, and 2004b; Moore, 1984.

6. With the exception of research by Kivivuori (1998) on adolescents engaged in shoplifting "phases" and Svensson's (2002) report that shoplifting failed to trigger a criminal career, the career patterns of shoplifters are unknown. For research on the criminal career see Blumstein, Cohen, Roth, and Visher, 1986; Piquero, Farrington, and Blumstein, 2007.

7. Cox, Cox, and Moschis, 1990.

8. Cox, Cox, Anderson, and Moschis, 1993.

9. Ray and Briar, 1988.

10. Dabney, Hollinger, and Dugan, 2004.

11. See Beck and Ajzen, 1991; Bradford and Balmaceda, 1983; Cao and Deng, 1998; Cromwell, Parker, and Mobley, 1999; Deng, 1997; Edwards and Roundtree, 1982; Francis, 1979; Goldman, 1991; Klemke, 1982; Klemke and Egger, 1992; Krasnovsky and Lane, 1998; Kraut, 1976; Lamontagne, Boyer, Hetu, and Lacerte-Lamontagne, 2000; McElroy, Pope, Hudson, Keck, and White, 1991; Moore, 1983; Ray, 1987; Ray and Briar, 1988; Sarasalo, Bergman, and Toth, 1997.

12. Moore, 1984.

13. Kleptomania is a psychiatric disorder as defined in the *DSM–IV* and afflicts only a fraction (estimated between 5 and 10 percent) of all shoplifters. It is an impulse-control disorder with the essential feature a recurrent failure to resist impulses to steal objects not needed for personal use or their monetary value. In other words, such shoplifting is an impulsive and irrational act. The individual suffering from kleptomania usually steals alone and without help from others and rarely keeps anything he or she steals. Rather, the kleptomaniac is likely to discard, give away, or bring back merchandise to stores. Emotionally, the kleptomaniac experiences an increasing sense of tension immediately before the act and then pleasure, gratification, or relief of tension during and after the theft. This theft is not a result of anger, resentment, or vengeance and is not in response to a delusion or hallucination. A kleptomania diagnosis follows only when an individual displays all of these criteria and if no other mental disorder can explain the theft. Shoplifters may fulfill one or more of the *DSM–IV* criteria for kleptomania, such as unplanned theft, stealing alone, giving items away, and experiencing thrill, but they usually express other motivations. Consequently, few shoplifters fulfill all criteria for kleptomania to be "true" kleptomaniacs. Because of this, kleptomania is rarely a definite diagnosis for shoplifting. Still, many shoplifters cannot explain their behaviors and express a helpless lack of control. For more on kleptomania see American Psychiatric Association, 1994; Bradford and Balmaceda, 1983; Dannon, 2002; Durst, Katz, Teitelbaum, Zislin, and Dannon, 2001; Goldman, 1991, 1998; McElroy, Hudson, Pope, and Keck, 1991; McElroy, Pope, Hudson, Keck, and White, 1991; Murray, 1992; Sarasalo, Bergman, and Toth, 1997.

14. Beck and McIntyre, 1977.

15. Ray, Solomon, Doncaster, and Mellina, 1983.

16. Babin and Babin, 1996.

17. Goldner, Geller, Birmingham, and Remick, 2000.

18. Arboleda-Florez, Durie, and Costello, 1977.

19. Katz, 1988.

20. Dabney, Hollinger, and Dugan, 2004.

21. Buckle and Farrington, 1984.

22. Weaver and Carroll, 1985; Carroll and Weaver, 1986.

23. Steffensmeier and Terry, 1973.

24. Tonglet, 2002.

25. Lo, 1994.

26. For research finding women's overrepresentation, see: Abelson, 1989; Bradford and Balmaceda, 1983; Cleary, 1986; Moore, 1984; Kivivuori,

1998; Ray, 1987; Ray, Solomon, Doncaster, and Mellina, 1983. Few studies report a predominance of males; see Buckle and Farrington, 1984; Sarasalo, Bergman, and Toth, 1997, Tonglet, 2002. See also research reporting similar rates of offending among women and men: Cox, Cox, and Moschis, 1990; Klemke, 1982. My research found women to be well overrepresented among adult shoplifters ordered to probation. In 1997, women comprised 82 percent among forty-four shoplifters on probation, and in 2002, I found that seven in ten (70 percent) of shoplifters ordered to probation over a seventeen-month period were women. See Caputo, 1998, 2004b.

27. See Cameron, 1964, Cohen and Stark, 1974; Ray, Solomon, Doncaster, and Mellina, 1983. In my 2002 study, I found that while county residents were primarily Hispanic (about 56 percent), the 224 shoplifters were disproportionately Hispanic (93 percent). See Caputo, 1998, 2004b.

28. See Belknap, 2001.

29. See Cameron, 1964

30. See Abelson, 1989; Cleary, 1986; Francis, 1979; Klemke and Egger, 1992; Moore, 1984; Caputo 1998; 2004b.

31. See Caputo, 1998.

32. See Cameron, 1964; and Cleary, 1986.

33. See Caputo, 1998.

34. See for example; Maher, 1997; Maher and Curtis 1992; Mathews, 1986; Miller, 1986; Rosenbaum, 1988; Williamson and Folaron, 2003.

35. For literature on critical, feminist, and intersectional research methods and analytic approaches, see Burgess-Proctor, 2006; Holsinger, 2000; Steffensmeier and Allan, 1996; Way, 2004; West and Fenstermaker, 1995. For more on grounded theory see Dey, 1999; Glaser, 1992; Glaser and Strauss, 1967.

36. On the sociology of work and occupations, see for example Caplow, 1954; Elliot, 1972; Pavalko, 1971. On the sociology of criminal occupations, see King with Chambliss, 1972; Klockars, 1974; Letkemann, 1973; Steffensmeier, 1986; Steffensmeier and Ulmer, 2004; Sutherland, 1937.

37. Polsky, 1969: 93.

Chapter 2: Early Life Trauma (pages 27–66)

1. For an excellent historical analysis of urban decline and its effects in Camden, see Gillette, 2006.

2. Webster and Bishaw, 2006.

3. New Jersey Department of Law and Public Safety, 2005.

4. U. S. Department of Justice, 2007.

5. See Crespi and Sabatelli, 1997. A National Household Survey on Drug Abuse found that 8 percent of children live with a parent who used alcohol daily and 9 percent with a parent who used illicit drugs over the past month. See U.S. Department of Health and Human Services, 1994.

6. Removing from analysis La Toya, who reported a drinking onset of age three, brings the average drinking age onset for women from drug abus-

ing homes to 12.4 years, nearly a match to women from homes with alcohol abuse alone.

7. As to drug use and socioeconomic class, the 1991 National Household Survey on Drug Abuse reported rates of drug use among parents with low incomes was higher (10 percent) than among parents living above the poverty line (5 percent). See U.S. Department of Health and Human Services, 1994.

8. For more on behavioral responses of children to alcoholism of parents see Crespi and Sabatelli, 1997; Crespi and Rueckert, 2006; Seixas and Youcha, 1985.

9. I excluded La Toya from computations of drinking onset for women directly abused since her reported age (three years) is well outside the mean.

10. For more on method and scholarship in feminist criminology, including pathways research, see Belknap, 2006; Belknap and Holsinger, 2006; Chesney-Lind, 1997; Chesney-Lind and Pasko, 2004a, 2004b; Daly, 1994; Daly and Chesney-Lind, 1988; Renzetti, Goodstein, and Miller, 2006. See also Chesney-Lind and Shelden, 2003, a book devoted to female youth in trouble with the law.

11. Kathleen Daly's research (1992, 1994) explored diversity among female offenders, as did Richie's (1996) work on women's violence.

12. After analyzing Bureau of Justice Statistics data from 1991, Peugh, and Belenko (1999) found that 80 percent of female inmates were drug involved. A 2006 Bureau of Justice Statistics report written by Mumola and Karberg (2006) puts the number of women in prison classified as addicted to drugs at 60 percent.

13. Sher, Walitzer, Wood, and Brent, 1991.

14. Reese, Chassin, and Molina, 1994.

15. Kilpatrick, Acierno, Saunders, Resnick, Best, and Schnurr, 2000.

16. Andrews, Hops, Arv, Tildesley, and Harris, 1993.

17. Biederman, Faraone, Monuteaux, and Feighner, 2000.

18. Duncan, Duncan, and Hops, 1995.

19. Ellickson, Tucker, Klein, and McGuigan, 2001.

20. For more on parental substance abuse and behaviors of girls and women, including drug use and crime, see Bloom, Owen, Rosenbaum, and Piper Deschenes, 2003; Kramer and Berg, 2003; Peugh and Belenko, 1999; Windle, 1996.

21. Kilpatrick, Acierno, Saunders, Resnick, Best, and Schnurr, 2000.

22. For more on violence in the home see Carlson, 2000; Fantuzzo, Depaola, Lambert, Martino, Anderson, and Sutton, 1991; Fergusson and Horwood, 1998; Fleming, Mullen, and Bammer, 1997; Kenning, Merchant, and Tomkins, 1991.

23. Greene, Haney, and Hurtado, 2000.

24. Pasko, 2006.

25. See Acoca, 1999; Acoca and Dedel, 1998; Belknap and Holsinger, 1998, 2006; Bloom, Owen, Rosenbaum, Piper Deschenes, 2003; Browne, Miller, and Maguin, 1999; Chesney-Lind and Rodriguez, 1983; Daly, 1992;

Dembo, Schmeidler, Chin Sue, Borden, and Manning, 1995; Dembo, Williams, and Schmeidler, 1993; Finkelhor, 1994; Flowers, 2001; Fullilove, Lown, and Fullilove 1992; Gavazzi, Yarcheck, and Chesney-Lind, 2006; Gilfus, 1992; Harlow, 1999; Miller, Trapani, Fejes-Mendoza, Eggleston, and Dwiggins, 1995; Owen, 1998; Owen and Bloom, 1995.

26. Bloom and Owen, 1995.

27. Cook, Smith, Poister Tusher, and Raiford, 2005.

28. Browne, Miller, and Maguin, 1999; Chesney-Lind and Rodriguez, 1983; Daly, 1992; Gaardner and Belknap, 2002; Harlow, 1999.

29. For more on gender and abuse, see Dembo, Schmeidler, Chin Sue, Borden, and Manning, 1995; Dembo, Williams, and Schmeidler, 1993; Gavazzi, Yarcheck, and Chesney-Lind, 2006; Miller, Trapani, Fejes-Mendoza, Eggleston, and Dwiggins, 1995.

30. Belknap and Holsinger, 2006.

31. Pasko, 2006.

32. See for example Acoca, 1999; Acoca and Dedel, 1998; Chesney-Lind and Rodriguez, 1983; Flowers, 2001; Fullilove, Lown, and Fullilove, 1992.

33. Finkelhor, 1994. For more on child sexual abuse, its causes and consequences including prevalence in the general population see Briere and Elliott, 1994; Cole and Putman, 1992; Fergusson, Woodward, and Horwood, 2000; Neumann, Houskamp, Pollock, and Briere, 1996; Finkelhor, 1993; Finkelhor and Araji, 1986.

34. Harlow, 1999.

35. Siegel and Williams, 2003.

36. Goodkind, Ng, and Sarri, 2006.

37. For more on pathways to prostitution including the role of prior sexual abuse and other precipitating factors see Brannigan and Fleischman, 1989; Goldstein, 1979; James and Meyerding, 1978; Kramer and Berg, 2003; Potterat, Rothenberg, Muth, Darrow, and Phillips-Plummer, 1988; Silbert and Pines, 1981, 1982, 1983; Silbert, Pines, and Lynch, 1982; Simons and Whitbeck, 1991; Widom and Kuhns, 1996. For literature reviews on sex work, see Farley and Kelly, 2000; Miller and Jayasundara, 2001.

38. Silbert, Pines, and Lynch, 1982.

39. See McClanahan, McClelland, Abram, and Teplin, 1999.

40. Potterat, Rothenberg, Muth, Darrow, and Phillips-Plummer, 1988.

41. Widom and Kuhns, 1996.

42. Simons and Whitbeck, 1991.

43. See Finkelhor, 1993; Jarvis, Copeland, and Walton, 1998; Kovach, 1983; Langeland and Hartgers, 1998; Malinosky-Rummell and Hangsen, 1993; Rosenbaum, 1989; U.S. Department of Health and Human Services, Administration on Children, Youth, and Families, 2007; Wilsnack, Vogeltanz, Klassen, and Harris, 1997.

44. Kilpatrick, Acierno, Saunders, Resnick, Best, and Schnurr, 2000.

45. Chandy, Blum, and Resnick, 1996.

46. Kendler, Bulik, Silberg, Hettema, Myers, and Prescott, 2002.

47. Medrano, Hatch, Zule, and Desmond, 2003.

48. Horowitz, Widom, McLaughlin, and White, 2001.

49. See Bloom, 1998; Green, Miranda, Daroowalla, and Siddique, 2005; Teplin, Abram, and McClelland, 1996.

50. Najavits, Weiss, and Shaw, 1997.

51. Oregon Youth Authority, 2002.

52. Wilsnack, Vogeltanz, Klassen, and Harris, 1997.

53. Kilpatrick, Acierno, Saunders, Resnick, Best, and Schnurr, 2000.

54. Spataro, Mullen, Burgess, Wells, and Moss, 2004.

55. U.S. Department of Health and Human Services, National Center on Child Abuse and Neglect, 1996.

56. See Beitchman, Zucker, Hood, DaCosta, and Akman, 1991; Finkelhor and Baron, 1986; Hyman and Williams, 2001.

57. Wenzel, Hambarsoomain, D'Amico, Ellison, and Tucker, 2006.

58. Moeller, Bachman, and Loeller, 1993.

59. At the forefront of theoretical advances in the psychological development of girls is Carol Gilligan's model of moral development. See Brown and Gilligan, 1992; Gilligan, 1983; Gilligan, Lyons, and Hanmer, 1989; Gilligan, Ward, and McLean Taylor with Bardige, 1988; Johnson, 1988.

60. In her study of the female inmate social system, Barbara Owen (1998: 41) described chronic physical, sexual, and emotional abuses simultaneously present in the childhood lives of women as a multiplicity of abuse.

Chapter 3: Coming of Age (pages 67–100)

1. Kaufman, Alt, and Chapman, 2001.

2. Andres-Lemay, Jamieson, and MacMillan, 2005.

3. See, for example, Belknap, Holsinger, and Dunn, 1997; Bloom, Owen, Rosenbaum, and Piper Deschenes, 2003; Browne, Miller, and Maguin, 1999; Chesney Lind, 1997.

4. American Correctional Association, 1990.

5. Silbert and Pines, 1981.

6. Snyder and Sickmond, 2006.

7. Hammer, Finkelhor, and Sedlak, 2002.

8. Simons and Whitbeck, 1991.

9. Whitbeck, Hoyt, Yoder, Cauce, and Paradise, 2001. On risk factors for sexual victimization of both female and male adolescents who are homeless and runaways see Tyler, Whitbeck, Hoyt, and Cauce, 2004.

10. Tyler, Hoyt, and Whitbeck, 2000.

11. Greene, Ennett, and Ringwalt, 1999.

12. Weber, Boivin, Blais, Haley, and Roy, 2004.

13. Seng, 1989.

14. Gilfus, 1992.

15. Harlow, 2003.

16. McCarthy and Hagan, 1995. For a study on drug use, involvement in street peer groups, and survival strategies of female homeless and adolescent runaways, see Chen, Tyler, Whitbeck, and Hoyt, 2004. On substance abuse among runaways see Greene, Ennett, and Ringwalt, 1997.

17. Letkemann, 1973.
18. Whitebeck, Hoyt, and Yoder, 1999.
19. Harrison, 1997.
20. McPherson, Lovin, and Cook, 2001:415.
21. Forsyth and Deshotels, 1997; Lewis, 2006; Maticka-Tyndale, Lewis, Clark, Zubick, and Young, 2000.
22. Bruckert, Parent, and Robitaille, 2003; Peretti and O'Connor, 1989; Ronai and Ellis, 1989; Thompson and Harred, 1992; Thompson, Harred, and Burks, 2003; Trautner, 2005; Wood, 2000.
23. Egan, 2005.
24. Sweet and Tewksbury, 2000.
25. Barton, 2002, 2006.
26. Thompson and Harred, 1992; Thompson, Harred, and Burks, 2003.
27. Raphael and Shapiro, 2004.
28. Ronai and Ellis, 1989.
29. During its golden years, according to Shteir (2004), striptease was more than pornography; it was a show of entertainment, of seduction, of interpretive art between a performer and her audience. Not anymore—the American appetite for sex and pornography is whetted everywhere, on television, in music, and striptease had to change too.
30. Baskin and Sommers, 2006.
31. Fagan and Freeman, 1999.
32. Farley, 2004, 2005.
33. Raphael and Shapiro, 2004.
34. Bruckert, Parent, and Robitaille, 2003: 15.
35. Wahab, 2004.
36. Jeffrey and MacDonald, 2006.

Chapter 4: Making Crime Specialization Work in the Urban Drug Culture (pages 101–140)

1. While literature on shoplifters' customers is undeveloped, for more on the outlets used by property crime offenders to dispose of stolen goods, see Johns and Hayes, 2003; Schneider, 2005; Steffensmeier, 1986; Steffensmeier and Ulmer, 2004.
2. For discussions of shoplifter typologies see Abelson, 1989; Cameron, 1964; Caputo, 1998, 2004b; Cleary, 1986; Francis, 1979; Klemke, 1992; Moore, 1984.
3. See Caputo, 1998, 2004b.
4. For discussions on changes in price for sex work and on prostitutes who trade sex for drugs or small amounts of money, see Elwood and Greene, 2003; Goldstein, Ouellet, and Fendrich, 1992; Inciardi, Lockwood, and Pottieger, 1993; Maher, 1996; Maher and Daly, 1996; Murphy and Rosenbaum, 1997; Ratner, 1993; Sterk, Elifson, and German, 2000.
5. For discussions of violence and degradation associated with living and working out of crack houses, see, for example, Inciardi, Lockwood, and Pot-

tieger, 1993; Inciardi and Surratt, 2001; Maher and Daly, 1996. For a good discussion of choices sex workers make about living arrangements, see Maher, Dunlap, Johnson, and Hamid, 1996.

6. Ruggiero and South, 1997.

7. On human and economic capital see Becker, 1964. On social and cultural capital, see Bourdieu, 1986; Portes, 1998.

8. Levy and Anderson, 2005.

9. Redlinger, 1975.

10. Caplow, 1954.

11. See Walby, 1986, 1990.

12. See Anderson, 2005; Bourgois, 1989; Bourgois and Dunlap, 1993; Fagan, 1994; Inciardi, Lockwood, and Pottieger, 1993; Inciardi and Surratt, 2001; Maher, 1997, 2004; Maher and Curtis, 1992; Maher and Daly, 1996; Miller, 1986, Miller, 1995.

13. Steffensmeier, 1983; Steffensmeier and Terry, 1986.

14. Steffensmeier and Terry, 1986.

15. Maher and Daly, 1996.

16. Sommers, Baskin, and Fagan, 1996.

17. A contemporary study of prestige in criminal occupations reports different results about the status of drug dealing and sex work compared to this larger body of literature. Matsueda, Gartner, Piliavin, and Polakowski (1992) used criminal offenders and drug addicts to rank the prestige they held toward offenders in different forms of criminal work. While shoplifting was not part of that research, sex work was. The results show that the highly and very highly respected jobs rank from the numbers banker at the top followed by hustler, gambler, numbers runner, loan shark, counterfeiter, prostitute, drug dealer, pimp, and purse snatcher. Criminal offenders and drug addicts also ranked how much they looked down upon offenders in these occupations, and results show that sex workers were looked down upon less than were drug dealers.

18. U.S. Department of Justice, 2006.

19. Miller, 1978: 239–240.

20. Letkemann, 1973.

21. Klockars, 1974.

22. Steffensmeier, 1986.

23. McCarthy and Hagan, 2001.

24. Rosenbaum, 1988: 79.

25. Jeffrey and MacDonald, 2006.

26. Maher, Dunlap, Johnson, and Hamid, 1996.

27. Polsky, 1969.

28. Letkemann, 1973.

29. Maher, 1996.

30. Massey, 1994:8. The quote refers to "places," which are open systems.

31. DeKeseredy, Alvi, Schwartz, and Tomaszewski, 2003.

32. See Anderson, 2000; Bell, 1973; Calster, Mincy, and Tobin, 1997; Castells, 1986, 1989; Harrington, 1962; Kasarda, 1989; Knox, 1991; Massey, 1984; Morrill and Wohlenberg, 1971; Schwirian, 1983; Wilson, 1987.

33. Calster, Mincy, and Tobin, 1997.
34. Rose, 1970.
35. Kodras, 1997.
36. Kodras, 1997: 81.
37. Anderson, 1990.
38. Anderson, 1990: 246.
39. Anderson, 1990: 239.

Chapter 5: Risk Management Strategies for Shoplifters and Sex Workers (141–184)

1. Most of the sex work specialists in my study were at some point approached by men on the streets who manage sex work (pimps), but only about 5 percent of them ever worked for a pimp, preferring independence instead. The decline of pimp prostitution is noted in other research, see Miller, 1995; Weitzer, 2005; Williamson and Clues-Tolar, 2002. The pimps women in my study talk about are different than one might expect; pimps are more like intimate partners, usually "husbands" who also care for children and other members of a sex worker's family.
2. Michie, 2002.
3. Michie, 2002.
4. Scott and Dedel, 2006.
5. Raphael and Shapiro, 2003.
6. O'Connell Davidson, 1998.
7. For more on violence and protective measures sex workers use, see Dalla, Xia, and Kennedy, 2003; Farley, Cotton, Lynne, Zumbeck, Spiwak, Reyes, Alvarez, and Sezgin, 2003; Miller, 1993; Monto, 2004; Rapheal and Shapiro, 2004; Weitzer, 2005; Williamson and Folaron, 2003.
8. Williamson and Folaron, 2001.
9. Surratt, Inciardi, Kurtz, and Kiley, 2004.
10. Farley and Barkan, 1998.
11. Maher, 1997.
12. Miller and Schwartz, 1995.
13. Valera, Sawyer, and Schiraldi, 2001.
14. Silbert and Pines, 1982.
15. Romero-Daza, Weeks, and Singer, 2003.
16. Lowman, 2000.
17. Potterat, Brewer, Muth, Rothenberg, Woodhouse, Muth, Stites, and Brody, 2004.
18. Williamson and Folaron 2001.
19. Dalla, Xia, and Kennedy, 2003:470.
20. Sanders, 2004a.
21. Scott and Dedel, 2006.
22. Neame and Heenan, 2003:8.
23. Williamson and Folaron, 2001.
24. Scott and Dedel, 2006:32–33.

25. Dalla, Xia, and Kennedy, 2003:470.
26. Kurtz, Surratt, Inciardi, and Kiley, 2004.
27. Kurtz, Surratt, Inciardi, and Kiley, 2004.
28. Dalla, Xia, and Kennedy, 2003:1380.
29. Kurtz, Surratt, Inciardi, and Kiley, 2004.
30. Sanders, 2004b.
31. For more on protective measures, see Farley, Cotton, Lynne, Zumbeck, Spiwak, Reyes, Alvarez, and Sezgin, 2003; Miller, 1993; Monto, 2004; Rapheal and Shapiro, 2004; Romero-Daza, Weeks, and Singer, 2003; Weitzer, 2005; Williamson and Folaron, 2003.

Chapter 6: Out in the Storm (pages 185–196)

1. See Bloom, Chesney-Lind, and Owen, 1994; Maur, 2004; Mauer and Chesney-Lind, 2002.
2. On intermediate sanctions see Caputo (2004a) and on drug courts see Belenko, 2001; Schmitt, 2006; Young and Belenko, 2002.
3. Treatment works. Effective treatment is structured, focused on specific criminogenic needs of an offending population, takes a multiple modality approach, including cognitive behavioral as well as vocational and educational components, and occurs in the community. See Andrews, 1994; Austin, Bloom, and Donahue, 1992; Bonta, 1997; Gendreau, 1993; National Institute of Corrections, 2000.

References

Abelson, E. S. 1989. *When ladies go a-thieving: Middle-class shoplifters in the Victorian department store.* New York: Oxford University Press.

Acoca, L. 1999. Investing in girls: A 21st century strategy. *Juvenile Justice, VI, Number 1.* Washington, D.C.: U.S. Department of Justice, Office of Justice Programs, Office of Juvenile Justice and Delinquency Prevention.

Acoca, L., and Dedel, K. 1998. *No place to hide: Understanding and meeting the needs of girls in the California juvenile justice system.* San Francisco: National Council on Crime and Delinquency.

American Correctional Association. 1990. *The female offender: What does the future hold?* Washington, D.C.: St. Mary's Press.

American Psychiatric Association. 1994. *Diagnostic and statistical manual of mental disorders,* 4th ed. Washington, D.C.: American Psychiatric Association.

Anderson, E. 2000. "The emerging Philadelphia African American class structure." *The Annals of the American Academy of Political and Social Science* 568: 54–77.

———. 1990. *Streetwise: Race, class, and change in an urban community.* Chicago: University of Chicago Press.

Anderson, T. L. 2005. "Dimensions of women's power in the illicit drug economy." *Theoretical Criminology* 9: 371–400.

Andres-Lemay, V. J., Jamieson, E., and MacMillan, H. L. 2005. "Child abuse, psychiatric disorder, and running away in a community sample of women." *Canadian Journal of Psychiatry* 50: 684–690.

Andrews, D. A. 1994. *An overview of treatment effectiveness. Research and clinical principles* (Draft). Washington, D.C.: National Institute of Corrections.

Andrews, J. A., Hops, H., Arv, D., Tildesley, E., and Harris, J. 1993. "Parental influence on early adolescent substance use." *The Journal of Early Adolescence* 13: 285–310.

Arboleda-Florez, J., Durie, H., and Costello, J. 1977. "Shoplifting—An ordinary crime?" *International Journal of Offender Therapy and Comparative Criminology* 21: 201–207.

Austin, J., Bloom, B., and Donahue, T. 1992. *Female offenders in the com-*

munity: An analysis of innovative strategies and programs. San Francisco: National Council on Crime and Delinquency.

Babin, B. J., and Babin, L. A. 1996. "Effects of moral cognitions and consumer emotions on shoplifting intentions." *Psychology & Marketing* 13: 785–802.

Barton, B. 2002. "Dancing on the Möbius Strip: Challenging the sex war paradigm." *Gender & Society* 16: 585–602.

———. 2006. *Stripped: Inside the lives of exotic dancers.* New York: New York University Press.

Baskin, D. R., and Sommers, I. 2006. "Women, work, and crime." In L. F. Alarid and P. Cromwell (eds.), *In her own words: Women offenders' views on crime and victimization* (pp. 189–202). Los Angeles: Roxbury.

Baumer, T. L., and Rosenbaum, D. P. 1984. *Combating retail theft: Programs and strategies.* Boston: Butterworth.

Beck, E. A., and McIntyre, S. C. 1977. "MMPI patterns of shoplifters within a college population." *Psychological Reports* 41: 1035–1040.

Beck, L., and Ajzen, I. 1991. "Predicting dishonest actions using the theory of planned behavior." *Journal of Research in Personality* 25: 285–301.

Becker, G. S. 1964. *Human capital: A theoretical and empirical analysis, with special reference to education.* Chicago: University of Chicago Press.

Beitchman, J., Zucker, K., Hood, J., DaCosta, G., and Akman, D. 1991. "A review of the short-term effects of child sexual abuse." *Child Abuse and Neglect* 15: 537–556.

Belenko, S. 2001. *Research on drug courts: A critical review 2001 update.* New York: National Center on Addiction and Substance Abuse at Columbia University.

Belknap, J. 2001. *The invisible woman: Gender, crime and justice,* 2nd ed. Belmont, CA: Wadsworth.

———. 2006. *The invisible woman: Gender, crime and justice,* 3rd ed. Belmont, CA: Wadsworth.

Belknap, J., and Holsinger, K. 1998. "An overview of delinquent girls: How theory and practice have failed and the need for innovative changes." In R. T. Zaplin (ed.), *Female offenders: Critical perspectives and effective interventions* (pp. 31–64). Gaithersburg, MD: Aspen.

———. 2006. "The gendered nature of risk factors for delinquency." *Feminist Criminology* 1: 48–71.

Belknap, J., Holsinger, K., and Dunn, M. 1997. "Understanding incarcerated girls: The results of a focus group study." *Prison Journal* 77: 381–404.

Bell, D. 1973. *The coming of post-industrial society: A venture in social forecasting.* New York: Basic Books.

Biederman, J., Faraone, S. V., Monuteaux, B. A., and Feighner, J. A. 2000. "Patterns of alcohol and drug use in adolescents can be predicted by parental substance abuse disorders." *Pediatrics* 106: 792–797.

Bloom, B. 1998. "Women with mental health substance abuse problems on probation and parole." *Offender Programs Report: Social and Behavioral Rehabilitation in Prisons, Jails, and the Community* 2: 1–13.

Bloom, B., Chesney-Lind, M., and Owen, B. 1994. *Women in prison in*

California: Hidden victims of the war on drugs. San Francisco: Center on Juvenile and Criminal Justice.

Bloom, B., and Owen, B. 1995. *Profiling the needs of California's female prisoners: A needs assessment.* Washington, D.C.: National Institute of Corrections.

Bloom, B., Owen, B., Rosenbaum, J., and Piper Deschenes, E. 2003. "Focusing on girls and young women: A gendered perspective on female delinquency." *Women & Criminal Justice* 4: 117–136.

Blumstein, A., Cohen, J., Roth, J. A., and Visher, C. A. (eds.). 1986. *Criminal careers and "career criminals,"* Vol. I. Washington, D.C.: National Academy Press.

Bonta, J. 1997. *Offender rehabilitation: From research to practice.* Ottawa, Ontario: Public Works and Government Services Canada.

Bourdieu, P. 1986. "The forms of capital." In J. G. Richardson (ed.), *Handbook of theory and research for the sociology of education* (pp. 241–258). New York: Greenwood Press.

Bourgois, P. 1989. "In search of Horatio Alger: Culture and ideology in the crack economy." *Contemporary Drug Problems* 16: 619–649.

Bourgois, P., and Dunlap, E. 1993. "Exorcising sex-for-crack: An ethnographic perspective from Harlem." In M. S. Ratner (ed.), *Crack pipe as pimp: An ethnographic investigation of sex-for-crack exchanges* (pp. 97–132). New York: Lexington.

Bradford, J., and Balmaceda, R. 1983. "Shoplifting: Is there a specific psychiatric syndrome?" *Canadian Journal of Psychiatry* 28: 248–254.

Brannigan, A., and Fleischman, J. 1989. "Juvenile prostitution and mental health: Policing delinquency or treating pathology." *Canadian Journal of Law and Society* 4: 77–98.

Briere, J. N., and Elliott, D. M. 1994. "Immediate and long-term impacts of child sexual abuse." *The Future of Children* 4: 54–69.

Brown, L. M., and Gilligan, C. 1992. *Meeting at the crossroads: Women's psychology and girls' development.* Cambridge, Mass.: Harvard University Press.

Browne, A., Miller, B., and Maguin, E. 1999. "Prevalence and severity of lifetime physical and sexual victimization among incarcerated women." *International Journal of Law & Psychiatry* 22: 301–322.

Bruckert, C., Parent, C., and Robitaille, P. 2003. *Erotic service/erotic dance establishments: Two types of marginalized Labour.* Ottawa: Law Commission of Canada.

Buckle, A., and Farrington, D. P. 1984. "An observational study of shoplifting." *British Journal of Criminology* 24: 63–73.

Burgess-Proctor, A. 2006. "Intersections of race, class, gender, and crime." *Feminist Criminology* 1: 27–47.

Calster, G., Mincy, R., and Tobin, M. 1997. "The disparate racial neighborhood impacts of metropolital economic restructuring." *Urban Affairs Review* 32: 797–824.

Cameron, M. O. 1964. *The booster and the snitch: Department store shoplifting.* London: The Free Press of Glencoe.

Cao, L., and Deng, X. 1998. "Shoplifting: A test of an integrated model of strain, differential association, and seduction theories." *Sociology of Crime, Law, and Deviance* 1: 65–84.

Caplow, T. 1954. *The sociology of work.* New York: McGraw-Hill.

Caputo, G. A. 1998. "A program of treatment for adult shoplifters." *Journal of Offender Rehabilitation* 27: 123–137.

———. 2003. *What's in the bag? A shoplifting treatment and education program.* Lanham, Md.: American Correctional Association.

———. 2004a. *Intermediate sanctions in corrections.* Denton: University of North Texas Press.

———. 2004b. "Treating sticky fingers: An evaluation of a treatment program for shoplifters." *Journal of Offender Rehabilitation* 38: 49–68.

Carlson, B. E. 2000. "Children exposed to intimate partner violence." *Trauma, Violence, & Abuse* 1: 321–342.

Carroll, J., and Weaver, F. 1986. "Shoplifters' perceptions of crime opportunities: A process-tracing study." In D. B. Cornish and R. V. G. Clarke (eds.), *The reasoning criminal: Rational choice perspectives on offending* (pp. 19–38). New York: Springer-Verlag.

Castells, M. 1986. "High technology, world development, and structural transformation: The trends and the debate." *Alternatives: Social Transformation and Human Governance* 11: 297–343.

———. 1989. *The informational city.* Oxford: Blackwell.

Chandy, J. M., Blum, R. W., and Resnick, M. D. 1996. "History of sexual abuse and parental alcohol misuse: Risk, outcomes and protective factors in adolescents." *Child and Adolescent Social Work Journal* 13: 411–432.

Chen, X., Tyler, K., Whitbeck, L. B., and Hoyt, D. R. 2004. "Early sexual abuse, street adversity, and drug use among female homeless and runaway adolescents in the Midwest." *Journal of Drug Issues* 34: 1–21.

Chesney-Lind, M. 1997. *The female offender: Girls, women, and crime.* Thousand Oaks, Calif.: Sage.

Chesney-Lind, M., and Pasko, L. J. (eds.). 2004a. *Girls, women and crime: Selected readings.* Belmont, Calif.: Sage.

———. 2004b. *The female offender: Girls, women, and crime,* 2nd ed. Thousand Oaks, Calif.: Sage.

Chesney-Lind, M., and Rodriguez, N. 1983. "Women under lock and key." *The Prison Journal* 63: 47–65.

Chesney-Lind, M., and Shelden, R. G. 2003. *Girls, delinquency, and juvenile justice.* Belmont, Calif.: West/Wadsworth.

Cleary, J., Jr. 1986. *Prosecuting the shoplifter.* Boston: Butterworth.

Cohen, L.E., and Stark, R. 1974. "Discriminatory labeling and the five-finger discount: An empirical analysis of differential shoplifting dispositions." *Journal of Research in Crime and Delinquency* 11: 25–39.

Cole, P. M., and Putman, F. W. 1992. "Effect of incest on self and social functioning: A developmental psychopathology perspective." *Journal of Consulting and Clinical Psychology* 60: 174–184.

Cook, S. L., Smith, S. G., Poister Tusher, C., and Raiford, J. 2005. "Self-reports of traumatic events in a random sample of incarcerated women." *Women & Criminal Justice* 16: 107–126.

Cox, A. D., Cox, D., Anderson, R. D. and Moschis, G.P. 1993. "Research note: Social influences on adolescent shoplifting—Theory, evidence, and implications for the retail industry." *Journal of Retailing* 69: 234–245.

Cox, D., Cox, A. D., and Moschis, G. P. 1990. "When consumer behavior goes bad: An investigation of adolescent shoplifting." *Journal of Consumer Research* 17: 149–159.

Crespi, T. D., and Rueckert, Q. H. 2006. "Family therapy and children of alcoholics: Implications for continuing education and certification in substance abuse practice." *Journal of Child & Adolescent Substance Abuse* 15: 33–44.

Crespi, T. D., and Sabatelli, R. M. 1997. "Children of alcoholics and adolescence: Individuation, development, and family systems." *Adolescence* 32: 407–417.

Cromwell, P., Parker, L., and Mobley, S. 1999. "The five-finger discount: An analysis of motivations for shoplifting." In P. Cromwell (ed.), *In their own words: Criminals on crime,* 2nd ed. (pp. 57–70). Los Angeles: Roxbury.

Dabney, D.A., Hollinger, R. C., and Dugan, L. 2004. "Who actually steals? A study of covertly observed shoplifters." *Justice Quarterly* 21: 693–725.

Dalla, R.L., Xia, Y., and Kennedy, H. 2003. "You just give them what they want and pray they don't kill you: Street-level sex workers' reports of victimization, personal resources, and coping strategies." *Violence Against Women* 9: 1367–1394.

Daly, K. 1992. "Women's pathways to felony court: Feminist theories of lawbreaking and problems of representation." *Southern California Review of Law and Women's Studies* 2: 11–52.

———. 1994. *Gender, crime, and punishment.* New Haven, Conn.: Yale University Press.

Daly, K., and Chesney-Lind, M. 1988. "Feminism and criminology." *Justice Quarterly* 5: 497–538.

Dannon, P. N. 2002. "Kleptomania: An impulse control disorder?" *International Journal of Psychiatry in Clinical Practice* 6: 3–7.

DeKeseredy, W. S., Alvi, S., Schwartz, M. D., and Tomaszewski, A. 2003. *Under siege: Poverty and crime in a public housing community.* New York: Lexington Books.

DeKeseredy, W. S., and Schwartz, M. D. In press. *Dangerous exits: Escaping abusive relationships in rural America.* New Brunswick, N.J.: Rutgers University Press.

Dembo, R., Schmeidler, J., Chin Sue, C., Borden, P., and Manning, D. 1995. "Gender differences in service needs among youths entering a juvenile assessment center: A replication study." *Journal of Correctional Health Care* 2: 191–216.

Dembo, R., Williams, L., and Schmeidler, J. 1993. "Gender differences in mental health service needs among youths entering a juvenile detention center." *Journal of Prison and Jail Health* 12: 73–101.

Deng, X. 1997. "The deterrent effects of initial sanction on first-time apprehended shoplifters." *International Journal of Offender Therapy and Comparative Criminology* 41: 284–297.

Dey, I. 1999. *Grounding grounded theory: Guidelines for qualitative inquiry.* San Diego: Academic Press.

Duncan, T. E., Duncan, S. C., and Hops, H. 1995. "An analysis of the relationship between parent and adolescent marijuana use via generalized estimating equation methodology." *Multivariate Behavioral Research* 30: 317–339.

Durst, R., Katz, G., Teitelbaum, A., Zislin, J., and Dannon, P. N. 2001. "Kleptomania: Diagnosis and treatment options." *CNS Drugs* 15: 185–195.

Edwards, D. W., and Roundtree, G. A. 1982. "Assessment of short-term treatment groups with adjudicated first time shoplifters." *Journal of Offender Counseling, Services & Rehabilitation* 6: 89–102.

Egan, R. D. 2005. "Emotional consumption: Mapping love and masochism in an exotic dance club." *Body Society* 11: 87–108.

Ellickson, P. L., Tucker, J. S., Klein, D. J., and McGuigan, K. A. 2001. "Prospective risk factors for alcohol misuse in late adolescence." *Journal of Studies on Alcohol* 62: 773–782.

Elliott, P. 1972. *The sociology of the professions.* London: Macmillan.

Elwood, W. N., and Greene, K. 2003. "Desperately seeking skeezers: Downward comparison theory and the implications for STD/HIV prevention among African-American crack users." *Journal of Ethnicity in Substance Abuse* 2: 15–33.

Fagan, J. 1994. "Women and drug use revisited: Female participation in the cocaine economy." *Journal of Drug Issues* 24: 179–225.

Fagan, J., and Freeman, R. B. 1999. "Crime and work." *Crime and Justice* 25: 225–290.

Fantuzzo, J. W., DePaola, L. M., Lambert, L., Martino, T., Anderson, G., and Sutton, S. 1991. "Effects of interparental violence on the psychological adjustment and competencies of young children." *Journal of Consulting & Clinical Psychology* 59: 258–265.

Farley, M. 2005. "Prostitution harms women even if indoors." *Violence Against Women* 11: 950–964.

———. 2004. "Bad for the body, bad for the heart: prostitution harms women even if legalized or decriminalized." *Violence Against Women* 10: 1087–1125.

Farley, M., and Barkan, H. 1998. "Prostitution, violence against women, and posttraumatic stress disorder." *Women & Health* 27: 37–49.

Farley, M., Cotton, A., Lynne, J., Zumbeck, S., Spiwak, F., Reyes, M. E., Alvarez, D., and Sezgin, U. 2003. "Prostitution and trafficking in 9 countries: Update on violence and post-traumatic stress disorder." In M. Farley (ed.), *Prostitution, trafficking, and traumatic stress* (pp. 33–74). Binghamton, N.Y.: Haworth.

Farley, M., and Kelly, V. 2000. "Prostitution: A critical review of the medical and social sciences literature." *Women & Criminal Justice* 11: 29–64.

Fergusson, D. M., and Horwood L. J. 1998. "Exposure to interparental violence in childhood and psychosocial adjustment in young adulthood." *Child Abuse & Neglect* 22: 339–357.

Fergusson, D. M., Woodward, L. J., and Horwood, L. J. 2000. "Risk factors and life processes associated with the onset of suicidal behaviour during adolescence and early adulthood." *Psychological Medicine* 30: 23–39.

Finkelhor, D. 1993. "Epidemiological factors in the clinical identification of child sexual abuse." *Child Abuse and Neglect: The International Journal* 17: 67–70.

———. 1994. "Current information on the scope and nature of child sexual abuse." *The Future of Children* 4: 31–53.

Finkelhor, D., and Araji, S. 1986. *A sourcebook on child sexual abuse.* Beverly Hills, Calif.: Sage.

Finkelhor, D., and Baron, L. 1986. "Risk factors for child sexual abuse." *Journal of Interpersonal Violence* 1: 43–71.

Fleming, J., Mullen, P., and Bammer, G. 1997. "A study of potential risk-factors for sexual abuse in children." *Child Abuse and Neglect* 21: 49–58.

Flowers, R. B. 2001. *Runaway kids and teenage prostitution.* Westport, Conn.: Greenwood Press.

Forsyth, C. J., and Deshotels, T. H. 1997. "The occupational milieu of the nude dancer." *Deviant Behavior* 18: 125–142.

Francis, D. B. 1979. *Shoplifting—The crime everybody pays for.* New York: Elsevier/Nelson.

Fullilove, M., Lown, A., and Fullilove, R. 1992. "Crack hos and skeezers: Traumatic experiences of women crack users." *The Journal of Sex Research* 29: 275–287.

Gaardner, E., and Belknap, J. 2002. "Tenuous borders: Girls transferred to adult court." *Criminology* 40: 481–517.

Gauthier, J., and Pellerin, D. 1982. "Management of compulsive shoplifting through covert sensitization." *Journal of Behavior Therapy and Experimental Psychiatry* 13: 73–75.

Gavazzi, S. M., Yarcheck, C. M., and Chesney-Lind, M. 2006. "Global risk indicators and the role of gender in a juvenile detention sample." *Criminal Justice and Behavior* 33: 597–612.

Gendreau, P. 1993. *The principles of effective intervention with offenders.* Paper presented at the International Association of Residential and Community Alternatives, Philadelphia.

Gilfus, M. 1992. "From victims to survivors to offenders: Women's routes of entry into street crime." *Women and Criminal Justice* 4: 63–89.

Gillette, H., Jr. 2006. *Camden after the fall: Decline and renewal in a post-industrial city.* Philadelphia: University of Pennsylvania Press.

Gilligan, C. 1983. *In a different voice.* Cambridge, Mass.: Harvard University Press.

Gilligan, C., Lyons, N. P., and Hanmer, T. J. (eds.). 1989. *Making connections: The relational worlds of adolescent girls at Emma Willard School.* Cambridge, Mass.: Harvard University Press.

Gilligan, C., Ward, J. V., and McLean Taylor, J., with Bardige, B. (eds.) 1988. *Mapping the moral domain: A contribution of women's thinking to psychological theory and education.* Cambridge, Mass.: Harvard University Press.

Glaser, B. 1992. *Basics of grounded theory analysis.* Mill Valley, Calif.: Sociology Press.

Glaser, B., and Strauss, A. 1967. *The discovery of grounded theory.* Chicago: Aldine.

Goldman, M. J. 1991. "Kleptomania: Making sense of the nonsensical." *American Journal of Psychiatry* 148: 986–996.

———. 1998. *Kleptomania: The compulsion to steal—What can be done?* Far Hills, NJ: New Horizon Press.

Goldner, E. M., Geller, J., Birmingham, C. L., and Remick, R. A. 2000. "Comparison of shoplifting behaviours in patients with eating disorders, psychiatric control subjects, and undergraduate control subjects." *Canadian Journal of Psychiatry* 45: 471–475.

Goldstein, P. J. 1979. *Prostitution and drugs.* Lexington, Mass.: Lexington Books.

Goldstein, P. J., Ouellet, L. J., and Fendrich, M. 1992. "From bag brides to skeezers: A historical perspective on sex-for-drugs behavior." *Journal of Psychoactive Drugs* 24: 349–361.

Goodkind, S., Ng, I., and Sarri, R. C. 2006. "The impact of sexual abuse in the lives of young women involved or at risk of involvement with the juvenile justice system." *Violence Against Women* 12: 456–477.

Green, B. L., Miranda, J., Daroowalla, A., and Siddique, J. 2005. "Trauma exposure, mental health functioning, and program needs of women in jail." *Crime Delinquency* 51: 133–151.

Greene, J. M., Ennett, S. T., and Ringwalt, C. L. 1997. "Substance use among runaway and homeless youth in three national samples." *American Journal of Public Health* 87: 229–235.

———. 1999. "Prevalence and correlates of survival sex among runaway and homeless youth." *American Journal of Public Health* 89: 1406–1409.

Greene, S., Haney, C., and Hurtado, A. 2000. "Cycles of pain: Risk factors in the lives of incarcerated mothers and their children." *The Prison Journal* 80: 3–23.

Guidry, L. S. 1975. "Use of a covert punishing contingency in compulsive stealing." *Journal of Behavior Therapy and Experimental Psychiatry* 6: 169.

Hammer, H., Finkelhor, D., and Sedlak, A. 2002. *Runaway/thrownaway children: National estimates and characteristics.* NISMART: National Incidence Studies of Missing, Abducted, Runaway, and Thrownaway Children. Washington, D.C.: Office of Juvenile Justice and Delinquency Prevention.

Harlow, C. W. 1999. *Prior abuse reported by inmates and probationers.* Washington, D.C.: U.S. Department of Justice.

———. 2003. *Education and correctional populations.* Washington, D.C.: Bureau of Justice Statistics.

Harrington, M. 1962. *The other America: Poverty in the Unted States.* Baltimore, Md.: Peguin.

Harrison, R. S. 1997. *Drug & alcohol use among juvenile probationers in Utah—October, 1997.* Salt Lake City: Social Research Institute, University of Utah.

Hollinger, R. C. 2000. *2000 National retail security survey.* Gainesville: University of Florida.

Holsinger, K. 2000. "Feminist perspectives on female offending: Examining real girls' lives." *Women & Criminal Justice* 12: 23–51.

Horowitz, A. V., Widom, C. S., McLaughlin, J., and White, H. R. 2001. "The impact of childhood abuse and neglect on adult mental health: A prospective study." *Journal of Health and Social Behavior* 42: 184–201.

Hyman, B., and Williams, L. 2001. Resilience among women survivors of child sexual abuse. *Affilia* 16: 198–219.

Inciardi, J. A., Lockwood, D., and Pottieger, A. E. 1993. *Women and crack-cocaine.* New York: Macmillan.

Inciardi, J. A., and Surratt, H. L. 2001. "Drug use, street crime and sex-trading among cocaine dependent women: Implications for public health and criminal justice policy." *Journal of Psychoactive Drugs* 33: 379–389.

Jack L. Hayes International, Inc. 2006. *18th Annual retail theft survey.* Fruitland Park, Fla.

James, J., and Meyerding, J. J. 1978. "Early sexual experiences as a risk factor in prostitution." *Archives of Sexual Behavior* 7: 31–42.

Jarvis, T. J., Copeland, J., and Walton, L. 1998. "Exploring the nature of the relationship between child sexual abuse and substance abuse among women." *Addiction* 93: 865–875.

Jeffrey, L. A., and MacDonald, G. 2006. "It's the money honey: The economy of sex work in the Maritimes." *Canadian Review of Sociology and Anthropology* 43: 313–327.

Johns, T., and Hayes, R. 2003. "Behind the fence: Buying and selling stolen merchandise." *Security Journal* 16: 29–44.

Johnson, K. D. 1988. "Adolescents' solutions to dilemmas in fables: Two moral orientations—Two problem-solving strategies." In C. Gilligan, J. V. Ward, and J. McLean Taylor, with B. Bardige (eds.), *Mapping the moral domain: A contribution of women's thinking to psychological theory and education* (pp. 49–72). Cambridge, Mass.: Harvard University Press.

Kallis, M. J., and Dinoo, J. V. 1985. "Consumer shoplifting: Orientations and deterrents." *Journal of Criminal Justice* 13: 459–473.

Kasarda, J. 1989. "Urban industrial transition and the underclass." *The Annals of the American Academy of Political and Social Science* 501: 24–27.

Katz, J. 1988. *Seductions of crime: Moral and sensual attractions in doing evil.* New York: Basic Books.

Kaufman, P. J., Alt, M. N., and Chapman, C. D. 2001. *Dropout rates in the United States: 2000.* Washington, D.C.: National Center for Educational Statistics.

Kendler, K. S., Bulik, C. M., Silberg, J., Hettema, J. M., Myers, J., and Prescott, C. A. 2002. "Childhood sexual abuse and adult psychiatric and substance use disorders in women: An epidemiological and cotwin control analysis." *Archives of General Psychiatry* 57: 953–959.

Kenning, M., Merchant, A., and Tomkins, A. 1991. "Research on the effects of witnessing parental battering: Clinical and legal policy implications." In M. Steinman (ed.), *Women battering: Policy implications* (pp. 237–261). Cincinnati: Anderson.

Kilpatrick, D. G., Acierno, R., Saunders, B, Resnick, H. S., Best, C. L., and Schnurr, P. P. 2000. "Risk factors for adolescent substance abuse and dependence: Data from a national sample." *Journal of Consulting and Clinical Psychology*, 68: 19–30.

King, H., with Chambliss, W. J. 1972. *Boxman: A professional thief's journey.* New York: Harper & Row.

Kivivuori, J. 1998. "Delinquent phases: The case of temporally intensified shoplifting behavior." *British Journal of Criminology* 38: 663–680.

Klemke, L. W. 1982. "Exploring juvenile shoplifting." *Sociology and Social Research* 67: 59–73.

Klemke, L. W., and Egger, S. A. 1992. *The sociology of shoplifting: Boosters and snitches today.* Westport, Conn.: Praeger.

Klockars, C. B. 1974. *The professional fence.* New York: Free Press.

Knox, P. L. 1991. "The restless urban landscape: Economic and sociocultural change and the transformation of metropolitan Washington, DC." *Annals of the Association of American Geographers* 81: 181–209.

Kodras, J. E. 1997. "The changing map of American poverty in an era of economic restructuring and political realignment." *Economic Geography* 73: 67–93.

Kolman, A. S., and Wasserman, C. 1991. "Theft groups for women: A cry for help." *Federal Probation* 55: 48–54.

Kovach, J. A. 1983. "The relationship between treatment failures of alcoholic women and incestuous histories with possible implications for post-traumatic stress disorder symptomatology." *Dissertation Abstracts International* 44: 710–712.

Kramer, L. A., and Berg, E. C. 2003. "A survival analysis of timing of entry into prostitution: The differential impact of race, educational level, and childhood/adolescent risk factors." *Sociological Inquiry* 73: 511–528.

Krasnovsky, T., and Lane, R. C. 1998. "Shoplifting: A review of the literature." *Aggression and Violent Behavior* 3: 219–235.

Kraut, R. E. 1976. "Deterrent and definitional influences on shoplifting." *Social Problems* 23: 358–368.

Kurtz, S. P., Surratt, H. L., Inciardi, J. A., and Kiley, M. C. 2004. "Sex work and 'date' violence." *Violence Against Women* 10: 357–385.

Lamontagne, Y., Boyer, R., Hetu, C., and Lacerte-Lamontagne, C. 2000. "Anxiety, significant losses, depression, and irrational beliefs in first-offence shoplifters." *Canadian Journal of Psychiatry* 45: 63–65.

Langeland, W., and Hartgers, C. 1998. "Child sexual and physical abuse and alcoholism: A review." *Journal of Studies on Alcohol* 59: 336–348.

Letkemann, P. 1973. *Crime as work.* Englewood Cliffs, N.J.: Prentice Hall.

Levy, J. A., and Anderson, T. 2005. "The drug career of the older injector." *Addiction Research & Theory* 13: 245–258.

Lewis, J. 2006. "I'll scratch your back if you'll scratch mine: The role of reciprocity, power and autonomy in the strip club." *The Canadian Review of Sociology and Anthropology* 43: 297–311.

Lo, L. 1994. "Exploring teenage shoplifting behavior: A choice and constraint approach." *Environment & Behavior* 26: 613–639.

Lowman, J. 2000. "Violence and the outlaw status of street prostitution in Canada." *Violence Against Women* 6: 987–1011.

MacDevitt, J. W., and Kedzierzawski, G. D. 1990. "Structured group format for first offense shoplifters." *International Journal of Offender Therapy and Comparative Criminology* 34: 155–164.

Maher, L. 1996. "Hidden in the light: Occupational norms among crack-using street-level sex workers." *Journal of Drug Issues* 26: 143–173.

———. 1997. *Sexed work: Gender, race, and resistance in a Brooklyn drug market.* Oxford, England: Clarendon Press.

———. 2004. "A reserve army: Women and the drug market." In B. R. Price and N. J. Sokoloff (eds.), *The criminal justice system and women: Offenders, prisoners, victims, and workers,* 3rd ed. (pp. 127–146). New York: McGraw-Hill.

Maher, L., and Curtis, R. 1992. "Women on the edge of crime: Crack cocaine and the recent changing contexts of street-level sex work in New York City." *Crime, Law, and Social Change* 18: 221–258.

Maher, L., and Daly, K. 1996. "Women in the street-level drug economy: Continuality or change." *Criminology* 34: 465–491.

Maher, L., Dunlap, E., Johnson, B. D., and Hamid, A. 1996. "Gender, power, and alternative living arrangements in the inner-city crack culture." *Journal of Research in Crime and Delinquency* 33: 181–205.

Malinosky-Rummell, R., and Hansen, D. J. 1993. "Long-term consequences of childhood physical abuse." *Psychological Bulletin* 114: 68–79.

Massey, D. 1984. *Spatial divisions of labor: Social structures and the geography of production.* London: MacMillian.

———. 1994. *Space, place, and gender.* Minneapolis: University of Minnesota Press.

Mathews, F. 1986. *Mirror to the night: A psychosocial study of prostitution.* Doctoral dissertation. Toronto: University of Toronto.

Maticka-Tyndale, E., Lewis, J., Clark, J., Zubick, J., and Young, S. 2000. "Exotic dancing and health." *Women & Health* 31: 87–108.

Matsueda, R. L., Gartner, R., Piliavin, I., and Polakowski, M. 1992. "The prestige of criminal and conventional occupations: A subcultural model of criminal activity." *American Sociological Review* 57: 752–770.

Maur, M. 2004. *Lessons of the "Get Tough" movement in the United States.* Washington, D.C.: The Sentencing Project.

Mauer, M., and Chesney-Lind, M. 2002. *Invisible punishment: The collateral consequences of mass imprisonment.* New York: New Press.

McCarthy, B., and Hagan, J. 1995. "Getting into street crime: The structure and process of criminal embeddedness." *Social Science Research* 24: 63–95.

———. 2001. "When crime pays: Capital, competence, and criminal success." *Social Forces* 79: 1035–1060.

McClanahan, S. F., McClelland, G. M., Abram, K. M., and Teplin, L. A. 1999. "Pathways into prostitution among female jail detainees and their implications for mental health services." *Psychiatric Services* 50: 1606–1613.

McElroy, S. L., Hudson, J. I., Pope, H. G., and Keck, P. E. 1991. "Kleptomania: Clinical characteristics and associated psychopathology." *Psychological Medicine* 21: 93–108.

McElroy, S. L., Pope, H. G., Jr., Hudson, J. I., Keck, P. E., Jr., and White, K. L. 1991. "Kleptomania: A report of 20 cases." *American Journal of Psychiatry* 148: 652–657.

McPherson, M., Lovin, L. S., and Cook, J. M. 2001. "Birds of a feather: Homophily in social networks." *Annual Review of Sociology* 27: 415–444.

Medrano, M. A., Hatch, J. P., Zule, W. A., and Desmond, D. P. 2003. "Childhood trauma and adult prostitution behavior in a multiethnic heterosexual drug-using population." *The American Journal of Drug and Alcohol Abuse* 29: 463–486.

Michie, S. 2002. "Causes and management of stress at work." *Occupational and Environmental Medicine* 59: 67–72.

Miller, D., Trapani, C., Fejes-Mendoza, K., Eggleston, C., and Dwiggins, D. 1995. "Adolescent female offenders: Unique considerations." *Adolescence* 30: 429–435.

Miller, E. M. 1986. *Street women.* Philadelphia: Temple University Press.

Miller, G. 1978. *Odd jobs: The world of deviant work.* Englewood Cliffs, NJ: Prentice Hall.

Miller, J. 1993. "Your life is on the line every night you're on the streets: Victimization and the resistance among street prostitutes." *Humanity & Society* 17: 422–446.

———. 1995. "Gender and power on the streets: Street prostitution in the era of crack cocaine." *Journal of Contemporary Ethnography* 23: 427–452.

Miller, J., and Jayasundara, D. 2001. "Prostitution, the sex industry, and sex tourism." In C. M. Renzetti, J. L. Edleson, and R. K. Bergen (eds.), *Sourcebook on violence against women* (pp. 459–480). Thousand Oaks, Calif.: Sage.

Miller, J., and Schwartz, M. D. 1995. "Rape myths and violence against street prostitutes." *Deviant Behavior: An Interdisciplinary Journal* 16: 1–23.

Moeller, T. P., Bachman, G. A., and Loeller, J. R. 1993. "The combined effects of physical, sexual, and emotional abuse during childhood: Long-term health consequences for women." *Child Abuse and Neglect* 17: 623–640.

Monto, M. A. 2004. "Female prostitution, customers, and violence." *Violence Against Women* 10: 160–188.

Moore, R. H. 1983. "College shoplifters: Rebuttal of Beck and McIntyre." *Psychological Report* 53: 1111–1116.

———. 1984. "Shoplifting in middle America: Patterns and motivational correlates." *International Journal of Offender Therapy and Comparative Criminology* 28: 53–64.

Morrill, R., and Wohlenberg, E. 1971. *The geography of poverty in the United States.* New York: McGraw-Hill.

Mumola, C., and Karberg, J. C. 2006. *Drug use and dependence, state and federal prisoners, 2004.* Washington, D.C.: Bureau of Justice Statistics.

Murphy, S., and Rosenbaum, M. 1997. "Two women who use cocaine too much." In C. Reinarman and H. Levine (eds.), *Crack in America: Demon drugs and social justice* (pp. 98–112). Berkeley: University of California Press.

Murray, J. B. 1992. "Kleptomania. A review of the research." *The Journal of Psychology* 126: 131–138.

Najavits, L. M., Weiss, R. D., and Shaw, S. R. 1997. "The link between substance abuse and posttraumatic stress disorder in women: A research review." *American Journal on Addictions* 6: 273–283.

National Institute of Corrections. 2000. *Promoting public safety using effective interventions with offenders.* Washington, D.C.: National Institute of Corrections.

Neame, A., and Heenan, M. 2003. *What lies behind the hidden figure of sexual assault? Issues of prevalence and disclosure.* Melbourne: Australian Institute of Family Studies, Australian Centre for the Study of Sexual Assault.

Neumann, D. A., Houskamp, B. M., Pollock, V. E., and Briere, J. 1996. "The long-term sequelae of childhood sexual abuse in women: A meta-analytic review." *Child Maltreatment* 1: 6–16.

New Jersey Department of Law and Public Safety. 2005. *Crime in New Jersey: 2005 Uniform crime reports.* Trenton: Office of the Attorney General, New Jersey Department of Law and Public Safety.

O'Connell Davidson, J. 1998. *Prostitution, power and freedom.* London: Polity Press.

Ordway, J. A. 1962. "Successful court treatment of shoplifters." *Journal of Criminal Law, Criminology, and Police Science* 8: 27–29.

Oregon Youth Authority. 2002. *Mental health and female offenders in custody of the Oregon Youth Authority.* Salem: Oregon Youth Authority.

Owen, B. A. 1998. *In the mix: Struggle and survival in a women's prison.* Albany: State University of New York Press.

Owen, B., and Bloom, B. 1995. "Profiling women prisoners: Findings from national surveys and a California sample." *The Prison Journal* 75: 165–185.

Pasko, L. J. 2006. *The female juvenile offender in Hawaii: Understanding gender differences in arrests, adjudications, and social characteristics of juvenile offenders.* Research and Statistics Branch, Crime Prevention and Justice Assistance Division, Department of the Attorney General, State of Hawaii.

Pavalko, R. M. 1971. *Sociology of occupations and professions.* Itasca, Ill.: F. F. Peacock.

Peretti, P. O. and O'Connor, P. 1989. "Effects of incongruence between the perceived self and the ideal self on emotional stability of stripteasers." *Social Behavior and Personality* 17: 81–92.

Peugh, J., and Belenko, S. 1999. "Substance-involved women inmates: Challenges to providing effective treatment." *The Prison Journal* 79: 23–44.

Piquero, A. R., Farrington, D. P., and Blumstein, A. 2007. *Key issues in criminal career research.* New York: Cambridge University Press.

Polsky, N. 1969. *Hustlers, beats, and others.* New York: Doubleday & Company.

Portes, A. 1998. "Social capital: Its origins and applications in modern sociology." *Annual Review of Sociology* 24: 1–25.

Potterat, J. J., Brewer, D. D., Muth, S. Q., Rothenberg, R. B., Woodhouse, D. E., Muth, J. B., Stites, H. K., and Brody, S. 2004. "Mortality in a long-term open cohort of prostitute women." *American Journal of Epidemiology* 159: 778–785.

Potterat, J. J., Rothenberg, R. B., Muth, S. Q., Darrow, W. W., and Phillips-Plummer, L. 1988. "Pathways to prostitution: The chronology of sexual and drug abuse milestones." *Journal of Sex Research* 35: 333–340.

Raphael, J., and Shapiro, D. L. 2003. *Sisters speak out: The lives and needs of prostituted women in Chicago, A research study.* Chicago: Center for Impact Research.

———. 2004. "Violence in indoor and outdoor prostitution venues." *Violence Against Women* 10: 126–139.

Ratner, M. 1993. *Crack pipe as a pimp: An ethnographic investigation of sex-for-crack exchanges.* New York: Lexington Books.

Ray, J. 1987. "Every twelfth shopper: Who shoplifts and why?" *Social Casework: The Journal of Contemporary Social Work* 68: 234–239.

Ray, J., and Briar K. H. 1988. "Economic motivators for shoplifting." *Journal of Sociology & Social Welfare* 15: 177–189.

Ray, J. B., Solomon, G. S., Doncaster, M. G., and Mellina, R. 1983. "First offender adult shoplifters: A preliminary profile." *Journal of Clinical Psychology* 39: 769–770.

Redlinger, L. 1975. "Marketing and distributing heroin: Some sociological observations." *Journal of Psychedelic Drugs* 7: 331–353.

Reese, F. L., Chassin, L., and Molina, B. S. G. 1994. "Alcohol expectancies in early adolescents: Predicting drinking behavior from alcohol expectancies and parental alcoholism." *Journal of Studies on Alcohol* 55: 276–284.

Renzetti, C. M., Goodstein, L., and Miller, S. L. (eds.). 2006. *Rethinking gender, crime, and justice: Feminist readings.* New York: Oxford University Press.

Richie, B. E. 1996. *Compelled to crime: The gender entrapment of battered black women.* New York: Routledge.

Romero-Daza, N., Weeks, M., and Singer, M. 2003. "Nobody gives a damn if I live or die: Violence, drugs, and street-level prostitution in inner-city Hartford, Connecticut." *Medical Anthropology* 22: 233–259.

Ronai, C. R., and Ellis. C. 1989. "Turn-ons for money: Interactional strategies of the table dancer." *Journal of Contemporary Ethnography* 18: 271–298.

Rose, H. M. 1970. "The development of an urban subsystem: The case of the Negro ghetto." *Annals of the Association of American Geographers* 60: 1–17.

Rosenbaum, J. 1989. "Family dysfunction and female delinquency. Special issue: Women and crime." *Crime & Delinquency* 35: 31–44.

Rosenbaum, M. 1988. *Women on heroin.* New Brunswick, N.J.: Rutgers University Press.

Ruggiero, V., and South, N. 1997. "The late-modern city as a bazaar: Drug markets, illegal enterprises and 'barricades.'" *British International Journal of Sociology* 48: 54–70.

Russell, M. 1978. "Groups for women who shoplift." *Canadian Journal of Criminology* 20: 73–74.

Sanders, T. 2004a. "Controllable laughter: Managing sex work through humour." *Sociology* 38: 273–291.

———. 2004b. "The risks of street prostitution: Punters, police and protesters." *Urban Studies* 41: 1703–1717.

Sarasalo, E., Bergman, B., and Toth, J. 1997. "Theft behavior and its consequences among kleptomaniacs and shoplifters: A comparative study." *Forensic Science International* 86: 193–205.

Schmitt, G. R. 2006. *Drug courts: The second decade.* Washington, D.C.: National Institute of Justice.

Schneider, J. L. 2005. "Stolen-goods markets." *British Journal of Criminology* 45: 129–140.

Schwirian, K. P. 1983. "Models of neighborhood change." *Annual Review of Sociology* 9: 83–102.

Scott, M. S., and Dedel, K. 2006. *Street prostitution,* 2nd ed. Washington, D.C.: U.S. Department of Justice, Office of Community Oriented Policing Services.

Seixas, J. S., and Youcha, G. 1985. *Children of alcoholism.* New York: Harper & Row.

Seng, M. J. 1989. "Child sexual abuse and adolescent prostitution: A comparative analysis." *Adolescence* 24: 665–675.

Sher, K. J., Walitzer, K. S., Wood, P. K., and Brent E. E. 1991. "Characteristics of children of alcoholics: Putative risk factors, substance abuse and abuse, and psychopathology." *Journal of Abnormal Psychology* 4: 427–448.

Shteir, R. 2004. *Striptease: The untold history of the girlie show.* New York: Oxford University Press.

Siegel, J. A., and Williams, L. M. 2003. "The relationship between child sexual abuse and female delinquency and crime: A prospective study." *Journal of Research in Crime and Delinquency* 40: 71–94.

Silbert, M. H., and Pines, A. M. 1981. "Sexual child abuse as an antecedent to prostitution." *Child Abuse and Neglect* 5: 407–411.

———. 1982. "Entrance into prostitution." *Youth & Society* 13: 471–500.

———. 1983. "Early sexual exploitation as an influence in prostitution." *Social Work* 28: 285–289.

Silbert, M. H., Pines, A. M., and Lynch, T. 1982. "Substance abuse and prostitution." *Journal of Psychoactive Drugs* 14: 193–197.

Simons R. L., and Whitbeck, L. B., 1991. "Sexual abuse as a precursor to prostitution and victimization among adolescent and adult homeless women." *Journal of Family Issues* 12: 361–379.

Snyder, H. N., and Sickmond, M. 2006. *Juvenile offenders and victims: 2006 national report.* Washington, D.C.: Office of Juvenile Justice and Delinquency Prevention.

Solomon, G. S., and Ray, J. B. 1984. "Irrational beliefs of shoplifters." *Journal of Clinical Psychology,* 40: 1075–1077.

Sommers, I., Baskin, D., and Fagan, J. 1996. "The structural relationship between drug use, drug dealing, and other income support activities among women drug sellers." *Journal of Drug Issues* 26: 975–1006.

Spataro, J., Mullen, P. E., Burgess, P. M., Wells, D. L., and Moss, S. A. 2004. "Impact of child sexual abuse on mental health: Prospective study in males and females." *The British Journal of Psychiatry* 184: 416–421.

Steffensmeier, D. J., 1983. "Organizational properties and sex-segregation in the underworld: Building a sociological theory of sex difference in crime." *Social Forces* 61: 1010–1032.

———. 1986. *The fence: In the shadow of two worlds.* Totowa, N.J.: Rowman and Littlefield.

Steffensmeier, D. J., and Allan, E. 1996. "Gender and crime: Toward a gendered theory of female offending." *Annual Review of Sociology* 22: 459–487.

Steffensmeier, D. J., and Terry, R. M. 1973. "Deviance and respectability: An observational study of reactions to shoplifting." *Social Forces* 51: 417–426.

———. 1986. "Institutional sexism in the underworld. A view from the inside." *Sociological Inquiry* 56: 304–323.

Steffensmeier, D. J., and Ulmer, J. T. 2004. *Confessions of a dying thief: Understanding criminal careers and illegal enterprise.* New Brunswick, N.J.: Adline Transaction.

Sterk, C. E., Elifson, K. W., and German, D. 2000. "Female crack users and their sexual relationships: The role of sex-for-crack exchanges." *Journal of Sex Research* 37: 354–360.

Surratt, H. L., Inciardi, J. A., Kurtz, S. P., and Kiley, M. C. 2004. "Sex work and drug use in a subculture of violence." *Crime & Delinquency* 50: 43–59.

Sutherland, E. 1937. *The professional thief.* Chicago: University of Chicago Press.

Svensson, R. 2002. "Strategic offenses in the criminal career context." *British Journal of Criminology* 42: 395–411.

Sweet, N., and Tewksbury, R. 2000. "What's a nice girl like you doing in a place like this? Pathways to a career in stripping." *Sociological Spectrum* 20: 325–343.

Teplin, L. A., Abram, K. M., and McClelland, G. M. 1996. "Prevalence of psychiatric disorders among incarcerated women. I. Pretrial jail detainees." *Archives of General Psychiatry,* 53: 505–512.

Thompson, W. E., and Harred, J. L. 1992. "Topless dancers: Managing stigma in a deviant occupation." *Deviant Behavior* 13: 291–311.

Thompson, W. E., Harred, J. L., and Burks, B. E. 2003. "Managing the stigma of topless dancing: A decade later." *Deviant Behavior* 24: 551–570.

Tonglet, M. 2002. "Consumer misbehaviour: An exploratory study of shoplifting." *Journal of Consumer Behaviour* 1: 336–354.

Trautner, M. N. 2005. "Doing gender, doing class: The performance of sexuality in exotic dance clubs." *Gender Society* 19: 771–788.

Tyler, K. A., Hoyt, D. R., and Whitbeck, L. B. 2000. "The effects of early sexual abuse on later sexual victimization among female homeless and runaway adolescents." *Journal of Interpersonal Violence* 15: 235–250.

Tyler, K. A., Whitbeck, L. B., Hoyt, D. R., and Cauce, A. M. 2004. "Risk factors for sexual victimization among male and female homeless and runaway youth." *Journal of Interpersonal Violence* 19: 503–520.

U.S. Department of Health and Human Services. 1994. *Substance abuse among women and parents.* Washington, D.C.: U.S. Department of Health and Human Services.

U.S. Department of Health and Human Services, Administration on Children, Youth and Families. 2007. *Child maltreatment 2005.* Washington, D.C.: U.S. Department of Health and Human Services.

U.S. Department of Health and Human Services, National Center on Child Abuse and Neglect. 1996. *The third National Incidence Study of Child Abuse and Neglect NIS-3.* Washington, D.C.: U.S. Department of Health and Human Services.

U.S. Department of Justice, Federal Bureau of Investigation. 2005. *Crime in the United States, 2004.* Washington, D.C.: U.S. Department of Justice.

———. 2006. *Crime in the United States, 2005.* Washington, D.C.: U.S. Department of Justice.

———. 2007. *Crime in the United States, 2006.* Washington, D.C.: U.S. Department of Justice.

Valera, R. J., Sawyer, R. G., and Schiraldi, G. R. 2001. "Perceived health needs of inner-city street prostitutes: A preliminary study. *American Journal of Health Behavior* 25: 50–59.

Walby, S. 1986. *Patriarchy at work: Patriarchal and capitalist relations in employment.* Cambridge: Polity Press.

———. 1990. *Theorizing patriarchy.* Cambridge, Mass.: Basil Blackwell.

Wahab, S. 2004. "Tricks of the trade: What social workers can learn about sex workers through dialogue." *Qualitative Social Work* 3: 139–160.

Way, L. B. 2004. "Missing faces: Is historical institutionalism the answer for conducting intersectional research?" *Women & Criminal Justice* 15: 81–98.

Weaver, F. M., and Carroll, J. S. 1985. "Crime perceptions in a natural setting by expert and novice shoplifters." *Social Psychology Quarterly* 48: 349–359.

Weber, A. E., Boivin, J. F., Blais, L., Haley, N., and Roy, E. 2004. "Predictors of initiation into prostitution among female street youths." *Journal of Urban Health* 81: 584–595.

Webster, B. H., and Bishaw, A. 2006. *Income, earnings, and poverty data from the 2005 American Community Survey.* Washington, D.C.: U.S. Census Bureau.

Weitzer, R. 2005. "New directions in research on prostitution." *Crime, Law & Social Change* 43: 211–235.

Wenzel, S. L., Hambarsoomain, K., D'Amico, E. J., Ellison, M., and Tucker, J. S. 2006. "Victimization and health among indigent young women in the transition to adulthood: A portrait of need." *Journal of Adolescent Health* 38: 536–543.

West, C., and Fenstermaker, S. 1995. "Doing difference." *Gender and Society* 9: 8–37.

Whitbeck, L. B., Hoyt, D. R., and Yoder, K. A. 1999. "A risk-amplification model of victimization and depressive symptoms among runaway and homeless adolescents." *American Journal of Community Psychology* 27: 273–296.

Whitbeck, L. B., Hoyt, D. R., Yoder, K. A., Cauce, A. M., and Paradise, M. 2001. "Deviant behavior and victimization among homeless and runaway adolescents." *Journal of Interpersonal Violence* 16: 1175–1204.

Widom, C. S., and Kuhns, J. B. 1996. "Childhood victimization and subsequent risk for promiscuity, prostitution, and teenage pregnancy." *American Journal of Public Health* 86: 1607–1612.

Williamson, C., and Cluse-Tolar, T. 2002. "Pimp-controlled prostitution: Still an integral part of street life." *Violence Against Women* 8: 1074–1092.

Williamson, C., and Folaron, G. 2001. "Violence, risk, and survival strategies of street prostitution." *Western Journal of Nursing Research* 23: 463–475.

———. 2003. "Understanding the experiences of street level prostitutes." *Qualitative Social Work* 2: 271–287.

Wilsnack, S. C., Vogeltanz, N. D., Klassen, A. D., and Harris, T. R. 1997. "Childhood sexual abuse and women's substance abuse: National survey findings." *Journal of Studies on Alcohol* 58: 264–271.

Wilson, W. 1987. *The truly disadvantaged.* Chicago: University of Chicago Press.

Windle, M. 1996. "On the discriminative validity of a Family History or Problem Drinking Index with a national sample of young adults." *Journal of Studies on Alcohol* 57: 378–386.

———. 1998. "Substance use and abuse among adolescent runaways: A four-year follow-up study." *Journal of Youth and Adolescence* 18: 331–344.

Windle, M., Windle, R. C., Scheidt, D. M., and Miller, G. B. 1995. "Physical and sexual abuse and associated mental disorders among alcoholic patients." *American Journal of Psychiatry* 152: 1322–1328.

Wood, E. A. 2000. "Working in the fantasy factor: The attention hypothesis and the enacting of masculine power in strip clubs." *Journal of Contemporary Ethnography* 29: 5–31.

Young, D., and Belenko, S. 2002. "Program retention and perceived coercion in three models of mandatory drug treatment." *Journal of Drug Issues* 32: 297–328.

Index

Page numbers in *italics* refer to tables.